Children's Literature

Volume 27

Founder and Senior Editor: Francelia Butler (1913–98)

Editor-in-Chief: R. H. W. Dillard

Editor: Elizabeth Lennox Keyser

Book Review Editor: Christine Doyle

Advisory Board: Janice M. Alberghene, Ruth B. Bottigheimer, Beverly Lyon Clark, Barbara Garner (representing the ChLA), Margaret Higonnet, U. C. Knoepflmacher, Alison Lurie, Roderick McGillis, Mitzi Myers, Albert J. Solnit, M.D.

Consultants for Volume 27: Gillian Adams, Hamida Bosmajian, Ruth B. Bottigheimer, Donna Campbell, John Cech, Beverly Lyon Clark, Christine Doyle, Richard Flynn, Hugh Keenan, Millicent Lenz, Claire L. Malarte-Feldman, Leonard Marcus, Jean Marsden, James Holt McGavran, Jr., Roderick McGillis, Nina Mikkelsen, Miriam Youngerman Miller, Claudia Nelson, Perry Nodelman, Julie Pfeiffer, Anne K. Phillips, Suzanne Rahn, Annette Sampon-Nicholas, Sarah Smedman, Karen Patricia Smith, J. D. Stahl, Joseph Stanton, C. W. Sullivan III, Roberta Seelinger Trites, Tim Wolf

The editors gratefully acknowledge support from Hollins University.

Editorial correspondence should be addressed to The Editors, *Children's Literature,* Department of English, Hollins University, Roanoke, Virginia 24020.

Volume 27

Annual of
The Modern Language Association
Division on Children's Literature
and The Children's Literature
Association

Yale University Press

New Haven and London

1999

Children's Literature

Manuscripts submitted should conform to the style in this issue. An original on non-erasable bond with two copies, a self-addressed envelope, and return postage are requested. Yale University Press does not accept dot-matrix printouts, and it requires double-spacing throughout text and notes. Unjustified margins are required. Writers of accepted manuscripts should be prepared to submit final versions of their essays on computer disk in XyWrite, Nota Bene, or WordPerfect.

Volumes 1–7 of *Children's Literature* can be obtained directly from John C. Wandell, The Children's Literature Foundation, P.O. Box 370, Windham Center, Conn. 06280. Volumes 8–26 can be obtained from Yale University Press, P.O. Box 209040, New Haven, Conn. 06520-9040, or from Yale University Press, 23 Pond Street, Hampstead, London NW3 2PN, England.

Copyright © 1999 by Hollins University.

Set in Baskerville type by Tseng Information Systems, Inc., Durham, N.C.
Printed in the United States of America by Vail-Ballou Press, Binghamton, N.Y.

Library of Congress catalog card number: 79-66588
ISBN: 0-300-07775-0 (cloth), 0-300-07776-9 (paper); ISSN: 0092-8208

A catalogue record for this book is available from the British Library.

The paper in this book meets the guidelines for permanence and durability of the Committee on Production Guidelines for Book Longevity of the Council on Library Resources.

10   9   8   7   6   5   4   3   2   1

Contents

From the Editor

This volume features nine substantial essays that cover a wide range, both generically and chronologically, of American literature for young people. As always, I am grateful to the many readers who helped me select these essays and their authors to revise them. I am also grateful to Christine Doyle for a superb job during her first year as book review editor, and again I would like to thank Pamela Harer for the twenty-five-year cumulative index, which I hope will prove a valuable bibliographical tool, and Rachel Fordyce for her invariably helpful feature. I look forward to collaborating on the next volume, for the year 2000, with my Hollins University colleague Julie Pfeiffer. She, like Cynthia Wells and the other Yale University Press editors I have worked with over the years, has proved a great source of moral support. Finally, I would like to thank the eager and enthusiastic contributors, many of whom are new to these pages as well as to the profession.

Katharine Capshaw Smith, in her ground-breaking essay on black pageantry, quotes W. E. B. Du Bois as declaring, "I do not care a damn for any art that is not used for propaganda." According to Capshaw Smith, "the political, the didactic, the reformative all coalesced for Du Bois in the pageant format." Volume 27 of *Children's Literature* has also finally coalesced around the idea of "the political, the didactic, the reformative," as well as the formative—the stages or process through which the infant, child, preadolescent, and adolescent passes on his (in this volume more often her) way to maturity. Although the literature discussed in these essays transcends propaganda, it does have what today we would call an agenda, whether it be defending the authority of the Bible against heretical interpretations, as in the case of Eliza Bradburn's *The Story of* Paradise Lost, *For Children,* or arguing for the rights of nonhuman life, as in the case of Phyllis Reynolds Naylor's *Shiloh.* More interesting than these overt agendas, however, are the strategies for their communication that the contributors so ably discuss. And perhaps most fascinating of all are the ways in which the authors can be found to subvert not only the values they would transform or reform but also aspects of their own apparent programs.

Julie Pfeiffer opens volume 27 with an analysis of Bradburn's early-nineteenth-century adaptation of *Paradise Lost* for children. Bradburn, who attempts to maintain a delicate balance between extolling the work's poetic virtues and exposing its doctrinal flaws, adopts a framing technique common to much of the literature discussed in this volume. Pfeiffer describes how what has often been taken to be a patriarchal poem is domesticated by Bradburn's female narrator, a mother who introduces the poem simultaneously to her own children and to the child reader. Bradburn's Mamma, according to Pfeiffer, follows Milton's Raphael in instructing children to "solicit not thy thoughts with matters hid" and "dream not of other worlds." Yet in their discussion of Eve's responsibility for the Fall, Mamma and her female children prove themselves to be resisting readers and proto-feminists.

Lydia Maria Child, the "omnipresent" aunt of Etsuko Taketani's essay, frames the vision of antebellum America portrayed in her magazine *The Juvenile Miscellany*. Opposing the common view that children were depicted as depoliticized and ahistorical in early American children's literature, Taketani argues that in Child's work, at least, "the body and voice of the child serve as a site on which the discourse of domestic colonialism is examined, if not always disrupted." By associating children with disenfranchised groups such as Native Americans, the Irish, and freed slaves, Child, according to Taketani, subtly but devastatingly critiques domestic colonialism and patriarchy. A century later W. E. B. Du Bois and other creators of black pageantry for children also used child characters and actors to expose as a construct the canonical view of American history. Interestingly, many of the pageant creators were black female schoolteachers, according to Capshaw Smith, and their characteristic use of a female narrator served to perpetuate a matriarchal oral tradition. The figure of the child in black pageantry, however, was used not only, or primarily, to expose the evils of the past but to represent the race's hope for the future.

Daddy-Long-Legs, published during what Capshaw Smith calls "the great age of American pageantry," seeks no less than black pageantry to empower its audience. As Anne K. Phillips writes, "*Daddy-Long-Legs* is an unabashed campaign on behalf of women's colleges and the benefits for women of the college experience." And, as in black pageantry, the female voice is paramount. Placing the novel in both the epistolary and the college novel traditions, and employing contemporary feminist developmental theory, Phillips convincingly argues against the view that the heroine's college career is no more than preparation for marriage to her benefactor, John Smith-Jervis Pendleton. Alice Mills, on the other hand, in her witty psychoanalytic reading of Eleanor Porter's *Pollyanna* and *Pollyanna Grows Up*— novels that, like *Daddy-Long-Legs*, deal with an orphan girl's adoption and education, sentimental and otherwise—finds Pollyanna hopelessly enmeshed in and doomed to relive an oedipal past, as indicated by her compulsive rehearsing of an equivalent to a primal scene and her involvement with her dead mother's former suitor, John Pendleton. If the "Glad Game," for which the *Pollyanna* books are famous, is Porter's propaganda, she consistently subverts it by portraying Pollyanna's voracious appetite for victims with whom she can favorably compare herself. In Pollyanna's case, the way in which she consistently reframes her experience suggests, despite the title of the sequel, her inability to grow up.

The theoretically informed essays of Karen Coats and Roberta Seelinger Trites also discuss stages and issues of identity formation. Coats's Lacanian reading of E. B. White's classic *Charlotte's Web* illuminates difficult Lacanian concepts as much as it does the text itself. Trites employs the theoretical insights of Roland Barthes, Marianne Hirsch, and Susan Sontag as well as Lacan to explore how the protagonists of young adult fiction, through their own and others' photography—through framing and being framed—learn to see themselves as both subjects and objects. Like Phillips in her reading of *Daddy-Long-Legs*, Coats and Trites are concerned with how the self is constituted by language and identity bound up with acquiring a voice. Although the novels analyzed by Coats and Trites are less obviously didactic than other literature considered in this volume, they still serve an educative function by providing developmental models. And Trudy Krisher's *Spite Fences*, one of the novels discussed by Trites, reiterates a concern for the politically and economically disenfranchised.

Philip Nel, like Karen Coats, revisits an author who has become a household word. Nel's project is to recuperate the radical Dr. Seuss and obliterate the "*Book of Virtues* version" that has begun to prevail. In other words, Nel, like Taketani, does not so much want to dispel the image of a children's writer as didactic as to argue for a far more sophisticated and complex kind of didacticism. As Nel writes, although the books "are didactic, . . . instead of delivering a lecture to their readers Seuss's works teach by encouraging subversive thoughts and behaviors." By reconnecting Seuss to other avant-garde artists, Nel makes a strong case for his countercultural stance.

Finally, Claudia Mills brings her philosophical training, as well as her own experience as a fiction writer, to bear on Phyllis Reynolds Naylor's Newbery Award–winning *Shiloh*. As Mills convincingly demonstrates, *Shiloh* teaches far more than that animals have feelings worthy of consideration; instead its greatness lies in its revelation that children face moral dilemmas that defy resolution even by trained ethical thinkers. Although Naylor's hero cannot, like the children Eliza Bradburn portrays, rely on the absolute authority of the Bible, his efforts to grapple with the dilemma he confronts ultimately celebrate the moral life. All of the works considered here, with the possible exception of *Pollyanna* (which teaches indirectly through the pathos of Pollyanna's seeming triumphs), do what Philip Nel claims Dr. Seuss's do—"license the imagination as a realm in which one can at least *imagine* another world—if not actually realize that world." Thus they all, to use the terminology of *Paradise Lost*, recognize a postlapsarian world to which Raphael's injunction "Dream not of other worlds" does not apply. Instead, to paraphrase Mark Twain's Satan at the end of "The Mysterious Stranger," they are enjoined to dream other worlds—and better.

Elizabeth Lennox Keyser

At the copyediting stage of volume 27, the editors learned that Francelia Butler, founding editor of Children's Literature, *had died. We haven't the time or space here to do much more than acknowledge her passing, but we hope in the year 2000 to do greater justice to her memory. As an advocate for children, their literature, and world peace, Francelia was indeed one who dreamed better worlds and helped to make them a reality.*

Articles

"Dream not of other worlds": Paradise Lost and the Child Reader

Julie Pfeiffer

> *With very many [children] the easy neatness or pompous sounds of verse [in] Paradise Lost, have an ineffable charm. . . . We need hardly remind those concerned in [children's] welfare, that Homer, Shakespeare, Milton and Addison, are enjoyable and appreciable from a very early age, and that the child's store of such reading is one of the richest legacies the adult can inherit.*
>
> —Elizabeth Rigby

Milton's importance to adult readers of the nineteenth century is un-questioned,[1] even as his role in the education of their children has been ignored by twentieth-century critics.[2] Milton's work was seen as significant enough in the nineteenth century to justify not only the inclusion of his poetry in schoolbooks but also the publication of two versions of *Paradise Lost* intended especially for children. In particular, Eliza Weaver Bradburn's 1828 retelling, *The Story of* Paradise Lost, *For Children,* allows us to examine Milton's role as an educator of nineteenth-century children.[3] This text reinforces the belief that *Paradise Lost* was an essential component of a child's education, but it also suggests the ways in which adults of that time were unsettled by the poem. Written in the context of the Romantic fascination with Milton, Bradburn's text demonstrates Milton's complex roles for these readers as cultural icon, educator, and heretic. *The Story of* Paradise Lost, *For Children* reflects two nineteenth-century perspectives: the epic as good medicine that needs only to be made palatable for

Children's Literature 27, ed. Elizabeth Lennox Keyser (Yale University Press, © 1999 Hollins University).

young minds, and the epic as a dangerously tempting drug that requires the mediation of adult explication.

The first perspective relies on the nineteenth-century commonplace that *Paradise Lost* is a literary text of central importance and a source of pleasure and a treasure trove for children. As Thomas De Quincey wrote in 1839, John Milton "is not an author amongst authors, not a poet amongst poets, but a power amongst powers; and the 'Paradise Lost' is not a book amongst books, not a poem amongst poems, but a central force amongst forces" (777). Thomas Keightley focused on the child's interaction with this cultural icon with his comment that "the reading of *Paradise Lost* for the first time forms or should form, an era in the life of every one possessed of taste and poetic feeling. . . . [Since childhood] the poetry of Milton has formed my constant study,—a source of delight in prosperity, of strength and consolation in adversity" (Nelson 3–4). Writers including Thomas Cooper and Sara Coleridge emphasized the importance of their childhood readings of *Paradise Lost* (Nelson 5; Cruse 11). Emily Shore listed hearing the first installment of *Paradise Lost* as a reason to feel "very much pleased" with her governess (Cockshut 384).

The renowned actress Sarah Siddons claimed that at the age of ten "she used to pore over 'Paradise Lost' for hours together" (Campbell 20). After her retirement from the theater she continued giving readings from Milton both in public and in her home, and her lifelong interest in Milton's poetry culminated with the publication, in 1822, of *An Abridgement of* Paradise Lost. The preface to Siddons's abridgment reveals that she was motivated to produce this volume not simply by her own pleasure in Milton's text but also by the educational potential *Paradise Lost* offered the interested young reader. She wrote, "A taste for the sublime and beautiful is an approach to virtue; and I was naturally desirous that [children's] minds should be inspired with an early admiration of Milton. The perfection of his immortal Poem is seldom appreciated by the young; and its perusal is, perhaps, very generally regarded rather as a duty than a pleasure. This has been attributed by Dr. Johnson to *the want of human interest*" (iii, emphasis in original). Her solution was to select the passages "which relate to the fate of our first parents" and to remove "every thing, however exquisite in its kind, which did not immediately bear upon their affecting and important story" (iii–iv). In keeping with the ideals of Romanticism, Siddons linked "sublimity" with "virtue" and sees in the beauty of Milton's poetry and story an essential opportunity. With her abridgment children will see reading the poem more as a "pleasure" and less as a "duty."

Eliza Bradburn's *Paradise Lost* begins with this assumption of pleasure but quickly moves to highlight the epic's potential to educate (either well or ill). The significance of *The Story of* Paradise Lost, *For Children* lies in Bradburn's insistence that the poem be framed and even translated rather than simply abridged for children. As the daughter of Samuel Bradburn, the famous Methodist minister, and Sophia Cooke, an early advocate for Sunday schools, Bradburn viewed Milton's epic—like the fruit of the forbidden tree that so tempted Eve and then Adam—as itself an object of temptation. Without guidance, Bradburn feared, children would be swept away by Milton's poem and tempted to believe in his version of "the story of our first parents" even when it conflicts with (her reading of) the Bible. If we reconsider the enthusiasm with which both De Quincey and Rigby praised Milton's epic we see a vagueness that develops, in Eliza Bradburn's retelling, into full-fledged concern. According to De Quincey, *Paradise Lost* is a "force amongst forces"; Rigby speaks of the "ineffable charm" of the sounds of Milton's verse: but what exactly is the result of that force, that charm? These enthusiastic responses to *Paradise Lost* fail to define the nature or consequences of its power. Even while celebrating the poem, these critics emphasize its amorphous character; *Paradise Lost* is not a single entity, and children, it follows, could not be expected to take from it a unified impression. How, then, to encourage a child's curiosity to delve further into this cultural icon and reap the rewards of "sublimity" while protecting her from the dangers of a text that itself probes into the danger of knowing too much? How to make the poem more accessible while shaping and selecting the readings that a child might find in it? Bradburn's solution is to embed Milton's text in a dialogue between a mother and her three children (the eldest of whom is ten years old); thus through "mamma's" paraphrasing and explicit commentary she strives to mitigate the dangers lurking in this "central force among forces."

The theme of Bradburn's *Paradise Lost, For Children* is that Milton, like mamma, can provide instruction as well as delight; unlike mamma's text, though, Milton's is dangerous in that his fiction may appear to be truth. The dialogue between mamma and Eliza, William, and Emily begins with the children's delight in the poem (they have overheard their mother reading aloud to a friend) but immediately moves to its possible danger. According to Bradburn, *Paradise Lost* is

potentially subversive because it is fiction that carries the implication
of divine authority. Milton's text could replace authentic understanding of Christian doctrine—which is only to be found in the Bible—
with artistic speculation. The youngest daughter, Emily, wonders early
in the text if Milton's assertion that a toad (Satan in disguise) speaks
to Eve is "an untruth" since "nothing is said of a toad" in the Bible.
Mamma answers: "An untruth, my love, is anything that is said with an
intention to deceive. Now Milton never expected people would think
he related what you allude to as a fact: yet I feel a degree of fear, that
after hearing his account of the fall of man, &c, you will confound
fiction with truth, and think and speak of descriptions and discourses
in this poem, as if they were written by the inspiration of God, and,
therefore, to be believed" (7). Bradburn's text sends a double message: early exposure to Milton is a pleasure and a cultural necessity,
but a literal acceptance of Milton's story is potentially damaging to a
child's piety.

Here Bradburn draws on a notion of the dangers of the written
word that is at least as old as Plato. The written word can be misunder-
stood or misread as authoritative, and these misunderstandings may
go uncorrected. A dialogue, in contrast, provides the opportunity for
reflection and revision. In conversation with her children mamma can
check their understanding against her own and correct as necessary.

Throughout her version of the poem, Bradburn addresses the
issue with which Siddons and Rigby began: children's enjoyment and
understanding of the work. But whereas Siddons believed that the
sublimity of Milton's language will lead to virtue, Bradburn argues
that right understanding of the poem must precede an unadulterated
reading of the text. The reason for this is not the child's inability to enjoy Milton's poetry but the misunderstandings that might arise from
an independent reading. Mamma tells the three children: "When you
are acquainted with the story, I shall read to you many beautiful passages, for it is an advantage to have the ear early accustomed to the
sound of good poetry: and as Milton's language tends to improve the
style, I shall express myself as much as possible in his words, while attempting to give you in prose the substance of *Paradise Lost*" (14). In
fact, the majority of the text is mamma's prose rather than Milton's
poetry.[4] Whereas the children repeatedly return to a fascination with
Milton's language, mamma emphasizes its difficulty and her essential
role as mediator. Mamma is necessary to this text both to translate
ideas from one realm (Milton's *Paradise Lost*) to another (her parlor)

and to ensure that these ideas are properly understood. At the end of Bradburn's *Paradise Lost,* Eliza describes Milton's genius in terms of his ability to appeal to people of all ages: "That is what I call being truly clever. He writes poetry which is admired, mamma says, by the most wise and learned men, and by people who have real poetical taste; and yet when the sense of it is expressed in easy words, even children understand and like it very much" (67).[5] Although Bess Porter Adams may have found "this great poem much too difficult for young readers" (263) because she thought of Milton's language as integral to the poem, Bradburn's child characters testify otherwise. When imparted through the "easy words" of a sensitive re-teller, Bradburn insists, *Paradise Lost* can please "even children."

Paradoxically, however, Bradburn tells us that it is Milton's verse that has initially attracted the children, and they continue to plead for more of Milton's own poetry. Mamma's "easy words" may in fact be more useful as a way of shaping the children's understanding of Milton's story than they are a way of making the poetry accessible to them. William asserts, "I understand, too, and like very much the few lines of poetry you have repeated; they seem to give me the same kind of pleasure that music does" (13), and Eliza, who is allowed to hear more of Milton's verse because she is the oldest, remarks, "I have observed, mamma, that when I perfectly understand a good verse, it makes a deeper impression on my mind than the same sense does when expressed in prose; and I always remember it better" (99). The ability of *Paradise Lost,* through its poetry, to make a "deeper impression" on a child's mind emphasizes, for Bradburn, the importance of presentation. Bradburn's focus, then, is on explaining how to understand the poem correctly, so that it reinforces (rather than challenges) biblical truth.

Thus, Bradburn transforms a potential risk of reading *Paradise Lost* into an educational opportunity. Mamma's ability to use this poem both as positive and negative example succeeds largely because the impetus for this retelling is the children's own interest in the poem. Eliza provides a hint of the proper place of *Paradise Lost* in a child's education by reminding her mother that they will hear selections from *Paradise Lost* only occasionally, whereas they read from the Bible twice a day. William demonstrates his awareness of the relative importance of Miltonic and biblical texts with the assertion that "However entertaining books may be, I am determined never to believe anything in them which is contrary to the Bible" (9). Here Bradburn introduces another argument in defense of her project. She has Eliza point out that William cannot be so sure of his own powers of discernment. "But while you are a little boy, William, you might read and believe things without knowing they are false; so it is well you have some one to set you right. I think, mamma, it is better for you to tell us all Milton says, and explain in what respect he is wrong, than to miss those parts [that contradict the Bible]; for when we are old enough to read Paradise Lost, by ourselves, we might be puzzled at some things, without having an opportunity of asking you questions" (10). The opportunity to have their mother read *Paradise Lost* aloud and explain as she goes will serve as a kind of inoculation against the day when they will be old enough to read this epic alone. Bradburn warns her adult readers and parents: *Paradise Lost* is a powerful and potentially dangerous text; explain it to your children yourselves or run the risk that they will be entranced into forgetting that only the Bible is the authoritative source of Christian doctrine.

As Bradburn's text unfolds, we see that at several points in her retelling mamma is concerned to ensure that her children have properly understood a theological issue (the fortunate fall, Adam's relationship with Eve, Christ's relationship to the Father) and are aware of the epic's faults (Milton's depiction of the wicked and the heavenly angels). In fact, the dialogue begins with a caution about too enthusiastic a reception of Milton's theology. Mamma warns her children: "I shall begin with giving you the poet's account of a rebellion in heaven before the creation of the world; and I particularly wish you all to bear in mind that it is a fiction, and that something is said in it concerning Jesus Christ, which implies that he was not the great and eternal God, as St. Paul says he was" (8). This passage emphasizes a principle that will be repeated throughout Bradburn's text: when *Paradise Lost* and the Bible disagree, readers must remember that Milton's text is fiction, biblical text, truth.

Bradburn must concern herself, however, not only with Milton's explicit divergence from her reading of the Bible but also with nineteenth-century secular responses to *Paradise Lost*. The most famous such response is, of course, that of the Romantic poets who suggested that Satan is, in fact, the hero of the epic. Shelley writes (in *A Defense of Poetry*, 1821) that

> Milton's Devil as a moral being is as far superior to his God as one who perseveres in some purpose which he has conceived to be excellent in spite of adversity and torture, is to one who in the

cold security of undoubted triumph inflicts the most terrible revenge upon his enemy, not from any mistaken notion of inducing
him to repent of a perseverance in enmity, but with the alleged
design of exasperating him to deserve new torments. Milton has
so far violated the popular creed (if this shall be judged to be
a violation) as to have alleged no superiority of moral virtue to
his God over his Devil. And this bold neglect of a direct moral
purpose is the most decisive proof of the supremacy of Milton's
genius. (498)

Whereas Shelley shares Bradburn's assessment of Milton's literary excellence, his rationale emphasizes Milton's heresy over his Christianity. If when reading *Paradise Lost* we find ourselves sympathizing with
Satan and condemning God for his harshness, then Milton's Christian message has gone astray. Shelley's reaction to the poem—a typical Romantic response—was one that left nineteenth-century parents
who sought a Christian education for their children with a dilemma:
How might they help their children to learn from the virtues of *Paradise Lost* without risking moral disintegration?

Bradburn deals with this celebration of Satan by having mamma,
or one of her children, point out the moments where God appears
vindictive or Satan insufficiently miserable and contrast these images
with lines from the Bible. For example, after setting the scene for
Satan's disobedience (his jealousy of Christ), mamma describes Satan
before his fall with Milton's lines:

> Great indeed
> His name, and high was his degree in heaven;
> His countenance, as the morning star that guides
> The starry flock. (11)

She continues with her summary and follows it with Milton's own
words:

> He so successfully used his amazing powers of eloquence, that
> he infused bad influence into the minds of his associates and
> their inferior spirits, and with lies drew after him the third part
> of heaven's host.
>
> God the Father is then represented as making a speech to his
> blessed Son, in which are these lines:—

> Such a foe
> Is rising, who intends to erect his throne

Equal to ours, throughout the spacious north;
Nor so content, hath in his thought to try
In battle, what our power is, or our right.
Let us advise, and to this hazard draw
With speed what force is left, and all employ
In our defense, lest unawares we lose
This our high place.

Eliza is here the one to make the correction: "I do not like that, mamma. God never could have such a thought: he is, and must always have been *Almighty,* and therefore it is impossible he should have any fear of being conquered by the wicked angels" (11–12). Mamma agrees and continues with her narration, having succeeded in communicating to her children (and Bradburn's readers) both the beauty of Milton's verse and its theological pitfalls. Whereas Shelley and many of his contemporaries may have found in Satan the true hero of *Paradise Lost,* mamma sees him as the ultimate representative of "the abominable sin of unbelief" and claims that "to this day he tempts all people to disbelieve the power, the wisdom, or the mercy of God" (14). From mamma's viewpoint, a perspective such as Shelley's represents Satan's success on earth rather than plausible literary analysis.

In this debate over how to reconcile the place of Milton's epic in relation to the Bible, issues of knowledge and curiosity—so crucial to any reading of *Paradise Lost*—begin to surface. Eliza muses, "I never before thought what a mercy it is to have such a book as the Bible to which we can refer. It does not, certainly, always satisfy our curiosity about things which are not necessary for us to know, but it does not leave us in doubt how we are to be saved" (10). Though Eliza has yet to hear the story of Adam and Eve's fall, here she shows that she already shares their interests. Just as Raphael warns Adam in Book 8 of *Paradise Lost,* "Solicit not thy thoughts with matters hid, / Leave them to God above. . . . Think only what concerns thee and thy being; / Dream not of other worlds" (167–75), mamma warns her children against excessive questioning. At the moment of proclaiming her comfort in what the Bible does provide—the requirements for salvation—Eliza brings up what it does not provide—a salve for curiosity. Like Adam and Eve, Eliza is curious about things that she does not need to know. Their story can potentially allow her to exercise that curiosity without paying their price. There is a curious duality here: Eliza's emphasis on believing only the Bible is coupled with her admission that there are things she would like to know that she cannot learn from it. So *Para-*

dise Lost attracts these children not only because it is entertaining (its style) but because it provides information (the story). And although mamma's children are quick to assent to her commentary on Milton's heresies, the fact that she must explicitly remind them, for example, that Christ is co-equal with God and that there is no pleasure to be found in hell suggests that mamma's reading of *Paradise Lost* is not the only reading.

Bradburn repeatedly draws our attention to the beauty of Milton's verse and warns us against the dangers of a too-literal reading of his tale. Mamma is on one hand "highly gratified to observe you are all interested by the poem which, from childhood, has delighted me" (31) and, on the other, concerned that the story of *Paradise Lost* (which has led the children to consider playing at Satan, Death, and Sin) will intoxicate them with improper thoughts. (The children, like Shelley, find Milton's description of the fallen angels to be the most compelling source for their own imaginative play.) She tells them: "The fall of man is a most important subject, and nothing connected with it should be turned into a sport. I fear your minds have been too strongly excited the last few days with what you have heard; I am therefore rather pleased that it will not be in my power for some time to proceed with the story" (36).

By virtue of its attraction to children, *Paradise Lost* becomes a moral force not only for Milton's Christian message but for the doctrinal flaws in his depiction of the fall of man; these flaws allow Mamma to emphasize correct interpretation and use the book as a disciplinary tool: children who behave get to listen to the next installment of *Paradise Lost*. But although mamma is certainly able to maintain control over her children, both by explicating the text and by denying un-mediated access to it (these children hear *Paradise Lost,* but never read it themselves), Bradburn's description of reading *Paradise Lost* with children gives us a glimpse beyond the borders of the text and the confines of the parlor where mamma sits with her obedient children. As adult readers of *Paradise Lost* point out, the legacy of a childhood reading of Milton's epic continues long past childhood. It extends beyond the moment of reading, which mamma can control, to the ideas that reading inspires, which she can only attempt to control. We know that these children take this text with them as they leave mamma's physical domain. Whether her psychological and spiritual guidance will prove stronger than the power of Milton's language and themes remains in question.

The difference in strategy between Siddons's "abridgement" and

Bradburn's Paradise Lost, *For Children* reveals two ways of dealing with the extratextual effects of this poem. Siddons is more subtle: she simply removes passages and with them the ideas they might spawn. But Bradburn is already thinking ahead to future readings of *Paradise Lost* and chooses therefore to shape all readings of the poem by carefully structuring the first. What her concern demonstrates is that *Paradise Lost* is not necessarily a prop in the construction of Christian virtue. Bradburn is not alone in her concern, and as Ruth B. Bottigheimer points out, the Bible itself was refashioned in numerous way to support the cultural values of a given place in time. Bottigheimer's discussion of "the socializing uses to which religious narrative for children could be and have regularly been put" (xii) helps us see the almost inevitable need to refashion *Paradise Lost*. If even the Bible— that text to which Bradburn gives ultimate authority—can be shaped by the values and beliefs of a culture, how much more vulnerable is Milton's secular text? And Milton's epic came under increasing scrutiny in the nineteenth century as Milton's role as supreme literary and moral arbiter began to be challenged.[6] The publication of *Christian Doctrine* in 1825 (one hundred and fifty years after it was written) forced even the most generous of Milton's critics to admit that his theology could not be extolled with the same enthusiasm as his intellectual powers. In *Christian Doctrine* Milton aligns himself with Arianism, the religious belief that the Son is second rather than co-equal to God the Father. This is a position considered heretical by most nineteenth-century Christians and which Eliza Bradburn's father had specifically and dramatically denounced in 1779 (Blanshard 82–85). It is not surprising that Bradburn would begin her retelling of Milton's epic with a warning against his depiction of Father and Son.

She finishes her narration of *Paradise Lost* with a discussion of the faults of Milton's epic and the caution that "Great license is allowed to poets, but they should confine themselves to probability" (83). Though Milton manages to instill the most fantastic of events with a sense of inevitability, he does move outside of the realm of probability. His description of hell is insufficiently dismal, and particularly disturbing is the notion that the wicked angels could possibly enjoy themselves in hell. Milton writes,

> In discourse more sweet,
> (For eloquence the soul, song charms the sense)
> Others apart sat on a hill retired,

> In thoughts more elevate; and reason'd high
> Of Providence, &c.   (83)

The children provide both the critique of this passage and its biblical
antidote:

> William: It seems to me very unlikely, that where the land was
> firm fire, and the sea liquid flames, the wicked angels could
> sing[,] play on the harp, or have "sweet discourse."

> Eliza: It is enough to make one suppose, that after enduring
> the heat a great while, it becomes bearable; and that there is
> a possibility of even being entertained among the evil spirits. —
> O mamma, this is nothing like the spiritual account of hell.

> Mamma: Repeat, my dears, the verses you know, descriptive of
> this place or state of *everlasting punishment.*

> Eliza: It is called *the lake which burneth with fire and brimstone.*

> Emily: And *the bottomless pit.*

> William: It must be very dark; for you know, Eliza, you learned
> a verse about the angels being *reserved in everlasting chains, under
> darkness.* (83–84, emphasis in original)[7]

Similarly, mamma points out that Milton's concept of the angels still
in heaven is insufficiently refined, as in, for example, the scene where
the angels looking down from heaven laugh as the fallen angels are
confounded by the tower of Babel.

> Great laughter was in heaven,
> And looking down, to see the hubbub strange,
> And hear the din.   (85)

Mamma shifts the blame for these faults from Milton himself to "the
bad taste of the age in which he lived" (83) and implies thereby that
her own cultural context allows for a more accurate and more Christian understanding of the true nature of angels, both fallen and pure.

Bradburn's own context is not simply that of the early nineteenth
century. The success of this volume came because Bradburn was able
to please a more specialized public—advocates of the Methodist Sunday School Union. It is remarkable that Bradburn's Paradise Lost,
For Children was accepted for publication by the Methodist Sunday
School Press. In general, this press accepted only "thinly fictionalized,

real-life experiences," and the "books were meant for children's improvement, not their entertainment" (Gillespie 5). As the daughter of one of the early proponents of the Sunday School project, Bradburn was well aware of the expectations that organization had for children's books. That *Paradise Lost,* a fictional retelling of biblical history, was considered appropriate for this audience speaks to Milton's exceptional status in nineteenth-century culture; that Bradburn repeatedly cautioned the reader against confusing biblical truth with fiction speaks to a moral policy applied even to Milton.

But whereas Bradburn's perspective on the Trinity, hell, and angels follows in a conservative Methodist tradition, her perspective on Eve's place in Christian history is less conservative. In *The Bible for Children* Bottigheimer sees the depiction of Eve's responsibility for the Fall as an indicator of "sexist orientation." She writes: "If biting into the apple is viewed by an author or editor as the act that set the clock going for Jesus' eventual redemptive appearance, then transgressing God's prohibition and biting into the fruit of the tree of knowledge of good and evil has been portrayed as Adam's act. If, on the other hand, the fatal bite is interpreted solely as the precipitating event for the emergence of sin, death, and the loss of Paradise, then it has usually been argued that Eve alone was responsible" (205). Siddons simply removes the complexities of the fortunate fall (a focus on the notion that the Fall makes possible repentance and redemption) from her retelling of *Paradise Lost* by removing Adam's soliloquy on the wonder that sin has enabled his new understanding of God's grace:

> O goodness infinite, goodness immense!
> That all this good of evil shall produce,
> And evil turn to good; more wonderful
> Than that which by creation first brought forth
> Light out of darkness! Full of doubt I stand,
> Whether I should repent me now of sin
> By mee done and occasion'd, or rejoice
> Much more, that much more good thereof shall spring.
>   (*PL* 12:469–76)

This passage is crucial as a balance to one that comes about seventy-five lines later, where Adam tells us: "Henceforth I learn, that to obey is best, / And love with fear the only God" (12:561–62). The "good" that Adam celebrates in the first of these passages looks back to his and Eve's sin in book 9. There Eve names the forbidden tree "the tree of knowledge, knowledge both of good and evil" (9:751–52). Her description of the tree sets up the argument that we know good and evil simultaneously, that Adam's understanding of God's goodness comes only with a realization of his own disobedience. By removing Adam's celebration of the "Light out of darkness" from her abridgment of *Paradise Lost,* Siddons follows the second of the patterns Bottigheimer identifies: Eve remains primarily responsible for the Fall, and the Fall is primarily defined as the entrance of sin into the world rather than as an opportunity to know God's goodness.

Bradburn, on the other hand, focuses explicitly on both the fortunate fall and Eve's nature before and after the Fall. And rather than taking either of the paths that Bottigheimer describes as typical in children's Bibles, Bradburn insists both that the Fall was fortunate and that Eve was primarily responsible. In the dialogue that centers on how to understand the Fall, each child takes on a different theological perspective. William cries, "O, Mamma, I wish Adam and Eve had taken the kind angel's advice; how happy we might all have been at this very moment. . . . It is owing to their wickedness that we are all inclined to sin" (45). Emily has more compassion for Adam and Eve and expresses her relief that since someone had to be the first to sin, it wasn't she. Eliza introduces the position that the Fall, with the possibilities of grace and redemption it introduces, is in fact something to be grateful for: "For my part, if I get to heaven, I shall certainly be more thankful than I ever could have been, if I had always lived a holy life in Eden. Jesus Christ would not then have suffered and died for me; and of course I could not have loved him as my Redeemer" (45). Mamma reinforces the message of the fortunate fall with the assertion that no happiness could exceed that of "the bliss of a poor wretched sinner, who is received into the kingdom of heaven; because the Son of God, the Lord of life and glory, loved him so much as to suffer, in his stead, the dreadful punishment due to sin" (45–46). In the context of a culture that emphasized male superiority we might expect to find Adam responsible for the Fall in Bradburn's text. Instead, Bradburn's dialogue, with Eliza (the oldest daughter) as primary instigator, suggests a twentieth-century feminist preoccupation with Eve's role and rights in the poem.

Mamma's discussion of the Fall is located at the point in Milton's story where Raphael has entered Eden to educate Adam and Eve. Eliza shifts the focus of the dialogue from the Fall to Raphael's conversation with the question: "Is nothing said of Eve's talking with

the angel?" Mamma replies, "Milton tells us that Eve, as well as her
husband, was attentive to the story; but no mention is made of her
speaking in the presence of the angel" (46). In fact, mamma has little
actual support for Eve's attentiveness. In the course of Raphael's conversation with Adam (which spans books 5–8 of *Paradise Lost*) Eve
is mentioned only twice, first as she "Minister'd naked" (5:444) at
the feast set before Adam and Raphael and then as she withdraws
from "where she sat retir'd in sight" (8:41) to tend to her "Fruits
and Flowr's" (8:44). Despite the fact that mamma skims over almost
three books of *Paradise Lost* in six pages of dialogue, she does include
both mentions of Eve. And just as Eliza voices her discontent with
Eve's lack of participation as the conversation with Raphael begins,
so she complains that "I do not like her [Eve] going away, just as
if she had not sense enough to understand such conversation" (50).
Mamma provides Milton's explanation that "her husband the relator
she preferr'd / Before the angel" (50), but the subject does not end
here. Eliza calls even the doctrine of Eve's sin into question, saying:
"If God had not inspired Moses to write the account of her disobedience, I should think it a most improbable thing that Eve believed
a serpent rather than the Lord" (55). Eliza suggests that the problem
is mistranslation, a speculation that mamma is quick to squash both
in word—"In general I do not like to hear the common translation
criticized, especially from the pulpit: it tends to raise doubts in the
minds of ignorant people respecting passages of importance" (56)—
and in deed—she ends the day's telling "to prepare for the long walk
I promised to take you" (56). In Bradburn's version of the text, the
Fall centers around Eve's disobedience and her consequent temptation of Adam.

The result of Eliza's discomfort with Milton's portrayal of Eve is an
extended discussion of Eve's relation to Adam before and after the
Fall. Eliza argues that despite the moments in Milton's epic where
Eve appears to be inferior to Adam, she is in fact his equal until God
pronounces her punishment: to "bring forth children in sorrow, and
to submit to her husband's will" (61). Mamma agrees with Eliza's assessment (as does the youngest child, Emily) and goes a step further,
quoting from an unnamed source: "'In the creation, Adam and Eve
were formed with equal rights, and the woman had as much right
to *rule* as the man; but subjection to the will of her husband is one
part of her curse; and so very capricious is this will often, that a sorer
punishment no human being can well have . . .'" (62, emphasis in

original). In the context of other nineteenth-century renditions of the Fall, Bradburn's emphasis on the Fall as fortunate (she does include Adam's "Light out of darkness" soliloquy), Eve's responsibility for that fall, and the horrors of Eve's curse amounts to a radical revision of sexual politics. In Bradburn's retelling, Eve not only is responsible for the *fortunate* fall, but her curse is the means of criticizing a social order that authorizes a woman's subjection to her husband.

Bradburn thus uses *Paradise Lost* both to support her own theology and to critique her culture. Throughout her text, the focus is on the potential that a dialogue on *Paradise Lost* offers for education—a perspective appropriate to Milton's own goals in the poem. Milton uses two angelic narrators, Raphael and Michael, to teach Adam and Eve (and the reader). Bradburn uses "mamma" to impart information and shape her children's understanding of that information. The method of *Paradise Lost* would seem to be one entirely in accord with the nineteenth-century desire to educate as well as its suspicion about the effects of education. Yet, as Kathleen Swaim has pointed out, each angelic teacher uses a different method to instruct his pupils, suiting his educational theory to the lapsarian state of Adam and Eve.

Whereas Raphael can ground his instruction in Adam and Eve's innocence and appreciation for the wonders that surround them, Michael must move the postlapsarian Adam from a state of despair and disorder to the willingness to actively pursue Truth. The pre- and postlapsarian approaches to education that we see in *Paradise Lost* parallel the two strategies Milton lays out in his prose works *On Education* and *Areopagitica.* Whereas *On Education* suggests a course of study for children and youths that relies first on visible things and progresses from that understanding to a grasp of the invisible, *Areopagitica* insists that knowledge cannot be instilled but must be discovered by the individual. As Swaim argues, prelapsarian Adam and Eve are very like the children Milton seeks to educate in *On Education;* postlapsarian Adam and Eve must choose for themselves much as Milton would have adults judge information without censorship. Like the fallen Adam and Eve, the adult who would have knowledge must be willing to question the beliefs that form the basis of that knowledge. As Milton writes in *Areopagitica,* "Truth is compared in Scripture to a streaming fountain; if her waters flow not in a perpetual progression, they sicken into a muddy pool of conformity and tradition. A man may be a heretic in the truth; and if he believe things only because his pastor says so, or the Assembly so determines, without knowing other reason, though his belief be true, yet the very truth he holds becomes his heresy" (739). Milton suggests here that Truth cannot be told; it must be learned and kept current through questioning and research. Although he certainly believes in the primacy and ultimate authority of the Bible, he asserts the need for the individual to interpret Scripture.

Paradise Lost demands of its adult readers skepticism and self-questioning, but is the same true for child readers? If children are to begin with "solid things"—facts that can be memorized without being open to question—does the exhortation to exercise "faith and knowledge" apply to those who are at the very beginning of the learning process? Milton's description of the goal of education in *On Education* focuses more on ends than it does on means. He writes: "The end of learning is to repair the ruins of our first parents by regaining to know God aright, and out of that knowledge to love him, to imitate him, to be like him, as we may the nearest by possessing our souls of true virtue, which being united to the heavenly grace of faith makes up the highest perfection" (631). Raphael admonishes prelapsarian Adam to "think only that which concerns thee and thy being" as he distinguishes between the body of knowledge that is allowed Adam and Eve and that which is accessible to the angels and God. The parallel between these two kinds of knowledge and adult and childhood knowledge suggests that children are to learn what they are offered but not to experiment with knowledge that is properly that of an adult world. From this perspective, *Paradise Lost* can be told to children as a moral tale like the didactic tales of the early nineteenth century. Adam and Eve, as the children of the story, disobey their Father, are racked with physical and emotional pains, and are exiled from his house. This is the reading of *Paradise Lost* that reinforces a simple moral lesson and that suits the child in need of "solid things." It is not the reading that meets Milton's own strategy for avoiding heresy: "if he believe things only because his pastor says so . . . though his belief be true, yet the very truth he holds becomes his heresy." Presumably, the reader of *Paradise Lost* is not to trust its narrator any more than he does his pastor. Whatever truth Milton's retelling of biblical history offers, it is accessible only to the questioning reader.

It is a belief that even young children can profit from an investigation into Milton's epic that motivates Eliza Bradburn's retelling of *Paradise Lost*. But *On Education* proposes that students be introduced to great religious poetry only after several years of study—a perspective more in keeping with Bess Porter Adams's assessment of the poem than Bradburn's manipulation of it. Milton writes in *On Education* that the delay before introducing poetry "would make [the students] soon perceive what despicable creatures our common rhymers and play-writers be, and show them what religious, what glorious and magnificent use might be made of poetry, both in divine and human things" (637). The students to whom Milton refers are boys between the ages of twelve and twenty-one, and the reading of religious poetry comes at the end of the nine-year course of study he lays out. So for Milton, the very concept of reshaping a religious poem to make it fit for young children is nonsensical. Although he and Eliza Bradburn would probably agree about the goals of a child's education, they disagree about how—and when—to achieve this end.

Milton would argue that the poem can be understood only after mastery of the "solid things": grammar, languages (Latin, Greek, Hebrew), mathematics, agriculture, natural philosophy, moral philosophy, economics, and Scripture. The ability to judge right from wrong, to decipher the paradoxes that *Paradise Lost* forces us to experience, to consider the epic from a postlapsarian perspective, comes only after years of education.

Bradburn proposes that the epic is of great enough cultural significance to justify reformatting it for the education and enjoyment of much younger children (the eldest of mamma's children is ten). But she also recognizes that the poem requires a new format if it is to engage children actively. Rather than simply shortening Milton's epic structure, as Siddons does, Bradburn shapes the poem into a dialogue that can function as a catechism. This allows her not only to increase a child's enjoyment of the poem (through the story of a mother conversing with her children) but also to insist on the necessity for engagement with a text. Her strategy here matches that of many advocates of the catechism as a means of fulfilling a parent's duty toward his or her children. As Patricia Demers reflects, "it seems to me that the catechism, whether dialogue, picture, or sermon, has always been a springboard for more advanced or interpretive expressions. . . . Far from being inhibiting, the catechetical preliminaries enlist learners in the ranks of those seeking, finding, and, at times, making their own answers" (57). From this perspective Bradburn is able to fulfill Milton's ultimate goal for education with an audience much younger than the one he addresses. Mamma's insistence that the children refer to the Bible to support her critique of Milton's

theology, her explicit condemnation of Satan and the temptation he
represents, Eliza's questioning of Eve's role in the poem, and the children's discussion of the fortunate fall all point toward a strategy that
asks that children involve themselves with the poem. According to
C. John Sommerville, by the seventeenth century "both the opponents and proponents of catechizing had, it seems, accepted as their
goal the religious development rather than the religious stasis of the
child" (138), and this trend had gathered force and momentum by
the nineteenth century. At the same time, while a dialogue format
provides a model of textual interaction, it also allows the translator—
in this case Eliza Bradburn—to harness the force of a powerful literary document for her own ends.

Associated with nature and thus purity, nineteenth-century children were expected to need a different kind of stimulus than the
adults around them.[8] They also required careful guardianship as they
entered into a world of sin. The innocence that protected them as
babies needed to be replaced with a careful moral code as they passed
through childhood to adulthood. Thus, whereas Milton wrote *Paradise Lost* for adults (and considered religious poetry suitable only for
the already educated youth) and encouraged his readers to experience the Fall with Adam and Eve—to acknowledge their own falls as a
way of comprehending the first sin and repentance—Eliza Bradburn
transforms Milton's text into a safer one, a less controversial retelling
of biblical history. The boundaries Bradburn provides for children
reading *Paradise Lost* are consistent with the strategies Milton sets up
for Adam and Eve's prelapsarian education and that of children in *On
Education:* they attempt to protect children from falling, even fiction-
ally. Mamma's transformation of epic into dialogue and catechism
acts as a safety net that aims at protecting children from the power of
not only this first reading but all readings of *Paradise Lost.*

Bradburn's text remains in the realm of prelapsarian education
as the child characters she creates question and recite within the
boundaries of mamma's careful catechism. Bradburn makes Milton's
revolutionary poem accessible to a much younger audience than he
intended; she simultaneously privileges prelapsarian obedience over
the streaming—and uncontrolled—fountain of postlapsarian truth.
As Raphael warns Adam to "solicit not thy thoughts with matters hid, /
Leave them to God above," Bradburn has mamma identify "what it
is necessary for us to know." Yet Raphael's admonition to "dream not
of other worlds" introduces both the possibility of dreaming and the

existence of other knowledge even as it seeks to restrict access. By reshaping "the story of our first parents" to focus on Satan's disobedience and man's salvation rather than "man's first disobedience / And the fruit of that forbidden tree," Bradburn creates a model of textual interpretation that goes beyond conservative theology to cultural critique. Although the structure of Bradburn's text insists on obedience, its content celebrates the consequences of curiosity and reveals the existence of (forbidden) other worlds. The "legacy" of a childhood reading of Paradise Lost, *For Children* moves beyond the virtue to be gained from exposure to sublime language to a confrontation with the possibilities as well as the restrictions of textual interpretation.

Notes

1. For a detailed analysis of Milton's influence on adults in the nineteenth century, see Leslie Brisman, *Milton's Poetry of Choice and Its Romantic Heirs,* James G. Nelson, *The Sublime Puritan: Milton and the Victorians,* and George F. Sensabaugh, *Milton in Early America.* For close textual evidence of Milton's influence on the Romantics, see Joseph Wittreich's *The Romantics on Milton.*

2. Although Lee Jacobus has analyzed Milton's *Comus* as an example of children's literature, *Paradise Lost* has not been critically discussed as a book read by children. Milton's epic is usually completely ignored in twentieth-century anthologies and encyclopedias of children's literature; when mentioned, the poem is used as an example of epic form rather than discussed in terms of its literary merit. Bess Porter Adams writes in *About Books and Children* that "The best of the modern literary epics is *Paradise Lost* by John Milton, the great literary figure of the Puritan period in England. . . . This great poem is much too difficult for young readers. Indeed it proves a sort of literary obstacle course to adults, if they have not acquired a background in the Bible and in classical mythology; however, there are memorable passages to repay the lover of poetry when he is ready to read them" (263). This is the most detailed description of *Paradise Lost* to appear in a twentieth-century discussion of children's literature. What Adams demonstrates, in part, is the difference between nineteenth- and twentieth-century readers. The background in the Bible that she considers an achievement for an adult reader would be expected of the nineteenth-century child reader. And any reader of the nineteenth century would look to find in *Paradise Lost* more than "memorable passages."

3. Eliza Weaver Bradburn's *The Story of Paradise Lost, For Children* was published in London (1828); printed in Portland, Maine, by Shirley and Hyde (1830); and reprinted four times in New York for the Sunday School Union of the Methodist Episcopal Church: by J. Emory and B. Waugh (1831), by Lane and Scott (1848, 1851), and by Carlton and Porter (1856).

4. Mamma claims that Milton's text is more appropriate for her oldest child than it is for her younger children; access to unadulterated text comes only with education. As *Paradise Lost, For Children* progresses, mamma relies more heavily on Milton's text. Whereas less than a quarter of the dialogue aimed at all three of the children is literal quotation from *Paradise Lost* (the proportion of Milton's words to mamma's increases even here as we move through the poem and the dialogue), in the last section, where mamma speaks privately with the oldest daughter, mamma reads verbatim her favorite passages from the epic without paraphrasing and with very little commentary.

5. Here Eliza paraphrases John Wesley's description of the value of Wesleyan hymns for children: "They contain strong and manly sense, yet expressed in such plain and easy language as even children may understand. But when they do understand them they will be children no longer, only in years and in stature" (*Works* 132).

6. For a detailed analysis of Milton's shifting status see George F. Sensabaugh, *Milton in Early America.*

7. The passages mamma and the children cite are primarily from the New Testament. See John 5.29, Mat. 25.46, Rom. 2.7, Rev. 21.8, 20.3, 17.8, 9.2, Jude 6.

8. I've found Karin Calvert's book, *Children in the House,* particularly useful for considering the differences between Puritan and nineteenth-century visions of childhood. Calvert interprets the material culture of childhood to come to general conclusions about changes in adult perspectives on childhood. She argues that before the middle of the eighteenth century "childhood was a period of inadequacy . . . maturity was a goal and a reward, no one looked back with much regret" (32), whereas nineteenth-century parents "accept[ed] the age's sentimental image of childish sweetness and innocence" and "sought physical barriers to protect their children from physical injury, temptation, and worldly contamination" (7–8). Just as the objects Calvert describes change to support the changing cultural image of children, the concept of how (or if) to present *Paradise Lost* to children shifts historically.

Works Cited

Adams, Bess Porter. *About Books and Children.* New York: Henry Holt, 1953.
Blanshard, Thomas W. *The Life of Samuel Bradburn, the Methodist Demosthenes.* London: Elliot Stock, 1870.
Bottigheimer, Ruth B. *The Bible for Children: From the Age of Gutenberg to the Present.* New Haven: Yale University Press, 1996.
Bradburn, Eliza Weaver. *The Story of Paradise Lost, For Children.* New York: Carlton and Porter, 1856.
Brisman, Leslie. *Milton's Poetry of Choice and Its Romantic Heirs.* Ithaca: Cornell University Press, 1973.
Calvert, Karin. *Children in the House: The Material Culture of Early Childhood, 1600–1900.* Boston: Northeastern University Press, 1992.
Campbell, Thomas. *Life of Mrs. Siddons.* London: Edward Moxon, 1839.
Cockshut, A. O. J. "Children's Diaries." In *Children and Their Books,* ed. Gillian Avery and Julia Briggs. Oxford: Clarendon, 1989. Pp. 381–98.
Cruse, Amy. *The Englishman and His Books in the Early Nineteenth Century.* London: George G. Harrap, 1930.
Demers, Patricia. *Heaven upon Earth: The Form of Moral and Religious Children's Literature, to 1850.* Knoxville: University of Tennessee Press, 1993.
De Quincey, Thomas. "On Milton." *Blackwoods Magazine* 46 (1839).
Gillespie, Joanna Bowen. "An Almost Irresistible Enginery: Five Decades of Nineteenth Century Methodist Sunday School Library Books." *Phaedrus* (spring-summer 1980): 5–12.
Jacobus, Lee. "Milton's *Comus* as Children's Literature." *Children's Literature* 2 (1973): 67–72.
Milton, John. *Complete Poems and Major Prose.* Ed. Merritt Hughes. New York: Macmillan, 1957.
Nelson, James G. *The Sublime Puritan: Milton and the Victorians.* Madison: University of Wisconsin Press, 1963.
Rigby, Elizabeth. "Children's Books." *Quarterly Review* 74 (1844): 1–26.
Sensabaugh, George F. *Milton in Early America.* Princeton: Princeton University Press, 1964.

Shelley, Percy Bysshe. "A Defense of Poetry." In *Shelley's Poetry and Prose,* ed. Donald H. Reiman and Sharon B. Powers. New York: Norton, 1977. Pp. 480–508.

Siddons, Sarah. *An Abridgement of* Paradise Lost. London: John Murray, 1822.

Sommerville, C. John. *The Discovery of Childhood in Puritan England.* Athens: University of Georgia Press, 1992.

Swaim, Kathleen M. *Before and After the Fall: Contrasting Modes in* Paradise Lost. Amherst: University of Massachusetts Press, 1986.

Wesley, John. *The Works of John Wesley.* Ed. F. Hildebrandt, O. A. Beckerlegge, and J. Dale. 7 vols. Oxford: Clarendon, 1983.

Wittreich, Joseph, ed. *The Romantics on Milton: Formal Essays and Critical Asides.* Cleveland: Press of Case Western Reserve University, 1970.

The "Omnipresent Aunt" and the Social Child: Lydia Maria Child's Juvenile Miscellany

Etsuko Taketani

> *NA-TION. Nation: people who are governed by the same laws, who live*
> *in the same country, and speak the same language, are called a* nation.
> —Eliza Robbins, *Primary Dictionary . . . for the*
> *Younger Classes in Schools* (1828)

The inaugural issue of the *Juvenile Miscellany* (September 1826), a pioneer in children's magazines,[1] inscribes in American history a moment in which children act as politically motivated social beings. In "The Little Rebels," for example, a drama "[f]ounded on fact" (48), colonial children in Boston claim from the British their right to fly kites and ice skate during the War of Independence. With this act, the children challenge their status as colonized objects and claim their position as self-governed subjects. As I will demonstrate, this drama and others like it in the *Juvenile Miscellany* significantly herald the conjunction of postcoloniality and American childhood.

As "The Little Rebels" suggests, the *Juvenile Miscellany* is marked by a decidedly nationalistic tenor,[2] a tenor that, furthermore, was primarily inscribed by women. Edited by Lydia Maria Child (1802–80), the periodical drew to its pages a number of popular women writers. Contributors included Eliza Leslie, Catharine Maria Sedgwick, Lydia Huntley Sigourney, Hannah Flagg Gould, Sarah Josepha Hale, Caroline Howard Gilman, and Anna Maria Wells (Karcher, *First Woman* 66–67). Child was also often a contributor, and she created for herself an alter ego known as "Aunt Maria."[3] As Thomas Wentworth Higginson later recalled in *Contemporaries* (1899), Child was an "omnipresent aunt, beloved forever by the heart of childhood" (108).

Children did indeed love "Aunt Maria" and her periodical. The popularity of the *Juvenile Miscellany* among children of the early national period was attested to by Caroline H. Dall in the *Unitarian Review* in 1883:

I would like to thank Patty Keefe Durso, Robert Levine, Carolyn Karcher, Ivy Goodman, and Victoria Clements, who read drafts of this essay. For numerous helpful comments I am indebted to Elizabeth Keyser and *Children's Literature*'s anonymous readers. *Children's Literature* 27, ed. Elizabeth Lennox Keyser (Yale University Press, © 1999 Hollins University).

No child who read the *Juvenile Miscellany* edited by [Lydia Maria Child] will ever forget the excitement that the appearance of each number caused. . . . The children sat on the stone steps of their house doors all the way up and down Chestnut Street in Boston, waiting for the carrier. He used to cross the street, going from door to door in a zigzag fashion; and the fortunate possessor of the first copy found a crowd of little ones hanging over her shoulder from the steps above. . . . How forlorn we were if the carrier was late! (525–26).

Although Child observed that subscriptions came in large part from the "rich and fashionable people" in Boston,[4] the children's republic founded in the *Juvenile Miscellany* does not duplicate that bourgeois social world of the northeastern United States. The "little rebels" in the periodical, for example, reproduce the nationalistic ideology of America's Founding Fathers by mimicking their own fathers' claim of independence, but the children's authority is ultimately limited. For the children in the *Juvenile Miscellany* are not always affiliated with their fathers, the dominant sociopolitical group, but are more often allied with marginalized groups such as Native Americans, Irish immigrants, free people of color, and women.

Child's concern with disenfranchised groups in general is well known. Indeed, as Carolyn L. Karcher observes, "Twice during her eight-year tenure as editor," Child "risked her reputation by espousing the cause of [racial] Others": first, with the 1829 publication of *The First Settlers of New England,* which attacked the U.S. government's Indian policy, and second, with the 1833 publication of *An Appeal in Favor of That Class of Americans Called Africans,* which crusaded against slavery (Karcher, *First Woman* 151–52).

I am particularly intrigued, however, by the effect of the association of children with "racial Others" in Child's *Juvenile Miscellany* and the way in which the figure of the child emerges as an "Other" in the early national period. The magazine, I suggest, politicizes the relation between adults and children by aligning children with marginalized groups, thereby both explicitly and implicitly offering a critique of domestic colonialism. In a familial representation of American society, the children function as the disenfranchised, held under the patriarchal custody of the dominant, enfranchised group. In this respect, I argue, provocative stories in the *Juvenile Miscellany* such as "The Little Rebels," "The Irish Emigrants," and "Mary French and Susan Easton" deploy the Otherness of children for a political end: to challenge the colonization of socially disruptive Others by and within a patriarchal, familial framework.

Children and Mimicry

As mentioned above, "The Little Rebels" is a drama about colonial children—the king's juvenile subjects—who act out their own American Revolution by mimicking the revolutionary fathers. Through this mimicry, the children reject their position as colonized objects and declare themselves independent subjects of history. Furthermore, as I illustrate below, at the same time that the "little rebels" mimic their Founding Fathers through the actions they take, they claim allegiance with Native Americans through the flag that they carry, thereby subverting the colonialist framework in which they operate.

In "The Little Rebels," a crowd of boys gathered around the skating pond on the Boston Common discover that the ice has been broken by the British soldiers. The boys now view these soldiers, accordingly, as transgressors. Lamenting their powerlessness in the face of such an outrage, one of the boys, James, remarks, "I wish we were not boys. If I were big enough to carry a sword and a musket, I would drive 'em out of the land" (48). Another, George, manfully advocates the inalienable rights of children: "And what if we are boys? I, for one, have no mind to bear this treatment any longer" (48). In response to this revolutionary assertion by George—who functions in this drama largely as George Washington—the boys form a procession and march toward the headquarters of General Howe.

Seeing the marching troop of a hundred boys preceded by drum and fife, the British sentinel, with a gun over his shoulder, wonders, "Are they up in arms again, in this rascally town? . . . An Indian painted on their flag, and no sign of the English Cross" (51). When they arrive at the British tent, young George, "with the standard in his hand" (51), asks for the general.

George: Is General Howe at home?

Sentinel: Who are you?

George: We are Boston boys, sir.

Sentinel: And what do you want here?

George: We come for our rights; and we wish to speak to the British general.

Sentinel: The British general has better business than listening to a parcel of ragamuffin little rebels; I shall do none of your messages.

George: As you please, sir; but here we wait till we see General Howe. We *will* see him; and he *shall* do us justice.

All: Hurra! hurra! hurra! (51)

The sentinel, offended by the children's audacity, threatens them with abusive words: "That, you little rascals, would be to hang you, and your cowardly countrymen" (51–52). When General Howe steps out of the tent at the sound of the disturbance, George—speaking for the rights of the colonized—presents their complaint to the general. The British soldiers, George charges, "break our kite strings, ruin our skating pond, and steal our drums from us" (52). Surprised at the "little rebels," General Howe cries, "Good Heavens! liberty is in the very air, and the boys breathe it" (52).

Although this scene seems to enact the American Revolution in microcosm, an illustration of the encounter between the sentinel and the troop of children (figure 1) does more than aid the child reader's understanding of the drama—it also points to another layer of the story. Significantly, the engraving does not depict either the American or the British national flag. Instead, the illustration of the colonial encounter between the British sentinel and the children's army foregrounds the sentinel's gun, which signifies patriarchal power and control over the children, and the children's standard, depicting a Native American drawing a bow, which points to their marginalized status as Others and alliance with "racial Others" such as Native Americans.

The children rebel against British despotism and patriarchy by claiming their rights; their relation to the British in this drama undergoes a substantial change, however, when General Howe appears. Howe, a paternal figure with authority, honors the children's right to play and promises that their "sports shall never be disturbed again, without punishment to the offender" (52). The general then asks patronizingly, "Does that satisfy you?" (52), to which a grateful George answers, "Yes, General Howe; and in the name of my company I present you thanks" (52). Howe thus gives the "rebels" exactly what they demanded. But by conferring on the children a right to their pond, the British general essentially invents an Other *within* his territory, thereby unwittingly contributing to the emergence of a republic of American children. Howe, impressed by the courage of the

Is General Howe at Home?.....Page 51.

Figure 1. From Lydia Maria Child, "The Little Rebels," *Juvenile Miscellany* 1.1 (September 1862). Rare Book and Special Collections, Library of Congress.

children, calls them brave "English" boys, in response to which they unanimously proclaim, "No sir, Yankees—Yankees—Hurra! Hurra!," as they march off "with flying colors" (53). Thus, in their rebellion, the Yankee boys band together as a body politic, through which they successfully define and regain their social territory.

At first glance, "The Little Rebels" would seem to recapitulate the nationalistic ideology of the Founding Fathers. Yet it is important to note that the boys do not faithfully duplicate the Founding Fathers' political acts. As noted above, the children in the story carry a flag depicting a Native American; in this way, they act as representatives of the disenfranchised. The voice of the colonial children in this 1826 drama is more subversive than playful, for this voice effectively alludes to and supports the inalienable rights of Native Americans, who were fighting at that same time against the federal government.[5] The children in "The Little Rebels" thus do not simply role-play as revolutionaries. Instead, their drama enacts the reinvention, in the American political arena, of Native Americans as children—as an Other—who dare to claim independence from their "father."

In the 1820s the Indians came to be viewed not simply as children to be governed (as the colonists considered them to be) but as children (the Other) who dared to claim independence *within* the U.S. territories. In order to counter such revolutionist acts on the part of the Indians (who thus subversively mimic the Founding Fathers), Presidents John Quincy Adams and Andrew Jackson tried to depoliticize them as "children of nature" or "children of the forest." In his fourth annual message (1828) to "Fellow-Citizens of the Senate and of the House of Representatives," John Quincy Adams said: "In the practice of European States, before our Revolution, [Indians] had been considered *as children* to be governed . . . [but now] we have unexpectedly found them forming in the midst of ourselves communities claiming to be independent of ours and rivals of sovereignty within the territories of the members of our Union" (Richardson 416, emphasis in original). In that same message, however, Adams tactfully refers to them as "children of *nature*" (Richardson 416; emphasis added).

Andrew Jackson, who succeeded Adams the following year, characterizes Native Americans in much the same way as Adams. In his first annual message, Jackson asks, "Would the people of Maine permit the Penobscot tribe to erect an independent government within their State? . . . Would the people of New York permit each remnant of the Six Nations within her borders to declare itself an independent people under the protection of the United States? Could the Indians establish a separate republic on each of their reservations in Ohio?" (Richardson 457). Furthermore, in his second annual message Jackson calls them "children of the forest" (Richardson 523), just as General Howe in Child's "The Little Rebels" tried to pat the colonial children on the head, sending them back to their proper sphere (pond) and away from the battlefield (politics).

On May 28, 1830, the Indian Removal Act was approved by Congress. The federal government subsequently forced the "colonization" of the Cherokee Indians in the territories west of the Mississippi. As Anthony F. C. Wallace points out, "By the 1820s, the term 'colonization' had become a popular label for the concept of solving social problems by the physical removal of undesirables" (39).

The figure of the child in the presidential messages noted above serves as an ideological apparatus to effect this colonization of Indians: when social minorities are represented as children under the paternal guardianship of the enfranchised, the hierarchical relationship that subordinates such minorities is made to appear natural rather than political. The parent-child analogy thus effectively effaces the violence of conquest and, at the same time, works to make what was ultimately a forced act appear natural.

Lydia Maria Child's "The Little Rebels" challenges this naturalization by aligning the colonial children, through the painting on their flag, with Native Americans. In 1824, two years before the publication of the story, Child published *Hobomok,* a novel that critiqued patriarchy and racism, and in 1828 Child and her husband David Lee Child "actively campaign[ed] against Andrew Jackson's Cherokee removal scheme, as well as against the war still being waged on the Seminoles in Florida" (Karcher, Hobomok *and Other Writings* 153). Child's "The Little Rebels," like *Hobomok* and her campaign for the Cherokees and the Seminoles, illustrates her support for the rights of marginalized groups. The Indian painted on the flag in "The Little Rebels" represents a silenced Other, written out of the nation, an Other to whom the colonial children give political voice through mimicry of the Founding Fathers. Thus children's mimicry significantly, if implicitly, subverts the colonialist discourse that operates in the 1820s.

Bourgeois Containment

In "The Little Rebels," Lydia Maria Child scripted a political drama in and through which American children emerge as historical subjects. The progress from the colonized object to the independent subject, however, is not as sequential or linear as Child's drama suggests. "The Irish Emigrants" (contributed by "L." from Rhode Island), published in the *Juvenile Miscellany* in 1830, unpacks, albeit unwittingly and more subtly than "The Little Rebels," the continuing process of children's ideological subjugation.

In "The Irish Emigrants," Henry, a young American boy, is imbued with Anglocentric xenophobia, which manifests itself particularly in a hatred of the Irish. Interestingly, as the author emphasizes, such xenophobia is represented largely through Henry's appropriation— or misappropriation—of a word his father uses. As I illustrate below, however, Henry's (mis)appropriation of the discourse of patriarchy ultimately, and ironically, links Henry with a young Irish immigrant child. Thus, as in "The Little Rebels," colonialist discourse is both reproduced and critiqued through the agency of children. Yet the closure of "The Irish Emigrants," as I show, suggests that Henry's xenophobia is actually rechanneled into a subtler form—that of bourgeois containment.

In "The Irish Emigrants," Henry and his sister Laura notice a little boy sitting on the steps as they amuse themselves on a January morning by sliding on a frozen piazza before school. Bare-legged and pale, the boy is apparently suffering from poverty and cold. Henry asks the stranger where he came from.

"Ireland," was the reply.

"Oh, you are an Irish vagabond; you had better run off," said Henry, with an air of consequence; "for my father don't like the Irish, at all."

The little boy's heart seemed full; but he only said as he walked away, "I am no vagabond; but a poor Irish boy seeking work, or food." (230–31)

Henry cannot resist "a desire to appear important" (231) in children's society by echoing his father's Anglocentric ethnic biases.

Laura later brings food for the Irish boy, only to find that he has left. When she asks her brother where the boy has gone, Henry answers, "Oh, *I sent him away*, Laura; you know Pa don't like the Irish at all. He says the country is *nundated* with them" (231, emphasis in original). Henry reproduces the father's vocabulary, dropping the *i* from the word *inundated*. On hearing the father's word thus spoken by Henry, Laura laughs and says, "*nundated!* what does that mean, master Henry?" (231). Henry, who plays "master" in children's society, then rehearses his patriarchal lines: "Pa said, only yesterday, that he wished there could be some stop put to the constant—something,— 'twas a big word, I never heard before but I know it meant bringing the Irish here; for he said, the country was *nundated* with them" (232). It is largely the father's "big word" that generates xenophobia in Henry and helps to create a juvenile power structure in this fictional children's republic.

Henry's father, Mr. Campbell, however, may or may not have used the term *inundated* with a nativist sentiment the previous day. When Henry and Laura come back from the piazza, Mr. Campbell asks Mrs. Campbell, together with John (a servant), to take a basket of wood and bread to an Irish family in the neighborhood. He had heard a tale of misery from an old grandmother he had met that day who was "a real object of charity," but Mr. Campbell at that time had "had nothing, but a large bill in [his] pocket" (233). He suggests to his wife that Henry and Laura should also go because "it may be useful for them to see by contrast how blessed their lot is" (233).

When the children and their mother visit the Irish family, who live in a cellar, their eyes meet a scene of misery characterized by "sickness and death" (236)—a scene that horrifies the American children. The Irish mother sobs, "Nobody cares for an Irish beggar" (236). Even her boy, who looks as "young and innocent-like" (236) as an American child, is marked by the social distinctions that work in the adult world. The Irish mother laments, "My poor old mother has been out seeking food for us these two days; and she has scarce got enough to keep us from starving, madam. This morning I sent Willy, there, thinking he was so young and innocent-like, nobody would be for calling him a cheat; but he was not used to the trade, ma'am; for as he sat trying to get courage to tell his story, a little boy sent him off, because his father hated the Irish" (236). Henry, with guilty tears in his eyes, confesses to his mother that it is he who dismissed Willy: "Oh, mother, that was I! Yes it was; I was so foolish as to think I understood father's conversation with uncle James; and I told him to run away" (236–37).

This tale ends rather expectedly with a moral—the importance of charity. The American children's visit to the Irish immigrant household is useful not so much because the predicament of the Irish family is alleviated but because the visit teaches the American children a lesson. The narrator emphasizes this, noting that "Laura and Henry never forgot the lesson they learnt from this poor family"— the lesson, that is, that they should be "kind, to their inferiors, and generous to the poor" (238). Noting that the Irish boy "flushed with pleasure" when Henry offered his hand, begging forgiveness in tears, the narrator observes, "So easy is it for the rich to give pleasure to the poor" (237). The virtue of a charitable heart sanctioned at the tale's end does not call into question the social distinctions that mark rich and native-born as superior and poor and immigrant as inferior. If anything, the closure of this tale, with its emphasis on benevolent paternalism, reinforces rather than unwrites the social hierarchy.

This hierarchy is also reinforced when Mrs. Campbell questions her Irish counterpart, asking, "Why didn't you apply to the alms-house?" (237), for this question calls attention to immigrant pauperism and its association with immorality, supposedly evidenced by intemperance and other antisocial behaviors. According to E. M. Guion, clerk of the alms-house in New York City, in an 1835 report, "The whole number of paupers supported in the Alms-House, during the year 1833, was 5,179," a number that is largely attributed to immigrants, for a "great number of aliens . . . are continually pouring into the city from all quarters, and their confirmed habits of intoxication are such, that if either head of a large family gets out of employ, they almost immediately come on the public for support" (Chipman 40–41). This association of immigrants with pauperism and immorality is illustrated in "The Irish Emigrants," when, for instance, the young Irish boy knocks on the door of a large house and the servant cries, "Get about your business, you little thieving paddy!" (237), as if stealing is inherent in his ethnicity and his poverty.

Nevertheless, according to the story's boastful narrator, "there is no place in the world where the people are more liberal to the poor than in New-York" (238). Indeed, once their need is known, the Irish family is "supplied with every necessary" and a plan is "devised to give them employment" by which to support themselves (238). New York, observes the historian M. J. Heale, "probably nurtured more such enterprises [as associated benevolence] than any other community"; the city embraced "societies to treat the sick, teach the children of the poor, aid widowed mothers . . . [and] find work for needy women" ("City Fathers" 23). But as much as the establishment of humanitarian institutions for the urban poor[6] was an act of benevolence, it was also, notes Heale, a way "of maintaining order in a mobile society" unsettled by the arrival of immigrants, "who now seemed to constitute an alien class," a class that respectable citizens regarded "with growing alarm" ("Patterns of Benevolence" 339, 347, 338). Those who provided management for these benevolent societies were merchants, lawyers, bankers, insurance brokers, and other wealthy businessmen, all playing the role of "city fathers," reinforcing the familial patriarchal framework that casts marginalized Others as children. The city fathers "sought to encompass the whole community within their benevolent embrace and to improve in a variety of ways the quality of urban life without disrupting the social structure from which they benefited" ("City Fathers" 41).

A father figure is notably absent from the Irish family in "The Irish Emigrants." The family is made up of a slender, pale mother with a sick infant in her arms, two other children, and an old grandmother. Significantly, then, the tale makes it clear that the family will manage to subsist only under the care of the city fathers, only through the paternalistic government of the rich that is represented by Mr. Campbell. The Irish immigrants are, in effect, orphans. This is clearly dramatized as the grandmother "sob[s] like an infant" (238) in gratitude for the aid the family receives. The humanitarianism prescribed by the tale employs the trope of an orderly (that is, patriarchal) family to make the social hierarchies unproblematic.

In this context, Henry's act of pretending to have mastered his father's word—"inundated"—so that he might appear important and consequential speaks to the paternalistic underpinnings of antebellum urban reform. The difference between the father's word—"inundated"—and the child's—"nundated"—does not simply demonstrate the child's misunderstanding of language. This child who drops the *i* from *inundated* uncritically and unselfconsciously mimics his father's sense of ethnic superiority and attitude of paternalism. The dropped *i* signifies loss of self and individuality; Henry was not thinking for himself but thinking as his father.

Rather than honoring this paternalism, however, "The Irish Emigrants" calls it into question. For Henry ultimately learns not to mimic his father without being sure of what he is saying: "Henry was careful never to repeat any of his father's observations, without being sure he perfectly understood them" (238). Even so, despite his more benevolent perspective, Henry's subjectivity remains restricted by the discourse of patriarchy. For Henry will simply replace xenophobic denunciation with bourgeois benevolence, which is no less pernicious. The tale suggests that Henry grows up only to assume the paternalistic prerogative of the ruling class that oversees "charitable" bourgeois society. In the end, it is this paternalism that seeks to contain Willy—the Irish immigrant Other—in a hegemonic familial framework, a framework in which Willy is destined to play the part of a perpetual child and Henry his benevolent father.

"Free" Children as Currency

"The Irish Emigrants" ultimately fails to critique domestic colonialist control. The violence of subjugation is not only effectively masked, operating as it does under the guise of bourgeois benevolence, but Henry and Willy, the American and Irish immigrant children, are concomitantly entrapped by "benign" colonialism as ruler and ruled, respectively. Lydia Maria Child's "Mary French and Susan Easton," which appeared in the *Juvenile Miscellany* in 1834, however, unmasks the very repressive strategies and practices that "The Irish Emigrants" attempts to make invisible.

"Mary French and Susan Easton" is a story of two kidnapped children. Mary, who is white, and Susan, who is black, live on "the western shores of the Mississippi River" and have only each other as playmates (186). The girls are kidnapped by a peddler and sold as slaves, and only one of them—Mary—is later recovered. Susan, the daughter of freed blacks, is forever lost; the child is literally remade into a slave.

To all appearances, Susan is an innocent victim of the domestic slave trade in the United States. As Carol Wilson observes, the domestic slave trade in antebellum America endangered innumerable free blacks, who "existed in legal limbo, neither slave nor citizen" (41). The "kidnapping of free blacks for sale as slaves was prohibited in most states, including those in the South": "Vermont enacted the first state antikidnapping law in 1787, and all northern states except Rhode Island followed with similar legislation. The majority of northwestern territories followed suit as they gained statehood. Five slave states (Delaware, Virginia, Tennessee, Georgia, Mississippi), as well as the District of Columbia, also had antikidnapping laws" (67–8). And yet, notes Wilson, kidnapping "flourished despite its illegality" (67) because of the economic temptations of the slave market.

According to a report submitted by the Committee on the Domestic Slave Trade of the United States to the New England Anti-Slavery Convention in May 1834 "the kidnapping of freemen is common all over this country, and prevails to an extent of which few are aware" ("Report" 90). The report was signed by D. Lee Child—Lydia Maria Child's husband—and four others. The committee resolved that "the Domestic Slave Trade of the United States is equally atrocious in the sight of God with the foreign, that it equally involves the crimes of murder, kidnapping and robbery, and is equally worthy with the foreign to be denounced and treated by human laws and tribunals as piracy, and those who carry it on as enemies of the human race" (91). Lydia Maria Child's "Mary French and Susan Easton," published concurrently with this report, pursues the same political agenda—that is, it indicts the domestic slave trade, particularly as it fostered kidnapping.[7]

As the author of *An Appeal in Favor of That Class of Americans Called Africans* (1833), Child, in "Mary French and Susan Easton" and other writings, gives a distinct voice to the free people of color of the antebellum North, people whose existence is often either rendered invisible or, at best, linked with that of slaves. "Mary French and Susan Easton," then, should be differentiated from Harriet Beecher Stowe's *Uncle Tom's Cabin* and other children's antislavery literature in that it specifically addresses the plights of free people of color.[8] Yet "Mary French and Susan Easton," it would seem, fails to offer a solution, except through, in the words of Karen Sánchez-Eppler, "the obliteration of blackness" (31). The concluding remarks of Child's story moralize that "the only difference between Mary French and Susan Easton is, that the black color could be rubbed off from Mary's skin, while from Susan's it could not" (202). "Despite her clear desire for a different answer," Sánchez-Eppler argues, "the only solution to racial prejudice Child's story can offer is rubbing off blackness" (31). Susan's skin color functions in antebellum American society as the indelible sign of Otherness.

On one level, Child's "Mary French and Susan Easton" does effect the erasure of the black body (Susan disappears midway through the story). But I argue that the story erases the black body in such a way as to show that just as easily as it is erased (kidnapped, or written out of the story), it is reinscribed on Mary's body, showing that Mary is, ironically, no more "free" than Susan. An anonymous peddler brutally abuses Mary, treating her as human capital, circulating his product in the marketplace as a slave. In order to sell Mary he remakes her outward appearance, making her look black, wiping out racial differences, and, above all, inculcating Mary with "better manners" (191), silence, and "obedience" (194). "Mary French and Susan Easton" is less about slavery than it is, I suggest, about the mechanism of its perpetuation—or to be more specific, the complicity between slavery and patriarchy.

At the outset of the tale, the reader finds Mary and Susan creating a matriarchal utopia in the woods. The children mimic their mothers by playing house in nature; they "set out the acorns, for cups and saucers," on a big flat rock under an oak (187). It is an egalitarian utopia founded on the sisterhood between the white girl and the black girl. Both children play mother; there are no fathers in this house. The children have a favorite companion in the woods, a little spotted rabbit that is both white and black, functioning as the emblem of what Carolyn Karcher calls "the biracial egalitarian society their friendship heralds" (*First Woman* 166). Mary and Susan "very often carried him in their aprons to the great oak tree, and placed him on the flat rock, while they gathered clover for him to eat" (187). Significantly, the rabbit—the only male in the girls' home—is a speechless creature.

This idealistic home, however, is soon violated by the peddler, who has a seductive mercantile voice. "Little girls, don't you want to buy something pretty?" he asks (188). The man gives Mary and Susan some candy and suggests that they go and see a funny little monkey he keeps in his cart down by the roadside. The girls, eager to see the monkey, leave their rabbit and follow the eloquent peddler. When they reach the middle of the thick woods, the man suddenly seizes the children. In the ensuing tale, the bodies and voices of the children become sites on which racial egalitarianism is unwritten and slavery—mercantile colonialism—is reinscribed.

Most notably, in "Mary French and Susan Easton" the black body is not perceived as the "natural" sign of difference, for Mary's white body is also repositioned as a sign of oppression and denigration as the peddler transforms it. Tying her arms behind her, he cuts off her hair and curls it with curling tongs so that it looks short and crispy like "wool." He rubs soot on her skin, making her "almost as good-looking a *nigger* as t'other one" (192, emphasis in original). The peddler then puts Mary into his cart. To the reader's dismay, racial associations of blacks with animals are reinforced by the positioning of Mary's "black" body in a cage with a monkey.

In order to enforce on the girls the behavioral codes of the patriarchy to which they are now subject, the peddler must silence their voices. He stuffs handkerchiefs in the girls' mouths; Mary and Susan "cried very much; but they could not speak" (189). When the peddler takes the handkerchiefs away to make them eat some bread and a piece of cold sausage, the two girls cry out, "I want to go home to my mother! I want to go home to my mother!" (189). The man threatens to whip them unless they shut their mouths and eat supper—the girls are silenced with the threat of physical violence; in this instance, submission and silence are inextricably linked.

The suppression of Mary's voice, one might add, is made complete by the appearance of third parties—both white and black—who unwittingly become the peddler's social, if not personal, accomplices. First, Mary calls out for help to a white man passing by the cart. When the man inquires about the troubled call, the peddler answers, "Oh . . . it is only a couple of young slaves, who are so refractory, I can't keep 'em still" (193). The man laughs and says, "Give 'em a touch of the whip: that will quiet their tongues" (193). Later, when carried into the "negro huts" and placed under the care of old Dinah, Mary appeals to her: "I *am* a white child, and I *was* stolen" (195, emphasis in original). The black woman, though "a kind hearted creature," does not believe Mary's story. She thinks "the child lied" (195), for Dinah herself "had told many a lie to save herself from a whipping; and she knew that all the slaves told lies, when they thought they could avoid any punishment by it" (195). Dinah laughs at the girl and stuffs Mary's mouth with food, telling her to "hold her tongue" (195). Mary's voice, which appears to be that of a young black girl because of her disguise, thus no longer functions as socially legitimate—the peddler, the white man, and the black woman all deny Mary's voice and seek to silence her.

Furthermore, the peddler's control of Mary's body is implicated in the fact that she is an object of exchange in a patriarchal economy. The peddler sells Mary to a plantation for fifty dollars. Mary is then transferred to the hands of the overseer in the fields, who is no less surveillant than the peddler, as he strikes Mary across the shoulders, for example, for "turn[ing] to look at a little bird that perched on the stump of an old tree" (197).

Mary, the captive child, repossesses her own body and voice only after her master, the owner of the plantation, finds out that the black color comes off from her face. Only then is he convinced that the child is not a black liar but is telling the truth. At the end of the tale, however, Mary is not really freed: the girl—who earlier cried, "I want to go home to my mother!"—is simply transferred from the hands of the planter to the hands of Mr. French, her father. He had put "an advertisement in the newspaper" (200) for Mary, an act that re-fashioned Mary once again into a commodity, and when she is finally returned he is happy to recover at last his "lost treasure" (201). On their reunion, poor Mary sobs "in her father's arms" (201), a scene that teaches the lesson that one should not leave the paternal roof.

Though the child cries for her "lost playmate" (202), this is a happy ending for Mr. French, whose house "was a house of joy" (202). But the house Mary set up with Susan in the woods remains deserted. "The acorn-cups still stood on the flat rock, as if arranged for a mimic tea-party" (200). Seduced away from her matriarchal home in nature, Mary was circulated as a "free" child—a piece of currency among men—the peddler, the planter, the overseer, and the father—thus revealing the ways in which the patriarchal economy crosses the boundaries between the North and the South. Child's political point, then, would seem to be that patriarchy is a bulwark of domestic colonialism, geared to the maintenance of the Union at the expense of women as free people (of color). The tale thus implies that as Mary matures she will be silenced and taught to obey.

Through the association of Mary with free people of color, "Mary French and Susan Easton" not only indicts the vice of domestic slave trading but politicizes the relationship between the girl and her father. Mary functions as a "free" child in the republic, but a child who nonetheless is coerced into reproducing the discourse of domestic colonialism and submitting to the ideology of the dominant class. As the narrator says, if Susan is "no doubt a slave, compelled to labor without receiving any wages for her hard work, and whipped whenever she dares to say that she has a right to be free" (202), Mary—her social double—is also subjected to the patriarchal institution of economy, in which she claims her own body and voice at the risk of being suppressed. Although, as Child puts it, "the black color could be rubbed off from Mary's skin" (202), the female markers on Mary's body—crucial signs of her Otherness—could never be obliterated.

Politicizing the Child

Anne Scott MacLeod argues that antebellum children's literature typically constructs the figures of children as ahistorical. According to this argument, children live in didactic abstraction rather than in historical specificity. "All juvenile fiction before 1860," she notes, "was much the same: simple narratives, always pointing to moral, featureless backgrounds, stock characters moving through patterned plots" (*American Childhood* 92). The most common settings for children's stories, MacLeod suggests, are "vaguely pastoral, with trees, streams and hills all described very generally" (*Moral Tale* 44). The social issues of slavery, industrialization, and urbanization are seldom, in this scenario, directly addressed. According to John C. Crandall, American children—future citizens of the republic—are even advised "to shun a career in politics" (21).

Children in Child's *Juvenile Miscellany*, however, are not pastoral creatures who live nowhere but are instead highly politicized agents who occupy a realistic American world. In Child's magazine, the body and voice of the child serve as a site on which the discourse of domestic colonialism is examined, if not always disrupted. The *Juvenile Miscellany* does not simply treat or depict children as pedagogical objects, receivers of the social values of their fathers' world. Instead, integral to the magazine is the problematization of the relations between children and adults. This is done, as I have shown, through the association of children with the disenfranchised—with Native Americans, Irish immigrants, free people of color, and women. Lydia Maria Child's *Juvenile Miscellany*, then, generates a subversive perspective on the ways in which bourgeois society seeks to contain a socially disruptive Other through the trope of family-nation. In the end, the "omnipresent aunt" deploys the Otherness of children in the service of unsettling the fathers' culture from within.

Notes

1. For an account of the periodical, see Karcher, *First Woman*, 57–79; MacDonald 258–62; Jordan 46–60.

2. As Alice M. Jordan notes, the *Juvenile Miscellany* is "distinguished from its faltering predecessors by its unabashed Americanism." The magazine devotes a great deal of space to American history and biography and contains "countless allusions to the American landscape," a focus that is "different from the English background of books hitherto available to children" (47).

3. By creating herself in a familial framework as an "aunt," however, Child significantly does not hierarchalize her relation to children, as one might expect an adult aunt to do. Instead, Child announces in the inaugural issue's "Address to the Young" that the children will be the critics and will guide her in the magazine's editorial policy: "You, my dear young friends, shall be my critics: What you find[ ] neither affords you amusement or does you good, I shall think is badly written" (iv).

4. See Child's letter of 6 January 1827 to her sister Mary Preston (Meltzer and Holland 8).

5. As Harmon notes, "The year of 1825 might be regarded as the year terminating the old federal Indian policy of peaceful persuasion and negotiation and beginning the new coercive policy" (171). For a history of the federal Indian policy, see Cohen, Harmon, Kappler, and Prucha.

6. For a historical analysis of the almshouse in New York, see Cray.

7. For a discussion of kidnapping in antebellum America, also see Torrey.

8. For a discussion of the role nineteenth-century children's literature played in the abolitionist movement, see Keller.

Works Cited

Child, Lydia Maria. "Address to the Young." *Juvenile Miscellany* 1, no. 1 (September 1826): iii–iv.

[Child, Lydia Maria]. "The Little Rebels." *Juvenile Miscellany* 1, no. 1 (September 1826): 48–53.

———. "Mary French and Susan Easton." *Juvenile Miscellany* 3d ser. 6, no. 2 (May-June 1834): 186–202.

Chipman, Samuel. *Report of an Examination of Poor-Houses, Jails, &c., in the State of New-York.* 3d ed. Albany: Executive Committee of the New-York State Temperance Society, 1835.

Cohen, Felix S. *Handbook of Federal Indian Law.* Charlottesville, Va.: Bobbs-Merrill, 1982.

Crandall, John C. "Patriotism and Humanitarian Reform in Children's Literature, 1825–1860." *American Quarterly* 21 (1969): 3–22.

Cray, Robert E., Jr. *Paupers and Poor Relief in New York City and Its Rural Environs, 1700–1830.* Philadelphia: Temple University Press, 1988.

Dall, Caroline H. "Lydia Maria Child and Mary Russell Mitford." *Unitarian Review* 19 (June 1883): 519–34.

Harmon, George Dewey. *Sixty Years of Indian Affairs: Political, Economic, and Diplomatic, 1789–1850.* Chapel Hill: University of North Carolina Press, 1941.

Heale, M. J. "From City Fathers to Social Critics: Humanitarianism and Government in New York, 1790–1860." *Journal of American History* 63 (1976): 21–41.

———. "Patterns of Benevolence: Charity and Morality in Rural and Urban New York, 1783–1830." *Societas* 3 (1973): 337–59.

Higginson, Thomas Wentworth. *Contemporaries.* 1899. Upper Saddle River, N.J.: Literature House, 1970.

Jordan, Alice M. *From Rollo to Tom Sawyer.* Boston: Horn Book, 1948.

Kappler, Charles J., comp. and ed. *Indian Affairs: Laws and Treaties.* Vol. 2. Washington, D.C.: Government Printing Office, 1904.

Karcher, Carolyn L. *The First Woman in the Republic: A Cultural Biography of Lydia Maria Child.* Durham: Duke University Press, 1994.

———, ed. Hobomok *and Other Writings on Indians by Lydia Maria Child.* New Brunswick: Rutgers University Press, 1986.

Keller, Holly. "Juvenile Antislavery Narrative and Notions of Childhood." *Children's Literature* 24 (1996): 86–100.

"L." "The Irish Emigrants." *Juvenile Miscellany* n.s. 3, no. 3 (January 1830): 228–38.

MacDonald, Ruth K. "*The Juvenile Miscellany.*" In *Children's Periodicals of the United States.* Ed. R. Gordon Kelly. Westport: Greenwood, 1984. Pp. 258–62.

MacLeod, Anne Scott. *American Childhood: Essays on Children's Literature of the Nineteenth and Twentieth Centuries.* Athens: University of Georgia Press, 1994.

———. *A Moral Tale: Children's Fiction and American Culture 1820–1860.* Hamden: Archon, 1975.

Meltzer, Milton, and Patricia G. Holland, eds. *Lydia Maria Child: Selected Letters, 1817–1880.* Amherst: University of Massachusetts Press, 1982.

Prucha, Francis Paul. *American Indian Policy in the Formative Years: The Indian Trade and Intercourse Acts, 1790–1834.* Cambridge: Harvard University Press, 1962.

"Report on the Slave Trade." *Liberator* 4 (June 7, 1834): 89–91.

Richardson, James D., comp. *A Compilation of the Messages and Papers of the Presidents, 1789–1897.* Vol. 2. Washington, D.C.: Government Printing Office, 1896.

Robbins, Eliza. *Primary Dictionary . . . for the Younger Classes in Schools.* 1828. New York: R. Lockwood, 1842.

Sánchez-Eppler, Karen. *Touching Liberty: Abolition, Feminism, and the Politics of the Body.* Berkeley: University of California Press, 1993.

Torrey, Jesse. *A Portraiture of Domestic Slavery, in the United States.* 1817. St. Clair Shores, MI: Scholarly, 1970.

Wallace, Anthony F. C. *The Long, Bitter Trail: Andrew Jackson and the Indians.* New York: Hill and Wang, 1993.

Wilson, Carol. *Freedom at Risk: The Kidnapping of Free Blacks in America, 1780–1865.* Lexington: University Press of Kentucky, 1994.

Constructing a Shared History: Black Pageantry for Children During the Harlem Renaissance

Katharine Capshaw Smith

In 1926 W. E. B. Du Bois called for a new kind of theater for African Americans, composed of dramas that were "about us, by us, for us, and near us" ("Krigwa" 134). Alongside the Krigwa and little theater movements,[1] which answered Du Bois's call, one must place pageantry for children, since African American pageants during the 1920s and 1930s responded to the young population's desire for a drama that represented black lives and black history with dignity and virtue. Staged in schools, community halls, and churches, pageants for African American children touched audiences of various ages, classes, and educations. These productions often addressed a specific community's needs, celebrating local anniversaries and confronting regional economic or racial tensions. The child was, of course, a topic of dramatic interest during the "New Negro," or Harlem, Renaissance. The plays for adults by Georgia Douglas Johnson and Angelina Weld Grimké, for example, depict despairing mothers unable to protect their children from the violent threat of a racist society. Pageants of the period directed at children, however, offer a contrasting depiction of the possibilities of black childhood. By revealing to children their race's past accomplishments, and by constructing the child as intelligent and capable in the face of racist social structures, the period's pageants are infused with the new life and sense of potential commonly associated with the black literary renaissance. African American pageant writers believed that the "New Negro" would ultimately arise from the young Negro and that building black nationhood and a new cultural identity depended on the education of the younger generation.

Du Bois imagined that the innovative black drama would address racial conflict and represent heroic black figures and their contributions to mainstream American society.[2] With these ideals in mind, Du Bois was able to proclaim famously in "Criteria of Negro Art" (1926), "I do not care a damn for any art that is not used for propaganda"

Children's Literature 27, ed. Elizabeth Lennox Keyser (Yale University Press, © 1999 Hollins University).

(296). Most of the children's pageants of the period adhere to Du Bois's didactic paradigm, since many of the pageant writers, often schoolteachers who were disenchanted with racist constructions of history, found that Du Bois shared their overtly educative perspective. In "The Drama Among Black Folk" (1916), Du Bois articulated the goals of his own pageant, "The Star of Ethiopia," in didactic terms: "to teach on the one hand the colored people themselves the meaning of their history and their rich, emotional life through a new theatre, and on the other to reveal the Negro to the white world as a human, feeling thing" (171). Pedagogic and propagandistic, and often directed at a dual audience of both blacks and whites, most African American pageants written for children in the 1920s and 1930s followed Du Bois's model.

The Harlem Renaissance arose during the great age of American pageantry (1905–25), a movement linked to the Progressive Era's sense of democratic optimism (Prevots 1). During a period marked by massive immigration and urban migration, pageantry unified communities around shared stories of their city or town, presenting in dance, song, pantomime, and verse images that would invest the audience in the life of their community and enable them to share dreams of a city's progress and reform. Performances required extensive local participation; for example, Boston's 1910 *Cave Life to City Life* brought together more than 1,200 local organizations in a pageant that reflected the community's cultural diversity and also inspired a shared vision of urban improvement (Prevots 29). But however inclusive and democratic the pageant effort purported to be, in the early part of the century virtually every citywide pageant excluded black participation. For example, of the 7,500 participants in the 1913 St. Louis pageant, only one African American appeared (Prevots 17). Certainly many of the pageant movement's ideals appealed to Harlem Renaissance thinkers. Urban black populations in the 1920s were far from homogeneous; migration from the country to the city and West Indian immigration created local populations with disparate educations, social customs, and economic backgrounds. Pageantry offered communities a means of shaping a common history, of affirming a rural heritage, and of forging common cultural and economic goals. Although black writers drew on mainstream white pageant conventions, black pageantry has its roots in a satirical African American tradition. In northern cities in antebellum America, blacks often staged pageants that parodied white power and social structures. In Connecticut, for example, Hartford's black community celebrated Election Day, which saw the selection of a black governor and judges who spoofed white legal power (Lott 47).

One of the first Harlem Renaissance figures to embrace pageantry was Du Bois, as the ideals of mainstream pageantry attracted him in fundamental ways. The founders of the American Pageantry Association (APA) envisioned the genre as "art of the people, by the people, for the people" (Prevots 1), a sentiment perhaps echoed in Du Bois's "Krigwa" plea for drama "about us, by us, for us, and near us" (134). Percy MacKaye, one of the APA's founders and leaders, wrote that pageantry "satisfies an elemental instinct for art, a popular demand for poetry. This instinct and this demand . . . are capable of being educated, refined, developed into a mighty agency for civilization" (quoted in Prevots 70). Du Bois also believed in a popular desire for art, writing that "the Pageant is the thing. This is what the people want and long for. This is the gown and paraphernalia in which the message of education and reasonable race pride can deck itself" ("Star" 91). Du Bois's belief in the popular desire for art stems from his recognition that black Americans in the late teens and 1920s yearned not simply for art but for a political art that made manifest the ties that joined black American to black American and the African American community to a national identity that had previously been coded as exclusively white. The political, the didactic, the reformative all coalesced for Du Bois in the pageant format, and he found, as did other pageant writers, an eager and responsive audience for his vision.

Du Bois staged his own all-black pageant, "The Star of Ethiopia," with much success. Performed in New York (1913), Washington, D.C. (1915), Philadelphia (1916), and Los Angeles (1924), the work used as many as 1,200 participants in one production. Noting the racist undercurrent in mainstream pageantry, Du Bois asserted that "the American Pageant Association has been silent, if not actually contemptuous" with respect to "The Star of Ethiopia" ("Drama Among" 173). Regardless of the APA's response, "The Star" was so popular among African Americans, and Du Bois's enthusiasm so strong, that afterwards he sought to form a nonprofit association that would promote black pageantry. Although such an organization failed to materialize, Du Bois never lost faith in the power of the black pageant; he published one for the bicentenary of George Washington in 1932, and he left in his papers several pageants in manuscript (Scott 266–67).

Large-scale pageantry declined along with the Progressive movement in the late 1910s and with a shift from the original grandeur
of APA presentations to pageants produced in schools (Prevots 102).
Once the APA lost power over such art, and schoolteachers and community members became creative artists, pageantry lost the prestige
it had once enjoyed. Since APA leaders decried school productions
and actively excluded African American adults and children from
APA efforts, black pageantry, which was often produced in schools,
defied the racist and antichild dictates of the white pageantry movement. No wonder its spokesmen were "silent" and "contemptuous"
before Du Bois's efforts.

In addition, although pageant leaders might have looked askance
at pageants produced in schools, pageantry had always been a "cross-
written" genre, addressing an audience of both children and adults.
In the hands of Harlem Renaissance figures, the child became an even
more pronounced and important part of the audience. Mary Church
Terrell, the civil rights activist and potent supporter of black pageantry, explains in an introduction to her 1932 "Historical Pageant-
Play Based on the Life of Phyllis Wheatley" that her main goal had
been to influence black children: "I wanted to increase the colored
youth's respect for his African ancestors. . . . [The pageant] would increase their pride in their racial group and thus strengthen their self
respect" (1–2). If pageants required the audience to look toward the
future, for Renaissance figures the child became increasingly important to accomplishing the goals articulated in the pageant. The child
was the hope for the future, and reaching the child audience became
a priority for black pageant writers.

In fact, the pageant format appealed specifically to children, children of this historical moment, in ways of which an adult audience may not have been aware. The child growing up during the
Harlem Renaissance was increasingly sensitive to the power of the
printed word; as education became increasingly available and culturally significant,[3] the black child entered a space where written records
superseded the oral, where stories and histories reproduced by a
white publishing establishment displaced accounts of her or his own
people. A current of dissatisfaction with conventional schoolbooks
runs through letters from children to Du Bois at *The Brownies' Book*
(1920–1921), the first periodical for African American children. In
1920 Pocahontas Foster from Orange, New Jersey, wrote, "I have
never liked history because I always felt that it wasn't much good. Just

a lot of dates and things that some men did, men whom I didn't know
and nobody else whom I knew, knew anything about" (54).[4] A New
York City mother complained in 1920 that after telling her daughter
accounts of black achievement, the daughter responded, "Well, that's
just stories. Didn't they ever do anything in a book?" (340). The children of the period learned the power of textual representation and
its ability to legitimate versions of history.

As schoolteachers and community playwrights shared the children's dissatisfaction with conventional historical representations,
they modeled their plays on classroom conventions in order to fulfill
the children's desire for "textbook" black history. The pageant genre
offered an instant analog to the textbook, since it enabled historical
figures who addressed the need for new racial and gender identities
to take the stage. The structure of Dorothy Guinn's popular "Out of
the Dark" (1924)[5] is typical of the period's black pageantry for children. Guinn's pageant represents itself as the lost pages of a textbook,
for the Chronicler, a frame character who reads from a scroll, regrets
the gap in blacks' written history: "My page is often blurred, for the
hate of race has caused many to blot out the achievements of these
people. (*Pause.*) But I am here to bring to light out of the dark the
record of the progress of these folk here in America" (311). As the
Chronicler, like so many others in black pageantry, reads from her
scroll of the "gleams of light shining out of the dark" (313), children
become crucial to a written history of the present and the future.
Guinn's Chronicler asks the "Children of Genius" to "complete the
tale . . . concerning my people" (319), and after Science, Art, Literature, and Music speak of contemporary black achievements, the
Chronicler asserts, "Now is my scroll complete" (323). And yet, the
epilogue impresses on the child audience a need for a continual written history by asserting, "My tale is done, kind friends (or shall I say
begun?), for though my record gives no more, yet this is but a beginning" (323). The written scroll of African American history can never
really conclude as long as there are children to continue writing it by
joining its parade of heroes.

The authors adapted pageant conventions, such as the central
speaker and voiceless tableaux, in order to imitate textbook and classroom conventions. In "Out of the Dark," as in other pageants for
Harlem Renaissance children, a central female figure describes the
history of each character as he or she appears onstage, a pattern
that parallels classroom discourse. The central female consciousness

is both reassuring and familiar to a child audience since she also authorizes the material: it is the teacher figure who makes the telling of black history "official" and part of the educational canon. In Guinn's pageant, the stage directions indicate that "the best possible person should be chosen for the Chronicler, since everything depends upon her interpretation" (329). For Guinn, the most mature, expressive child actress should take the role of the teacher, since the documentation of black history depends on an appearance of confidence and authority. Female messengers, chroniclers, and speakers populate black pageants for children, offering a familiar, authoritative, and powerful analog to the teacher at work.

A third way in which the authors adapt pageant conventions to replicate the classroom setting is in their use of tableaux. While the teacher figure describes the life of a famous African American, often a light or a drawn curtain reveals a child costumed as that character. These scenes recall illustration conventions of storybooks and textbooks, for often, after reading descriptions of people or events out loud, teachers direct children's attention to representative pictures. For example, in "Out of the Dark," the Chronicler's description of Booker T. Washington is followed by these stage directions: "Curtain opens on tableau of Booker Washington lifting the veil of ignorance from Negro Youth. Reproduction of statue at Tuskegee. Curtain drawn" (318). The statue, a popular image (we recall Ellison's use of it in *Invisible Man* [1952]), is an icon that becomes legitimized within mainstream education by virtue of its inclusion in Guinn's textbook pageant. In fact, while repeatedly raising the stage curtain to reveal tableaux of famous black Americans, the pageant itself brings the icon to life: the curtain lifts the veil of ignorance away from the child viewers, revealing luminous examples of black achievement.

Finally, the tableau's function as equivalent to a picture in a schoolbook becomes explicit in Guinn's depiction of Benjamin Banneker; her costuming directions connect the tableau to printed texts for children: "[Banneker is] dressed in colonial suit, carrying large hat. See picture in *Brownies' Book*, June, 1920, page 173; published by Dubois [*sic*] and Dill" (328). Without a black history textbook on which to model her pictures, Guinn turns to Du Bois's groundbreaking magazine—the first publication that printed black history for children—and to black cultural icons such as the "well-known picture[s]" of Phyllis Wheatley and Sojourner Truth and the "Booker Washington and Negro Youth . . . statue at Tuskegee" (328). In fact, black pageantry for children reenacts the interaction of teacher, text, and audience found in the classroom; in this way, the New Negro pageants legitimate for children the black history that they seek in specific textual forms codified by the conventions of classroom education.

What appears on this classroom figure's scroll and on the scrolls of dozens of other pageants for children? How did Harlem Renaissance pageant writers construct a common history for a child audience? Most important, pageant writers were empowered by their realization that history is a construct. They believed that a black history could be built and authorized by drawing on a scattered heritage of texts. The pageant writers (as did many artists and critics writing for adults) underscored their belief in the importance of a written history by forging their works from legal documents, speeches, newspaper reports, poems, historical accounts, and other texts. Whether an excerpt from a Wheatley poem in Guinn's "Out of the Dark," a passage from Frederick Douglass's "What to the Slave Is the Fourth of July?" in Dunbar-Nelson's "Douglass Pageant," or a quotation from Benjamin Banneker's letter to Thomas Jefferson in Du Bois's "Pageant for the Bicentenary," most pageants take pains to assemble the actual language of historical African Americans. At the conclusion of T. S. Eliot's "The Waste Land," a speaker asserts, "These fragments I have shored against my ruins." Black pageant writers used textual fragments to shore up against their own ruin, one of race prejudice, historical anonymity, and exclusion from an American identity.[6]

Overwhelmingly, pageants are concerned with the black's historical place in America. According to Christine R. Gray, many adult plays produced outside New York City for black audiences had a self-contained sense of audience and local subject matter (18). Most children's pageants of the period, however, do not appear to be exclusively addressed to black listeners. Of course, black children are the primary audience, and stories of African American achievement work to inspire racial pride, but these plays concurrently appear to address white child audiences, for as alternative textbooks they teach the majority culture as well as the black audience about African American history. Nowhere is that double audience more apparent than in texts that explicitly address the issue of American identity. Inez M. Burke, a teacher at the primarily African American Charles Young School in Washington, D.C., wrote "Two Races" (1930) to celebrate Negro History Week in the 1920s (Peterson 44).[7] In it, as in other pageants, both white and black children appear, a gesture that intimates white investment in the work. The piece explicitly reacts against traditional history books as Gilbert, a white boy, flaunts the record of his ancestors' achievements before his black companion, Sam: "Just see all in music, invention, art, and business that *my* people, *my* forefathers, have done" (297). Black accomplishments do not appear in the history books, Gilbert informs Sam. Sam's response typifies the experience of many black youths, for it reveals a rival mode of historical record that has been discredited: "Bu—bu—but—a—a—my grandmother said—W-e-ll, maybe you are right" (298).

The Spirit of Negro Progress, a "Kind lady" (298), appears and revives Sam from his dejection by telling stories of black adventurers, soldiers, speakers, poets, and artists. The breadth and depth of Burke's descriptions are impressive, for she includes such famous figures as Frederick Douglass and Booker T. Washington alongside more obscure ones such as Elijah McCoy, inventor of "an appliance for lubricating . . . engines on steamboats and railway locomotives" (299), and orators Mary Church Terrell and Mary McLeod. The spirit also insists that white culture has publicly acknowledged black achievement. Of Colonel Young and his black soldiers in the Spanish-American war, "Roosevelt . . . made a splendid speech in praise of their heroism. . . . The Negro has proved his bravery" (300). Whites listened to and praised Booker T. Washington, whose speeches "set the whole world thinking about the Negro" (300). Burke's strategy mirrors Du Bois's theory of black pageantry, for while she affirms black feats and oral tradition in order to create ethnocentric pride, she also illustrates white America's attention to and endorsement of black accomplishments, even if its memory may seem short.

Presenting itself as a counter schoolbook, "Two Races" assembles and interprets evidence of the black's historical role, and in doing so, positions blacks side by side with the whites of conventional American history. The Spirit of Adventure begins the history of famous blacks by describing an African presence at the nation's inception: "In 1492 some Negroes came with Columbus on his great adventure" (298). Similarly, the Spirit of Bravery moves from describing Crispus Attucks, the first casualty of the Revolution, to depicting blacks fighting alongside Jackson in 1815 at New Orleans, to picturing African American soldiers in the Civil War, the Spanish-American War, and World War I. By naming the state in which each inventor lived, the Spirit of Invention identifies them as palpably American. A final proof of blacks' intrinsic place in American culture is music, for black

music defines the nation; it "is regarded by fair-minded thinkers as
the greatest contribution of America to civilization" (301). The last
voice we hear in Burke's pageant is that of Uncle Sam, who asserts
that America will become an "outstanding country" and "the land
of the free" (302) only when white and black unite, and, Burke implies, when black people's contributions to America are universally
acknowledged. Carter G. Woodson asserts in his *Mis-Education of the
Negro* (1933) that black teachers should "revolutionize the social order
for the good of the community" (145). Burke's play does just that; it
dismisses biased history books' construction of blacks as "slaves on
the plantations" ("Two Races" 297) and reconstitutes a wide-ranging
black identity as brave, intelligent, creative, outspoken, and central
to a definition of America. After attending a performance of "Two
Races" by Burke's fifth-grade class in the early 1930s, Woodson explained the effect of the play's ending on its dual audience: "The
Negro boy, thus enlightened, became inspired to do something great;
and the white boy, rid of his prejudice, believed that the colored boy
had possibilities and joined hands with the lad to help him do his
part. Thus we see dramatized a new America" ("Introduction" iv). For
Woodson, education about black achievement and American identity
should not be confined to the black community, since racism could be
extinguished only by cooperation among America's diverse peoples
to shape a New Negro in a new America.

If, on one level, pageants dramatize versions of textbook history,
on another, the female chroniclers also validate and institutionalize a
matriarchal oral tradition. Thus, whereas early in "Two Races" Gilbert
would have Sam believe that written histories are more authoritative
than oral ones, the remainder of the play legitimizes black oral tradition by offering an oral account of the black American identity.
Pageant writers use their genre to address and affirm both forms of
African American historicity. Addressed to an adult audience, both
literate and illiterate, the plays affirm the importance of an education for their children without excluding parents lacking a formal
education. Addressed to a school-aged audience, the pageants satisfy
the yearning for textbook representations of black history without
undermining the authority of oral histories. Ultimately, of course, the
Spirit of Negro Progress in "Two Races" replicates the stories Sam's
grandmother told him. A sophisticated and multivocal genre, black
pageantry emphasizes textual history without estranging members of
its diverse audience.

Whereas "Two Races" and other pageants define a black American identity across many different fields, such as business, exploration, and the arts, some pageants focus on specific contributions by African Americans to the nation. The most popular arena for establishing black participation in American history is the military, perhaps in recognition of African American efforts in World War I. Pageants such as Mary Church Terrell's "Pageant-Play Depicting Heroism of Colored Soldiers in Revolutionary War" (n.d.) and P.S. 24's "Negro Achievement" (1937)[8] use black military accomplishment to define African Americans as essential contributors to the building of the nation. Crispus Attucks often takes center stage in such pageants.

A more complex issue arises in pageants about the founding of America that focus on the paired figures of George Washington and Phillis Wheatley. As Mary Church Terrell notes in her autobiography, *A Colored Woman in a White World* (1940), African Americans had traditionally felt some disappointment in George Washington because he owned slaves.[9] Terrell writes about her Phillis Wheatley pageant:

> I wanted to show colored children that George Washington had done something commendable for a representative of their group, so that they would feel they had at least one reason to revere his memory as the children of other groups did. . . . This was clearly and strongly brought out in my pageant, so that colored children might see that although the Father of His Country was a slaveholder, in accordance with the deplorable custom of his time, nevertheless, he was broad-minded, generous-hearted, and just enough to give credit where credit is due, to make written acknowledgement of the talent of an African girl and to pay homage to her while she was still being held as a slave. (411–12)

When the nation celebrated the bicentenary of Washington's birth in 1932, African Americans such as Terrell and W. E. B. Du Bois took the opportunity to use pageantry to identify Washington positively with black America. Both Terrell's "Historical Pageant-Play Based on the Life of Phyllis Wheatley" and Du Bois's "A Pageant for the Bicentenary, 1732–1932" take as their central passage the story of Washington's kind response to a poem Phillis Wheatley wrote in his honor. Although both pageants attempt, in the words of Terrell, to "teach our children that we are citizens of this country" ("Why I Wrote" 2) by revealing the historical connection between Wheatley and Washington, the pageants' most significant accomplishments diverge a bit from this goal in order to emphasize specific dimensions of the black American identity. Du Bois's pageant moves away from Washington into dynamic depictions of black military leadership, while Terrell's play contains sensitive depictions of African American slave life, depictions often absent from other pageants for children.

Du Bois chose to offer images of active, aggressive responses to oppression instead of exploring slavery's devastating nature. In fact, conventionally pageants celebrate the accomplishments of individual African-Americans; very few contend in depth with the history of slavery. Like Burke's "Two Races," most plays move away from depictions of blacks as "slaves on the plantations" (297) to depict black achievements. If they do depict slavery, they might pantomime the capture of slaves in Africa, as does Guinn's "Out of the Dark," but refuse to treat two centuries of slave life by assuming that the audience is familiar with their painful shared history: "You well know the horrors of slavery. But have you ever seen the gleams of light shining out of the dark?" ("Out of the Dark" 313). Moreover, most pageants do not stage slavery, but nearly all include the folk songs and spirituals emerging from slavery as a way of remembering their traumatic past and revering the music, a cultural triumph that emerged from suffering. Terrell's pageant is distinct in that it focuses on the daily life of a slave girl, albeit the outstanding, atypical example of Phillis Wheatley, in language that calls attention to the constructedness of racial identity.

Staged in Washington, D.C., as the only black pageant in a citywide celebration of George Washington,[10] Terrell's piece begins with a dramatization of slave capture in Africa. But unlike other pageants, which might skip to descriptions of Frederick Douglass or Harriet Tubman, Terrell begins act II in a slave market; the dialogue emphasizes the agonizing middle passage: "The ocean voyage was terrible, they say. There was an awful storm. The waves were so high they almost touched the sky. The people were packed in that ship like those little fishes you buy in a can" (1). Various characters repeat such descriptions: "They were packed in that ship. . . . They could hardly move. . . . Many of them died on the way over and were thrown overboard. . . . Hundreds of them died on the way over, you know" (2). Naked, shivering, hungry, and sick, young Phillis does not appear the one-dimensional heroine of other history pageants, for Terrell must depict the trauma of slavery; her actors wear the signs of oppression and repeat horrific stories of the middle passage.

Once Phillis enters the Wheatley home, however, Terrell necessarily backs away from depictions of American slavery, since the young girl led a somewhat privileged life as a servant to young white twins and was educated and encouraged to write. Instead, Terrell explores the construction of racial identity through dialogue between the twins, Nathaniel and Mary. When Nathaniel calls Native Americans "bloodthirsty savages" who "steal up upon poor, unsuspecting, white people, murder them and scalp them," Mary responds, "White people have committed some awful crimes against them, you know. White people came here and stole their land. This country is theirs, not ours" (4). Although not wholly acknowledging that the depiction of Native Americans as "blood-thirsty savages" is reductive, Mary suggests that Indians have the right to retaliate against exploitation, endorsing an active, aggressive response to white oppression.

In the same scene Nathaniel educates Mary about African American intelligence, employing language that recalls and corrects racist rhetoric. When Mary asks, "Did you ever see anything quite so funny in all your life?" as Phillis attempts to read, Nathaniel responds, "You can teach animals some things. Even they have a certain amount of intelligence" (4), evoking a bigoted justification that is echoed when Mary exclaims, "Many people say that Africans have no brains and there are ever so many who believe they have no souls. That's why it is all right to make them slaves" (4). Terrell, however, summons these racist explanations only to deflate them. Nathaniel asserts, "Africans are human beings, you know. There is no reason in the world why they could not be taught some things anyhow" (4). Although offering tentative qualifications, Nathaniel here collapses the racial stereotypes; Terrell then draws a parallel between constructions of blacks and of white women that compellingly underscores the fallacy of such ideals. Nathaniel says, "Father says women are a pain in Mathematics on general principles, no matter how hard they try to master it. The trouble is that there is something radically wrong in a woman's brain —in a white woman's brain, I mean" (5). Terrell's pageant amasses clichés about race and gender to reveal that, like a house of cards, they are built on nothing concrete and could easily topple and collapse.

Although she stresses their insubstantiality, Terrell acknowledges that social constructions are powerful tools of oppression. In the figure of Dorcas, the elderly black cook with whom Phillis trains, Terrell reveals the effects of the images articulated by the Wheatley children. Concerned that Phillis will become ill from studying and writing, Dorcas asserts, "That's what comes of learnin black folks to read and write. The Lord never intended black folks to learn to read and write. No good aint a goin to come of it neither. I certainly am glad I don't know how to read and write. I aint never goin to learn neither. If you don't come to bed right away, I'm going to tell Mrs. Wheatley on you. You see if I dont" (5). Dorcas has internalized the tools of her own oppression, for she models her own self-concept, her views on black intellectual potential, and her image of God on biased beliefs. In turn, Dorcas employs this philosophy to subjugate Phillis, replicating racist rhetoric more forcefully than do Mary and Nathaniel.

Terrell's astute pageant does not univocally celebrate the positive dimensions of a black American identity; instead, it realistically depicts dimensions of the psychological and physical experience of slave life in America. Although the pageant reveals the emptiness of racist discourse, it also emphasizes its profound power. In doing so, Terrell demonstrates Wheatley's triumph over oppressive conditions rather than simply describing it. Wheatley's meeting with General Washington, her sojourn in England with the Countess of Huntington, and the publication of her book become even more arresting and significant by virtue of the graphic, detailed backdrop Terrell provides.

Whereas Terrell's pageant allows its audience to reclaim a history that included slavery, W. E. B. Du Bois's "A Pageant for the Bicentenary, 1732–1932" attempts to invest children in America's military history by juxtaposing images of an impotent General Washington against examples of black activist leadership. Although Du Bois does not demonize Washington the slaveholder, the *Crisis* editor depicts the general and president as a straightjacketed leader; always listening to contradictory advisors, Washington is caught between powerful slaveholding factions and his own economic limitations. Unable to eliminate slavery at the Constitutional Convention, Washington lacks the personal strength to extinguish slavery in his own house: "I earnestly wish to liberate my slaves but I must keep them until I can find some other way of defraying my necessary expenses" (123). Only in death does Washington free his slaves; in the pageant's final scene, Du Bois has Alexander Hamilton read Washington's will to the audience. Du Bois also softens his portrait of Washington by dramatizing his gracious response to Wheatley's poetic tribute.

In counterpoint to Washington's ineffectual response to slavery, Du Bois offers numerous examples of black agency on behalf of the nation. Beginning with Crispus Attucks, Du Bois emphasizes the centrality of black revolutionary effort. Du Bois reminds the audience that Attucks's death "was publicly commemorated in Boston by an oration and other exercises every year until 1784, when the Fourth of July was substituted for the Fifth of March as our National Holiday" (121). Du Bois also suggests that Attucks, by his sacrifice, was the original father of the country: "The Fourth of July displaces the Fifth of March. Washington succeeds Crispus Attucks" (123). Establishing a contrast between Washington and black military leaders becomes the thrust of the pageant; in scene 3, "First at War," which takes place at Valley Forge, the dialogues place black military contributions next to those of whites: "We [white soldiers] seized Boston and Montreal. . . . And Negroes helped you. . . . We saved Rhode Island. . . . And Prince captured General Preston while black troops defended General Greene" (122). While the debate is resolved with the recitation of a poem by Paul Laurence Dunbar on black success in war, the scene concludes with an emphasis on Haiti's place in American history: "As the American army began to retreat, the British attacked the rear, determined to annihilate the Americans. It was then that the black and mulatto freedmen from Haiti . . . made the charge on the English and saved the retreating Americans" (122).

Haiti becomes especially important as a model for black leadership in the pageant's final scene. Shortly before Hamilton announces Washington's death, Du Bois underscores the significance of Toussaint L'Ouverture for black Americans as the greatest leader: "I would call him Washington, but the great Virginian held slaves. This man risked his entire empire rather than permit the slave trade in the humblest village of his dominions" (124). In the light of Washington's economically based hesitation to free his own slaves, L'Ouverture's revolutionary action appears much more decisive, bold, and heroic. Clearly Du Bois envisions the Haitian hero as the more appropriate example of military authority, ironically using Washington's bicentenary as an occasion to demonstrate black military strength in the face of weak white moral leadership. Du Bois does not dispel black Americans' disenchantment with the nation's first president; instead the pageant uncovers Washington's flawed, hesitant leadership and offers in its place the dynamic contributions of Crispus Attucks, black revolutionary soldiers, and Toussaint L'Ouverture.

One of the most interesting facets of Du Bois's pageant is its use of the frame character. Like other "textbook" pageants, Du Bois employs a female figure who reads from a "Book of Fate" (121). But Du

Bois's character differs from others in its biblical allusion; Du Bois names his frame figure "The Witch of Endor" after a passage in which Saul asks a fortune teller to conjure a vision of Samuel (1 Sam. 28). The story was quite popular; Benjamin West had painted a famous version, *Saul and the Witch of Endor,* in 1777. The passage is especially appropriate to black children's search for examples of leadership in a racist society, since Saul looks to the fortune teller for help fighting a losing battle against the Philistines. Also important is the role of children in Du Bois's pageant. Before each scene, a group of children rouse the sleeping Witch of Endor by dancing and offering gold and a vase of blood, signifying the agents that move historical events. That the children prompt the witch's visions suggests the black child's desire for representations of black contributions to America; the children's eagerness to listen to the witch's stories, which she reads from the Book of Fate, implies again the concurrent importance of oral and written histories. In addition, Du Bois's inclusion of this frame dynamic signifies, as in other pageants, a consciousness of history's constructed nature. In recognizing the gap in white histories—the omission of African American experience—children, in Du Bois's pageant and in others, initiate a reconstruction of American history that reinterprets white historical figures such as Washington and authorizes and inscribes black achievement.

In constructing this new history of America, pageant writers sought ways to validate the African American experience, a difficult task since documentation of black life and achievements was scarce. How, then, did pageant writers invest their version of history with authority recognized by mainstream America and by black children who were taught to value written texts? One strategy was the use of passages from legal history. In fact, a governing metaphor for some pageants was that of the legal system in action; enacting a legal decision represents the definitive conclusion of debate about the degree of blacks' contribution to American civilization. Edward J. McCoo's pageant "Ethiopia at the Bar of Justice" (1930), first produced in 1924,[11] depicts a courtroom scene where Ethiopia must defend herself against the figure of Opposition, who charges that Ethiopia is "drawing heavily upon the Bank of Civilization" while having "nothing on deposit there" (353). Justice evaluates witnesses such as History, First Slave, Civil War Veteran, World War Veteran, Labor, Business, and The Church, among others, who attest to Ethiopia's abundant accomplishments. Toward the pageant's end, the Declaration of Independence, the Anti-Lynch Law, and the Thirteenth, Fourteenth, and Fifteenth Amendments each appear and quote from their documents to prove that blacks are citizens of America with the same rights and privileges as whites.

Similarly, Alice Dunbar-Nelson's unpublished "A Pageant: The Negro in History" (n.d.) uses legal metaphor to imagine the contemporary position of African Americans: "Today, W. E. B. DuBois [*sic*], James Weldon Johnson, Kelly Miller are a few of those who plead our case before the world" (n.p.). Dunbar-Nelson differs from McCoo and others who simply piece together legal documents, however, for she directly connects literary arts to the legal metaphor, granting a political function to creative work. This belief that literary texts will be the works on the basis of which the world will judge African Americans reflects once again the period's overall confidence in the written word. Texts have the capacity to transform: they can reconstitute history and they can effect political change on the national stage. Yet later in Dunbar-Nelson's pageant, in the section titled "The Negro in the Arts," she includes a poem by her former husband, Paul Laurence Dunbar, that speaks to a parallel strand in Harlem Renaissance aesthetic thought. In "The Poet and His Song," Dunbar writes:

> There are no ears to hear my lays,
> No lips to lift a word of praise,
> But still, with faith unfaltering
> I live and laugh and work and sing.
> What matters yon unheeding throng?
> They cannot hear my spirit's spell,
> Sibee life is sweet and love is long,
> I sing my song and all is well.   (n.p.)

The poem, which concludes by asserting that "life is more than fruit or grain, / And so I sing," proclaims the joy in a purely aesthetic dimension of black literature, an attitude shared by many successful apolitical writers of the period, such as Alain Locke and his followers or Countee Cullen. Dunbar-Nelson's pageant is typical of those that reflect the intricate tensions characterizing the period's aesthetic theories. Inclusive and suggestive, such pageants amass disparate literary texts to make their case about black artistic accomplishment,[12] embracing spirituals and dialect poems as well as the works of contemporary writers such as Cullen, Langston Hughes, and James Weldon Johnson. Rarely simplistic or reductive, Harlem Renaissance children's pageants bring together multiple textual strands to form their arguments about the nature of black American identity.

As much as these pageants demand a textual representation of black achievements, they also highlight the artifice of history and acknowledge such history's constructedness. The pageant format itself enables a liberation from the temporal constraints of timeline history, for a pageant is a moment out of time where historical figures can meet. A stage at a pageant's conclusion might reveal Crispus Attucks standing next to Frederick Douglass, Phillis Wheatley next to Booker T. Washington. Pageantry enables writers to unsettle historical and evaluative hierarchies, for Harriet Tubman might be given equal time and space with Paul Laurence Dunbar or Benjamin Banneker.

Because of what might be called pageantry's "equalizing effect," feminist subtexts frequently emerge. In Guinn's "Out of the Dark," for example, students read poems by Phillis Wheatley and Georgia Douglas Johnson before selections from Paul Laurence Dunbar and Claude McKay. Although boys, the P.S. 24 writers privilege female achievement as well; Booker T. Washington asks Dunbar, "Do you know anything of one of our greatest Negroes?" Dunbar responds: "Do you mean Frederick Douglass?" Washington asserts: "Douglass is a great man but I am referring to Phyllis Wheatley" (23). Writers of black pageants for children during the Harlem Renaissance were, more often than not, female schoolteachers, women who used the pageant's timeline structure, enactment of an oral tradition, and female frame characters in order to construct a vision of black history that celebrates women's contributions and achievements.

Black pageantry's equalizing effect also contributes to its allegorical nature, for individual figures often become identified with each other to produce an abstract ideal of black identity. In Frances Gunner's "The Light of the Women" (1930),[13] Ethiopia, a queen, tells the Spirits of Service, Truth, and Beauty of black women's accomplishments in terms that even begin as an abstraction: "I bring good news, news of light among the women. Light amid darkness; light amid care and sorrow; light amid prejudice and ignorance; light amid oppression and cruelty . . . the light of the souls of good women; light from the Light of the World!" (336). The repetition of *light* underscores the governing movement of the pageant, for the play works to identify heroic black women with each other. Beginning with the "Slave Mother," Ethiopia describes the feats of black women in American history. As she speaks, Sojourner Truth, Harriet Tubman, Amanda

Smith, Phillis Wheatley, Frances Coppin, Katie Ferguson, and Frances Harper[14] progress across the stage, as well as the more generalized figures of "The Mother," "The Teacher," and "The Nurse in uniform" (340), among others. The pageant becomes a palimpsest of female heroism, for each figure evokes the previous ones, and all work together to demonstrate what the Spirit of Service calls "the light in the souls of good women, of women brave and true" (341), producing an abstracted female African American identity.

In fact, some pageants overtly acknowledge the process of telescoping time. In Du Bois's "Pageant for the Bicentenary," the Witch of Endor explains: "I am the black Witch of Endor. To me there is neither Time nor Space. I see all and know all, everywhere; both things that were and shall be. When gold and blood cross my palm, I speak, I recall, I prophesy. I read the Book of Fate" (121). In this work military figures become analogues of each other; at the play's conclusion, children lead "all the colored characters and soldiers" (124) in song. Such a staging makes it easy for any audience to identify the bravery and vitality of Crispus Attucks with that of revolutionary fighters and of Toussaint L'Ouverture. Of course, the presence of the past persists as a theme in contemporary African American literature. The middle passage section of Toni Morrison's *Beloved* makes that point clear when the ghostly child says, "All of it is now it is always now" (210), suggesting, as does children's pageantry, that African American history remains vitally present in the current moment.

Not only do pageant figures reinforce each other in order to shape an ideal of African American identity, but writers often use the pageants' analogizing strategy to define the character of a specific community. It is a commonplace in black theater scholarship that the early plays emphasize community and collective values.[15] Black pageantry, however, moves beyond description to force the audience's involvement in and commitment to a definition of their specific people.

Louise Lovett's "Forward" (1935) employs analogized characters in order to forge an identification between the audience and the subjects onstage.[16] Written during her tenure as a teacher of speech at Cardozo High School, "Forward" traces in five episodes the history of black business education in the District of Columbia from antebellum times to the present. Lovett depicts in intricate, sometimes overwhelming detail the struggles of nineteenth-century leaders, both black and white, to establish elementary and secondary schools for African American youth. Many of the scenes are taken from textual passages, speeches, and Board of Education documents, but all suggest a similar value: the passionate desire for education. Clearly Lovett hoped to identify historical blacks who worked for education with each other, for toward the pageant's conclusion, two "Pages," who represent actual textual leaves, summarize the progress of the pageant in a rapid-fire exchange of numbers and names. The dialogue begins:

> 1st Page: 1870: The Preparatory High School, housed in the 15th Street Presbyterian Church—One teacher, Miss Emma Hutchins —40 pupils.
> 2nd Page: 1871: The Preparatory High School. Place—Stevens School. One teacher, Miss M. J. Patterson, first Negro woman graduate of Oberlin College—46 pupils.
>
> 1st Page: 1872: The Preparatory High School. Place—Summer School. One teacher, Mr. Richard Greener, First Negro graduate of Harvard University. 103 pupils. (19)

The exchange continues to describe events through 1935. By reducing each character, each setting, each moment to its statistical frame, Lovett at once succinctly demonstrates the progress of black education and, by blurring any sense of individuation, makes each passage a mirror of the previous and the next. All descriptions point to the same meaning: black youth's love for education. Lovett encourages her audience to share in this self-definition by including current students in the pages' list: "Today, the enrollment of Cardozo High School is 985 students. There are 30 teachers" (19). By juxtaposing historical figures and drawing a continuity between the past and the present, Lovett implicates her audience in a specific self-definition, one that demands a continued commitment to education.

Alice Dunbar-Nelson's "Douglass Pageant" (1917)[17] asks its audience to embrace an identity built on the increasingly allegorical example of Frederick Douglass. Instead of analogizing various historical figures to create an abstracted ideal, this work recounts episodes in Douglass's life that point toward the orator's bravery. Most interesting, however, is the strategy of an "engaging narrator"[18] through which Dunbar-Nelson encourages her audience to identify with Douglass. The "Messenger" begins each episode by asking the assembled to listen; she then employs physical imagery, beginning with the sentimental and commonplace: "Listen all of you whose hearts beat in sympathy to the sorrows of our beloved Frederick Douglass"; "Listen, all of you who call yourself kin to our beloved Frederick Douglass" (n.p.). By the beginning of scene 7, mention of common blood becomes graphic: "Listen, all of you, in whose veins flows the blood which flowed in the veins of our beloved Frederick Douglass"; scene 8 forces the child listener to equate his whole body with that of his parents, who may have been slaves, and those under slavery: "Listen, all of you whose fathers and mothers toiled in the rice swamp and cotton field, whose bodies are your own because of the Emancipation Proclamation." An early pageant, Dunbar-Nelson's text speaks to a specifically black audience that may have considered itself somewhat distanced from slavery. She requires them to identify themselves with Douglass's bravery and the slaves' triumph over their situation. The corporeal language mounts in each of the nine scenes, forcing the audience to see in its own flesh the heir of Frederick Douglass.

A final level of allegory in pageantry emerges in the figure of the child. Although the performance may require a community to define itself in the pageant's terms, the child actor also assumes a dual role as both a historical figure and a readily identifiable member of the community. The child actor makes present the identity of the past, offering hope for continuance of the pageant's ideals. At the conclusion of "The Light of the Women," for example, a member of the Girl Reserves, a YWCA youth organization, exclaims, "How glad am I that I followed the light! I speak for the Girls of Today. We shall not be unworthy of our goodly heritage but shall strive to carry on the work which has been begun" (341). This looking to the child to perpetuate the ideals allegorized onstage exists in most pageants. In fact, Laura Knight Turner wrote in 1939 of children's identification with their historical roles: "I have seen children of the sixth grade become so engrossed in such an undertaking that they ceased using given names and unconsciously began addressing each other by the names of characters they were representing—such as Harriet Tubman, Crispus Attucks, Booker T. Washington or Frederick Douglass" (36). Through allegory, pageantry provided a common identity, an abstracted ideal of the past that became a communal definition for the present, and, in the figure of the child, a projection of black history and identity into the future.

Of all twentieth-century dramatic forms, the pageant for children is among the most ephemeral. Although some African American pageants of the 1920s and 1930s were preserved in schools and a few were published, many texts do not survive. What does remain, however, is a sense of black pageantry's critical impact on its audience, a community of both young and old, both unlearned and educated. In Du Bois's passion for the genre and in Woodson's patronage and publication of children's pageants a glimpse of black pageantry's cultural significance emerges. More pointedly, the texts themselves reveal a passionate commitment to revising the African American identity through an insistence on black achievement, female equality, and historical equity. A vital source for cultural production and sustenance, the black pageant for children enables us to recognize that the creation of a "New Negro" during the Harlem Renaissance began with the development of a New Negro child.

Notes

1. Du Bois began the Krigwa Players, an alliance of black community theater groups, in 1926 through the NAACP. The little theater movement, a term used by black playwright Randolph Edmonds (Keyssar 7), describes the escalating popularity of plays produced in community halls, schools, libraries, and churches in the 1930s.

2. Although Du Bois is usually identified with propagandistic drama, at times, according to Darwin T. Turner, Du Bois's *Crisis* writings "reveal the ambivalent sentiments or the inherent contradictions" (17) in this propagandistic stance.

3. Not only did Harlem Renaissance thinkers such as Du Bois, Locke, and Woodson emphasize the importance of education to the race's "progress," but with the rise of both industrial schools and college preparatory programs, education became popular as a means to escape poverty and illiteracy among families of most backgrounds.

4. Foster eventually became a contributor to *The Brownies' Book*.

5. Little is known about Guinn; she may have been associated with the YWCA, since they first published the pageant before it was collected in Richardson's *Plays and Pageants from the Life of the Negro* (1930). Richardson's introduction asserts that "the pageant was presented with great success in Bridgeport, Connecticut, and made an equally favorable impression in Atlanta, Georgia, where it was staged soon after. This pageant . . . has enjoyed wider production in popular circles than most of those which have been used" (xlvi).

6. Contemporary writers such as Virginia Woolf, whose *Between the Acts* (1941) takes a town pageant as its topic, recognized the modernistic qualities of a mosaic structure and points of narrative rupture in pageantry.

7. Very little information exists about Inez M. Burke. According to the District of Columbia School System, her records from the 1920s were destroyed in a fire. (The school system never responded to my inquiries about records from the 1930s and 1940s.) Burke did contribute to the *Negro History Bulletin* and may have been an associate of Carter G. Woodson. The *Bulletin* identifies her school as the Charles Young School and in March 1946 pictures Burke twice at a Negro History Week celebration for Woodson. She composed the lyrics to "Our Thanks" for Woodson.

8. This pageant is included in "Our Negro Achievement Book" (1937), written by the sixth-grade students of New York City's P.S. 24; it contains descriptions of famous African Americans as well as the short history play. The school, once located on 128th and Madison, has been demolished; because of redistricting, the present district

office has no idea where its records and yearbooks are housed. This school seems to have been an important point of intersection for children and the leaders and aspirations of the Harlem Renaissance, for the children describe with pride their principal, Gertrude Ayer, the first African American female to head a New York school, a trip to the Schomburg Center, and an upcoming visit from Langston Hughes.

9. Terrell also asserts, "As a rule, colored people have no great love for George Washington because from their youth up they are taught that he was a slave-holder" ("Colored Woman" 412). Terrell writes that her pageant was performed "by the pupils of the public schools of Washington for colored children, assisted by a few citizens . . . [and] by the Booker T. Washington Junior High School of Baltimore" (412).

10. At Howard University, several letters and documents attest to Terrell's determination to include black children in the celebrations. Terrell was on the Pageantry Committee of the George Washington Bicentennial Commission; a letter dated April 30, 1933, from Marie Moore Forrest, head of the "Section of Pageantry and the Drama in the Community Center Department, D.C. Public Schools," endorses the pageant, explaining that "the story of this wonderful negro girl should be known to every colored child as an incentive to the child to perfect its own life. . . . We hope that many cities will produce this beautiful pageant."

11. Gray's introduction to the 1993 reissue of Willis Richardson's *Plays and Pageants From the Life of the Negro* (1930) explains that McCoo was a minister at the A.M.E. Church in Newport, Kentucky, and suggests that the pageant was produced by church members (xxxiv). Richardson's 1930 introduction asserts, "With the assistance of Prof. John R. Hawkins [McCoo] presented this pageant as one of the features of the Quadrennial Conference of the A.M.E. Church in Louisville, Kentucky, in 1924. Since then the pageant has been used extensively in connection with Negro History Week" (xlvi). Although interesting in its use of legal metaphor, McCoo's text is not one of the more suggestive and complex pageants of the period.

12. Most children's pageants of the period, such as those of Guinn, McCoo, and Du Bois, include an aesthetic component, such as poetry readings or song.

13. Gunner, general secretary of the Brooklyn YWCA, originally published "The Light of the Women" through the YWCA's "Woman's Press," though the YWCA's archives have kept no record of the play or its publication date. Collected in Richardson, Gunner's pageant reflects the author's interest in offering role models for junior high and high school girls. Richardson writes, "She considered it especially unfortunate that Negro women knew nothing of those of their sex who have achieved so much as heroines of the critical period through which the race had to pass" (xlvi).

14. Amanda Smith (1837–1915) was a popular evangelical orator, Frances Coppin (1835–1912) an educator, and Catherine (Katie) Ferguson (1749?–1854) spearheaded the Sunday school movement in New York.

15. See, e.g., Helene Keyssar and Elizabeth Brown-Guillory.

16. Louise Johnson Lovett was born in Baltimore on July 30, 1906, graduating from Dunbar High School in 1922 and from Howard University in 1926. She earned an M.A. in speech from Northwestern University in 1938, for which her play "Jungle Lore" served as a thesis. She taught at Bennet College for Women in Greensboro, North Carolina (1926–27), Dillard High School in Goldsboro, North Carolina (1927–29), and Cardozo High School in Washington, D.C. (1929–?). Lovett worked for a time at Camp Pleasant in Dunfries, Virginia, which served underprivileged children.

17. Dunbar-Nelson's text is subtitled "A Pageant in Honor of His Centenary. Howard High School, April 5, 1917." Brief but effective, the pageant includes a unique section titled "The Childhood of Frederick Douglass" that depicts slaves working in a field, an overseer beating a slave woman, and the dramatic separating of young Fred from his grandmother. Like other pageants, the text includes many spirituals.

62 KATHARINE CAPSHAW SMITH

18. Robyn R. Warhol defines *engaging narrator* as that which "strives to close the gaps between the narratee, the addressee, and the receiver" (811).

Brown-Guillory, Elizabeth. *Their Place on the Stage: Black Women Playwrights in America.* New York: Greenwood, 1988.
Burke, Inez M. "Two Races." In *Plays and Pageants from the Life of the Negro.* Ed. Willis Richardson. Washington, D.C.: Associated, 1930. Pp. 295–302.
Du Bois, W. E. B. "Criteria of Negro Art." *Crisis* 32 (October 1926): 290–97.
———. "The Drama Among Black Folk." *Crisis* 12 (August 1916): 169–73.
———. "Krigwa Players Little Negro Theater." *Crisis* 32 (July 1926): 134–36.
———. "A Pageant for the Bicentenary, 1732–1932." *Crisis* 38 (April 1932): 121–24.
———. "The Star of Ethiopia." *Crisis* 11 (December 1915): 90–93.
Dunbar-Nelson, Alice. "Douglass Pageant." Alice Dunbar-Nelson Collection, box 20, folder 379. University of Delaware, Newark. Typescript.
———. "A Pageant: The Negro in History." Alice Dunbar-Nelson Collection, box 20, folder 369. University of Delaware, Newark. Typescript.
Forrest, Marie Moore. Letter to Mary Church Terrell. 30 April 1933. Mary Church Terrell Papers, box 102-2, folder 26. Moorland-Spingarn Research Center, Howard University, Washington, D.C.
Gray, Christine Rauchfuss. " 'So Now I'm Called the Father of Black Drama': Willis Richardson and the Development of African American Drama." Ph.D. diss., University of Maryland, 1995.
Greene, Lorenzo J. *Working with Carter G. Woodson, the Father of Negro History, 1928–1930.* Ed. Arvarh E. Strickland. Baton Rouge: Louisiana State University Press, 1989.
Guinn, Dorothy C. "Out of the Dark." In *Plays and Pageants from the Life of the Negro.* Ed. Willis Richardson. Washington, D.C.: Associated, 1930. Pp. 305–30.
Gunner, Frances. "The Light of the Women." In *Plays and Pageants from the Life of the Negro.* Ed. Willis Richardson. Washington, D.C.: Associated, 1930. Pp. 333–42.
Keyssar, Helene. *The Curtain and the Veil: Strategies in Black Drama.* New York: Burt Franklin, 1981.
Lott, Eric. *Love and Theft: Blackface Minstrelsy and the American Working Class.* New York: Oxford University Press, 1993.
Lovett, Louise J. "Forward: A Pageant in Five Episodes." William A. Joiner Papers, box 120-2, folder 100. Moorland-Spingarn Research Center, Howard University, Washington, D.C. Typescript.
McCoo, Edward J. "Ethiopia at the Bar of Justice." In *Plays and Pageants from the Life of the Negro.* Ed. Willis Richardson. Washington, D.C.: Associated, 1930. Pp. 345–73.
Morrison, Toni. *Beloved.* New York: Penguin, 1997.
New York City Public School 24, Class 6B3. "Negro Achievement: An Original Play." In *Our Negro Achievement Book.* New York: n.p., 1937. Pp. 21–24.
Peterson, Bernard L., Jr. *Early Black American Playwrights and Dramatic Writers: A Biographical Directory and Catalog of Plays, Films, and Broadcasting Scripts.* New York: Greenwood, 1990.
Prevots, Naima. *American Pageantry: A Movement for Art and Democracy.* Ann Arbor: University of Michigan Research Press, 1990.
Richardson, Willis, ed. *Plays and Pageants from the Life of the Negro.* Washington, D.C.: Associated, 1930.
Scott, Freda L. "*The Star of Ethiopia:* A Contribution Toward the Development of Black Drama and Theater in the Harlem Renaissance." In *The Harlem Renaissance: Revalua-

tions. Ed. Amritjit Singh, William S. Shiver, and Stanley Brodwin. New York: Garland, 1989. Pp. 257–69.

Terrell, Mary Church. *A Colored Woman in a White World.* Washington, D.C.: Ransdell, 1940.

———. "Historical Pageant-Play Based on the Life of Phyllis Wheatley." Mary Church Terrell Papers, box 102–6, folder 159. Moorland-Spingarn Research Center, Howard University, Washington, D.C. Typescript.

———. "Why I Wrote the Phyllis Wheatley Pageant-Play." Mary Church Terrell Papers, box 102–6, folder 156. Moorland-Spingarn Research Center, Howard University, Washington, D.C. Typescript.

Turner, Darwin T. "W. E. B. Du Bois and the Theory of a Black Aesthetic." In *The Harlem Renaissance Re-examined.* Ed. Victor A. Kramer. New York: AMS, 1987. Pp. 9–30.

Turner, Laura Knight. "The Problem of Teaching Negro History in the Elementary School." *Negro History Bulletin* (December 1939): 35–36, 39–40, 41.

Warhol, Robyn R. "Toward a Theory of the Engaging Narrator: Earnest Interventions in Gaskell, Stowe, and Eliot." *PMLA* 101, no. 5 (October 1986): 811–18.

Carter G. Woodson. "Introduction." In *Negro History in Thirteen Plays.* Ed. Willis Richardson and May Miller. Washington, D.C.: Associated, 1935. Pp. iii–v.

———. *The Mis-Education of the Negro.* New York: AMS, 1933.

"Yours most loquaciously": Voice in Jean Webster's Daddy-Long-Legs

Anne K. Phillips

Daddy-Long-Legs, Jean Webster's novel about an orphan who is sent to college by an anonymous benefactor, has remained in print since its publication in 1912. Commonly regarded as an American Cinderella tale, it is currently marketed solely as a children's book, although it was widely read by adults as well at the time of its publication. It is often included in discussions of other books of the era that focused on orphans, such as *Pollyanna* and *Anne of Green Gables*—books that James D. Hart dismisses as a "cheery cycle of stories simpering with delight and mawkish with pathos. . . .—no strain upon either adult or youthful reader" (213).[1] Although some critics praise Webster's novel for its compelling heroine and entertaining (if not surprising) plot,[2] historically much of the criticism has been derogatory. Characteristic of such evaluators, Mary Cadogan and Patricia Craig note in *You're a Brick, Angela!* that *Daddy-Long-Legs* is "so trivially girlish a book" (107).

Critics have noted that Webster's is an epistolary novel; however, to date no one has pursued its relation to other epistolary works or traced the significance of its genre, particularly within American literary history.[3] In fact, *Daddy-Long-Legs* is perhaps the most enduring example of a popular epistolary tradition of the nineteenth and early twentieth centuries that emphasized female voice and female education. In this respect, it combines key characteristics of the novel of letters with those of another popular contemporary genre: the college novel. Studying the way these traditions work together in Webster's novel, we learn much more about the significance of the protagonist's evolving voice. In addition, because feminist developmental theory, as exemplified in *Women's Ways of Knowing* by Mary F. Belenky, Blythe Clinchy, Nancy Goldberger, and Jill Tarule, focuses on and convinc-

I would like to thank Kansas State University for the research grant that enabled me to study Webster's papers in the McKinney Family Collection, Special Collections of Lockwood Library, Vassar College. In addition, Roberta Seelinger Trites and an anonymous reader offered perceptive and constructive suggestions that shape the final version of this essay.

Children's Literature 27, ed. Elizabeth Lennox Keyser (Yale University Press, © 1999 Hollins University).

ingly demonstrates the significance of voice, particularly in the first-person narratives of female college students, it is relevant to this analysis of Webster's novel. As the novel's protagonist, Judy, discovers and experiments with her own literary voice through the letters she writes, she also achieves a much greater authority in her significant relationships with others—an issue of special relevance because there has been such intense debate about the relationship between Judy and Jervis in *Daddy-Long-Legs.*

In *The Epistolary Novel,* Godfrey Frank Singer usefully traces the history of the genre from Ovid's *Heroides* through Richardson's *Pamela* and *Clarissa,* among others. American as well as English authors have produced this type of literature: as Singer notes, "undoubtedly the epistles of Benjamin Franklin of a familiar nature, in *Bagatelles,* and the open letters of Francis Hopkinson added something to the literary impulse for letter writing in America. . . . The first American novel, *The Power of Sympathy* [Boston, 1789], was in epistolary form" (195). Such well-known late-nineteenth-century authors as Henry James and (Webster's great-uncle) Mark Twain experimented with the epistolary genre. Singer particularly notes a "revival of novels in letters in the first decade of the twentieth century" (203), among them Jack London's *The Kempton-Wace Letters* and William Dean Howells's *Letters Home* (both published in 1903). According to Elizabeth C. Goldsmith, "Since the sixteenth century, when the familiar letter was first thought of as a literary form, male commentators have noted that the epistolary genre seemed particularly suited to the female voice" (vii), and there are certainly epistolary novels featuring female protagonists that might have served as inspiration for Webster. These include *The Familiar Letters of Peppermint Perkins* (1886), which, according to Singer, "presents the letters of a modern girl of its period. . . . Her reactions to life and people form the extremely amusing substance of the entire book" (202),[4] and (paralleling the development of the relationship in *Daddy-Long-Legs) Lauriel: The Love Letters of an American Girl* (1901), which depicts Laura Livingston's letters to her "friend, later lover, then husband, Rex Strong" (Singer 204). Webster's biographers, Alan and Mary Simpson, suggest that Webster herself "had experimented earlier in her career with telling a story through letters. The publication in 1910 of Eleanor Hallowell Abbott's story *Molly-Make-Believe,* in which Molly, of 'the Serial Letter Company,' is hired by the hero to send him love letters while he is ill, may have inspired her to repeat the experiment" (148).[5] Epistolary novels featuring up-

beat female protagonists, as this brief historical survey suggests, were
quite popular around the turn of the century.

In what ways does *Daddy-Long-Legs* participate in the epistolary
genre? Traditionally, as Janet Gurkin Altman asserts in *Epistolarity*,
"the content of letter novels divides into two basic categories—erotic
and educational. At the center of erotic correspondence stands the
lover-seducer; crucial to the educational sequence is the mentor or
guide" (196). The majority of works in the epistolary tradition follow the erotic pattern. Establishing the pattern, the *Heroides* contains
"fictional letters from abandoned heroines, who repeatedly bemoan
the distance separating them from their lovers" (Altman 13). Or, as
in Pierre-Ambroise-François Choderlos de Laclos's *Les Liaisons dangereuses* (1782), "the letter is an insidious device used by the seducer to
break down his victim's resistance" (Altman 15). Until now, almost all
of the critical commentary on *Daddy-Long-Legs* has interpreted it as an
erotic epistolary novel because it ends with the protagonist's marriage
to her benefactor and because her benefactor has been in a position
of knowledge and power throughout the novel.[6] But the protagonist's
optimistic, energetic letters about her life at a private women's college are hardly those of a despairing lover. We have no sense of Jervis
as a Valmont-like seducer as in *Les Liaisons dangereuses;* indeed, because the only letters contained in the novel are those Judy writes to
her benefactor, Jervis is effectively silenced. The only letter explicitly
identified by Judy as a real "love letter" (304) is the final one—after
she has discovered the secret her benefactor has been keeping—and
her letter emphasizes their equality at that stage of the relationship.

Daddy-Long-Legs adheres more substantially to the educational tradition in epistolary fiction, not only through its emphasis on "the
education of Judy Abbott" but in its depiction of a population still
somewhat unknown at the turn of the century: "college girls."[7] Educational epistolary novels, according to Singer, were established much
earlier in American literary history and describe diverse settings and
experiences in order to educate the reading public about some aspect
of contemporary culture (40). Exemplifying this strain of American
epistolarianism, *Memoirs of the Bloomsgrove Family: In a Series of Letters
to a Respectable Citizen of Philadelphia* (1790) contains "Sentiments on a
Mode of Domestic Education, suited to the present State of Society,
Government, and Manners, in the United States of America: and on
the Dignity and Importance of the Female Character, with a Variety
of Interesting Anecdotes" (Singer 196). In many ways a literary de-

scendant of the *Bloomsgrove* memoirs, Webster's novel provides for the reading population of her own era "sentiments on a mode of domestic education"; it also emphasizes the "dignity and importance of the female character," particularly of the female college student.

At the beginning of the twentieth century, college education for females was still a relatively new aspect of American society.[8] The first women's colleges had opened in the 1860s and 1870s. From their inception, there was considerable concern about, if not outright hostility toward, the notion of higher education for women. Representative of such public anxiety, which continued well into the twentieth century, was Dr. Edward Clarke's *Sex in Education* (1873), in which he argued that allowing women to acquire higher education would waste their reproductive capabilities. Other "experts" concurred in numerous articles in popular magazines that questioned the wisdom of allowing young women to leave the home in pursuit of higher education (for example, see S. Weir Mitchell's "When the College Is Harmful to a Girl"), while G. Stanley Hall and others published studies arguing that because (primarily white, upper-middle-class) women who attended college were not marrying and reproducing, America in effect was committing "race suicide."[9] In Webster's era, there remained many questions about the effect of college on women and thus on society.

Fiction published in the late nineteenth and early twentieth centuries about female college students is very much concerned with the effect of college on young American women.[10] As Caroline Zilboorg notes, the authors of this fiction attempted to "define this new experience for their female protagonists at a time when in life the experience and its significance were not yet conventional or clear" (29). Though one type of college novel identified by Zilboorg is comparable to the erotic epistolary novel in its emphasis on romance and marriage, her second type of college novel is, like the educational strain of epistolary tradition, much more focused on the development of the protagonist. This material is, according to Zilboorg, "aesthetically better and thematically more interesting . . . [w]hile still autobiographically based, in the tradition not of the romance of sentimental courtship but of the *Bildungsroman*" (32).[11] In its emphasis on the development of the protagonist and on her evolving voice, the "aesthetically better" college novel has much in common with the educational epistolary narrative.

Webster's novel responds to many of the concerns of her era about sending young women to college. *Daddy-Long-Legs* is an unabashed campaign on behalf of women's colleges and the benefits for women of the college experience; as Shirley Marchalonis asserts, it "exalts the power of the college to transform" (62). In contrast to earlier epistolary novels, which, according to Goldsmith, "tended to reinforce social restrictions on female enterprise" (ix), Webster's novel powerfully depicts the empowerment of Jerusha Abbott as she develops from an orphan-laborer into a successful, self-sufficient novelist. Webster "believed firmly in women's colleges, and . . . never lost an opportunity to parade for 'Votes for Women' " (Simpson and Simpson 132), and there is evidence that she conceived of her fiction as a useful vehicle for her beliefs:

> For all her flippancy, Jean was too responsive to the appeal of the great women reformers of England and America not to demonstrate her sisterhood with the front-line fighters. The kind of talk that Jane Addams had given at Vassar about "The College Woman and the Social Claim" was part of her implicit religion. She toyed with the idea of a Socialist play in 1909, where the woman who inherits a factory takes the side of the striking workers against her lawyers, and she was to make herself an expert on conditions in Sing Sing as well as in the "John Grier Homes" of America. (Simpson and Simpson 132)

In this context, *Daddy-Long-Legs,* written only two years after Webster's first "Socialist" literary experiment, becomes especially significant as a commentary on the rights of women. Its empowering depiction of a young woman in a distinctly female, nurturing environment may also explain why, of all the popular novels of its era, only *Daddy-Long-Legs* has endured.

Daddy-Long-Legs participates in the educational strains of both the epistolary and the college novel traditions through its specific and fascinating description of college life.[12] Webster demonstrates the effect of the women's college experience on, as Judy describes herself near the beginning of the novel, "a foreigner in the world" (36). Though the college described in the novel is not named,[13] it is clearly drawn from Webster's own experiences at Vassar College. Judy's dorm suite, for instance, is a most accurate description of the arrangement for students within Old Main, the central building on Vassar's campus at the time of Webster's attendance there. Beginning in their sophomore year, Judy, Sally, and Julia share a suite (and Judy provides an illustrated view of the suite in one of her letters). Helen Lefkowitz Horowitz writes in *Alma Mater* that the second president of Vassar, Samuel L. Caldwell, "increased the number of detached single rooms, the choice most in demand, and reduced the number of students sharing a suite from five to three, allowing each to have a separate bedroom" (91). That a wealthy student such as Julia Pendleton should be assigned to share a suite with Judy reflects Vassar's policy of egalitarian assignment of rooms to its students (whereas other colleges enabled cliques to stay together, according to their circumstances, throughout their college years). Judy's, and her roommate Sally's, interest in social work reflects the popularity of the social sciences documented by Barbara Miller Solomon in her study *In the Company of Educated Women.* She writes, "[f]rom the 1890s on, at both women's colleges and coeducational colleges, a significant proportion of the courses students chose were in these developing fields of the social sciences. Some attributed this trend to women's interest in social problems and the new social work field in which such studies as economics and sociology were useful" (82). Even the poem with which Judy is confronted in English class, Emily Dickinson's "I asked no other thing," reflects Webster's college experience. In Vassar English Professor Gertrude Buck's textbook, *A Course in Expository Writing* (1899), which she co-wrote with her colleague Elisabeth Woodbridge, she recommends that students "[i]nterpret the thought in the following poems. . . ." (151). Among four examples specifically identified by the authors is the Dickinson poem. Webster, who specialized in English and economics as an upperclassman, and who maintained a close relationship with her favorite professors after graduation, most probably included this assignment in her novel not only for verisimilitude but also as a teasing tribute to her former professor.[14]

As these brief summaries of *Daddy-Long-Legs* as epistolary and college novel suggest, genre shapes and reveals the trajectory of the novel. Ultimately, this is less a romance than a depiction of the way in which Judy is transformed by—and raises her voice about—her college experience. According to Altman, epistolary novels in which only one character functions as the writer of the letters "emphasize the subject's perspective on events" (205). Marchalonis writes that women's college fiction "emphasizes discovery and expansion of self, talent, and desire and glorifies the resulting happiness that comes from stretching the self and enjoyment of the process" (178). Thus, the evolution of the protagonist's voice in *Daddy-Long-Legs* is especially significant.

Several of the references to Judy's after-hours reading add to our understanding of her evolving sense of self and provide necessary cultural context—for instance, her discovery that she is "the only girl in college who wasn't brought up on 'Little Women'" and her resulting admission, "I just quietly went and bought it with $1.12 of my last month's allowance; and the next time somebody mentions pickled limes, I'll know what she is talking about!" (48). But in connection with her epistolary habit and her developing sense that her daily experiences are a worthy subject for her letters, one reference in particular stands out. Judy tells her benefactor, "We're reading Marie Bashkirtseff's journal. Isn't it amazing?" (123). Even though she notes the somewhat melodramatic tone of the work, the style of Judy's letters suggests that she has taken Bashkirtseff's philosophy to heart. Before her death from tuberculosis at twenty-four, Bashkirtseff, a Russian artist, composed a journal of more than eighty volumes. Prefacing her journal, she wrote, "[t]he record of a woman's life, written down day by day, without any attempt at concealment, as if no one in the world were ever to read it, yet with the purpose of being read, is always interesting" (viii); she also argued that "[s]uch a document is very interesting from a human standpoint" (iii). Her journal was translated into English and published in one volume in 1889, and as Margo Culley explains, it "became phenomenally popular": "a kind of Marie Bashkirtseff cult developed in America. Women from Old Deerfield, Massachusetts to Butte, Montana began keeping journals with the explicit expectation that their journals would make them famous, too. . . . Marie Bashkirtseff readily admitted to 'immense egotism' for which she was both adored and despised. But the wide popularity of her journal in America clearly gave American women 'permission' to pay that kind of sustained attention to the self" (7).[15] Like Bashkirtseff, Judy records the details of daily experience. Though her reports are technically letters to her benefactor, they are presented together to the reader in the form of a journal. It is also significant that later in the novel she dreams about going into a bookstore and purchasing her own "Life and Letters of Judy Abbott" (253). In essence, Judy's reading of Bashkirtseff's journal inspires her own telling of her life story.

In order to more effectively focus on the development of Judy's voice in the novel, I find it useful to employ the developmental stages identified by Belenky, Clinchy, Goldberger, and Tarule in *Women's Ways of Knowing*. For the purposes of this essay, I am less concerned with the ramifications for gender difference that they propose than I am in using their developmental paradigm to gauge Judy's evolving voice. Because *Women's Ways of Knowing* includes numerous interviews with female college students, at private women's colleges as well as at coeducational public institutions, and because it focuses specifically on the students' developing sense of self through the metaphor of voice, it is particularly relevant to this analysis of *Daddy-Long-Legs*. Belenky and her colleagues' case studies of real women's college experiences round out our understanding of Judy's progression through her college life. The narratives contained in *Women's Ways of Knowing*, like the numerous college-based novels of the turn of the century, form a body of information that is relevant and significant. Comparing the developmental paradigm of *Women's Ways of Knowing* with the trajectory of *Daddy-Long-Legs*, we see that Judy moves from feeling "silenced" in the beginning of the novel through a variety of experiential stages, ultimately reaching a sense of personal authority and confidence which Belenky et al. refer to as "constructed knowledge."[16] In that stage, she articulates her opinions clearly and powerfully; she also demonstrates an enhanced self-awareness in her acceptance of relationships with others.

The first stage described in *Women's Ways of Knowing* is "silence." According to Belenky et al., silence may be "a position in which women experience themselves as mindless and voiceless and subject to the whims of external authority" (18). The first section of Webster's novel, a brief passage of approximately fifteen pages, contains a third-person narrative in which we are introduced to the John Grier Home and learn more about "Blue Wednesday," the day the trustees make their monthly inspection. After that section, the novel is told from Judy's first-person perspective as she moves beyond the confines of the asylum. The construction of this opening section literally emphasizes Judy's silencing at the beginning of the novel. In addition, silence functions as a metaphor for powerlessness throughout the first section. When Tommy Dillon comes to tell Judy that the matron wants to see her, she goes "without comment" (7). Her greatest fear at that moment is that one of the younger charges for whom she is responsible has broken out of the silent mode that all orphans are expected to adhere to: "Had—O horrors!—one of the cherubic little babes in her own room F 'sassed' a Trustee?" (8). She responds to Mrs. Lippett's conversation only when Mrs. Lippett seems to expect it, not when she herself might be moved to contribute something, and her responses are not independently formed: "[s]he could only repeat Mrs. Lippett's words" (14). Belenky et al. note that silenced women tend to have grown up "in great isolation"; they tend to have experienced childhoods "with neither play nor dialogue" (32). Certainly Judy's experience at the John Grier Home conforms to these characteristics.

The second stage, according to *Women's Ways of Knowing,* is "received knowledge, . . . a perspective from which women conceive of themselves as capable of receiving, even reproducing, knowledge from the all-knowing external authorities but not capable of creating knowledge on their own" (18). Belenky et al. write that "women who rely on received knowledge think of words as central to the knowing process. They learn by listening. . . . Believing that truth comes from others, they still their own voices to hear the voices of others" (37). Experiencing some freedom for the first time, Webster's heroine changes her name (from "Jerusha" to "Judy"); she nonetheless chooses this particular "pet name" because it is "what Freddie Perkins used to call me before he could talk plain" (33). Judy tells us, "The trouble with college is that you are expected to know such a lot of things you've never learned. It's very embarrassing at times. But now, when the girls talk about things that I never heard of, I just keep still and look them up in the encyclopedia" (29). She accepts the other students' pronouncements as well as those of the professors as "right" or "true." She writes, "The English instructor said that my last paper shows an unusual amount of originality. She did, truly. Those were her words" (34). Later, she writes, "It isn't the work that is going to be hard in college. It's the play. Half the time I don't know what the girls are talking about; their jokes seem to relate to a past that every one but me has shared. I'm a foreigner in the world and I don't understand the language" (36). Ultimately she resorts to studying "cultural linguistics" on her own time; at night, she reads the books that her classmates were raised with. As she writes, "You wouldn't believe, Daddy, what an abyss of ignorance my mind is; I am just realizing the depths myself" (46).

Received knowers depend on authorities; when exams loom, Judy writes, "Some of the girls sell their text-books when they're through with them, but I intend to keep mine. Then after I've graduated I shall have my whole education in a row in the bookcase, and when I need to use any detail, I can turn to it without the slightest hesitation" (58–59). In addition, writing to her benefactor from Lock Willow, a Connecticut farm where she spends her summers, Judy unquestioningly accepts Master Jervie's opinion of the stories and poems she has been submitting to publishers: "Master Jervie read them—he brought in the mail, so I couldn't help his knowing—and he said they were dreadful. They showed that I didn't have the slightest idea of what I was talking about. (Master Jervie doesn't let politeness interfere with truth.) But the last one I did—just a little sketch laid in college—he said wasn't bad and he had it typewritten, and I sent it to a magazine" (192–93). It is understandable that given her background, and her complete lack of freedom or authority during her childhood and adolescence, Judy seems incapable at this point of forming or supporting an independent opinion of her own work.

The third stage, according to *Women's Ways of Knowing,* is "subjective knowledge, . . . a perspective from which truth and knowledge are conceived of as personal, private, and subjectively known or intuited" (15). Belenky et al. note that "[n]o matter what their pasts were, most subjectivist women found it difficult to reflect upon or even describe themselves clearly. Like so many other aspects of their lives that were changing, so, too, was the image they held of themselves" (81–82), stressing that "[t]he women we interviewed who moved far beyond the epistemological atmospheres depicted in their histories had much in common. . . . Each learned to immerse herself in at least one symbol system from a very early age. . . . Frequently they kept a diary" (162). Judy's letters constitute a diary of sorts—a record of her daily experiences and observations. Belenky et al. also write that most of the women in their study who established a healthy sense of self "found important, decent human relationships . . . in their neighborhood, school, or among distant relatives. A few created such relationships for themselves through the sheer power of their imaginations, by endowing their pets and imaginary playmates with those attributes that nourish the human potential" (162–63). Judy creates "Daddy-Long-Legs" according to her needs and through her "journal writing" creates herself as well. She exemplifies the process that Marlene Schiwy describes in "Taking Things Personally: Women, Journal Writing, and Self-Creation":

Frequently, journal writing has no explicit goal save that of deepened self-understanding; yet, paradoxically, it may yield many

significant benefits. It can encourage self-awareness and exploration of one's private and public selves, thereby expanding one's
sense of identity; allow for cathartic expression without fear of
censorship or recrimination; provide a safe testing ground for
questions and half-formed thoughts and insights; stimulate cre-
ativity and the flow of ideas by removing the fear of premature
critical judgment; and build confidence through the gradual
emergence and evolution of the diarist's written voice. Finally
and perhaps most fundamentally, the very process of rendering
her experience into language prompts the journal writer to take
herself, her life, her experience, and her written voice seriously.
Thus, in significant ways, journal writing can empower the writer.
(234–35)[17]

Judy appropriates the letter format and makes it thoroughly her own.
Originally "assigned" to write to her benefactor once a month, describing her studies, she instead writes several times a month; although she mentions her studies in passing, her letters are filled with
the details of her daily life. In contrast to the initial section in which
she is silenced, Judy practically bursts forth with voice through her
letters.

The fourth stage is described as "procedural knowledge," of which
Belenky et al. identify two strains. First there is "separate knowing," a
pattern common to women who have attended college, in which the
women practice seeing the world through the intellectual disciplines
they have studied. Judy identifies for us a few of those patterns; for
instance, she contrasts the chemistry professor's "painstaking passion
for detail" with the history professor's advice to "stand far enough
away to get a perspective on the whole" (128–30). We see diverse
modes of thinking as she practices them in her own discourse. One
letter begins, "Sir: Having completed the study of argumentation and
the science of dividing a thesis into heads, I have decided to adopt
the following form for letter-writing. . . ." (157). The letter that follows
is the only one in the novel to appear in outline form.

As a procedural knower, however, Judy is more easily identified
as a "connected knower." Belenky et al. advise us that "connected
knowers learn through empathy" (115). Judy, for instance, describes
her reading of *Jane Eyre* in the terms of a connected knower: "When
I was reading about little Jane's troubles in the charity school, I got
so angry that I had to go out and take a walk. I understood exactly

how she felt. Having known Mrs. Lippett, I could see Mr. Brockle-hurst" (151–52).[18] This form of procedural knowledge is manifested by Judy throughout the remainder of the novel. As she explains to her benefactor, "I think that the most necessary quality for any person to have is imagination. It makes people able to put themselves in other people's places. It makes them kind and sympathetic and understand-ing. It ought to be cultivated in children" (153). Even when she is arguing with him about whether she should accept a scholarship, she expresses herself as a connected knower: "I suppose you feel that when you set out to educate me, you'd like to finish the work, and put a neat period, in the shape of a diploma, at the end. But look at it just a second from my point of view. . . ." (197).

The fifth and final way of knowing is what Belenky et al. identify as "constructed knowledge." Constructivists "show a high tolerance for internal contradiction and ambiguity. They abandon completely the either/or thinking so common to the previous positions described. They recognize the inevitability of conflict and stress" (137). In addi-tion to her reliance on writing the self through her letters, one of the ways Judy achieves constructivism is through what we might call her support group. At college, she has found women who share her inter-ests; through her involvement with them, she has clearly found her voice. She speaks with enthusiasm of the conversations she has had with her friends: "We spend a whole evening in nothing but talk—talk—talk—and go to bed with a very uplifted feeling, as though we had settled permanently some pressing world problems" (216). Her great-est objection to a visit to the home of Julia Pendleton, Jervis's niece, is that "[t]he material atmosphere of that house was crushing; I didn't draw a deep breath until I was on an express train coming back. All the furniture was carved and upholstered and gorgeous; the people I met were beautifully dressed and low-voiced and well-bred, but it's the truth, Daddy, I never heard one word of real talk from the time we arrived until we left" (213–14). Significantly, Belenky et al. assert that "[t]he devotion of constructivists to 'real talk' as a way of connecting to others and acquiring and communicating new knowledge distin-guishes them in both their personal and professional lives" (145).

Additional evidence that Judy has become a constructivist lies in her commitment to settling "pressing world problems." Belenky et al. assert that "[c]onstructivist women aspire to work that contributes to the empowerment and improvement in the quality of life of others. More than any other group of women in this study, the constructivists feel a part of the effort to address with others the burning issues of the day and to contribute as best they can" (152). Though Judy comments frequently on religion, politics, and philosophy, she is, understandably, especially interested in the condition of dependent children. In her junior year she writes, "I've elected economics this year—very illuminating subject. When I finish that I'm going to take Charity and Reform; then, Mr. Trustee, I'll know just how an orphan asylum ought to be run" (205).

Finally, Judy's constructivism is particularly evident after she graduates from college and publishes her novel, achieving for herself a degree of financial independence. Belenky et al. write that once women reach the constructivist stage, they "no longer want to suppress or deny aspects of the self in order to avoid conflict or simplify their lives. . . . These women want to embrace all the pieces of the self in some ultimate sense of the whole—daughter, friend, mother, lover, nurturer, thinker, artist, advocate" (137). Manifesting this desire, Judy muses in a letter to Daddy-Long-Legs, "After having been educated to be a writer, I must at least try to be one; it would scarcely be fair to accept your education and then go off and not use it. But now that I am going to be able to pay back the money, I feel that I have partially discharged that debt—besides, I suppose I could keep on being a writer even if I did marry. The two professions are not necessarily exclusive" (293). Judy's attitude demonstrates the tendency of constructivist women in Belenky's study to perceive their goal as "a *life* foreseen rather than a single commitment foreseen" (150, emphasis in original).

It is disturbing that so little criticism of *Daddy-Long-Legs* focuses on Judy herself, as opposed to Jervis. Karen Alkalay-Gut implies that any agency apparent at the end of the novel is not Judy's but Jervis's: "the trustee has—by providing a literary education and an audience—literally given the orphan her own voice" (91–92). Alberghene writes that Judy

feels self-worth not only because of who she is or what she had done or can do, but because she has received a present. . . . Judy is scarcely able to distinguish her "sweet" self from the boxes of desirable bon bons which made her feel valuable for the first time; she herself is both a consumer and a deliciously consumable object. Such a conflation does not bode well, especially since the man Judy deals with is a spider, one who's waited on his web four years. ("Daddies' Girls" 76)

These and other readings evidently stem from the readers' interpretation of the novel primarily as a romance. Viewing it within the educational epistolary tradition, and the *Bildungsroman* tradition of the college novel, we might allow instead that Judy's voice is undeniably her own and that the choices she makes at the end of the novel, as a result of her empowering college experience, reflect her constructivist desire to "embrace all of the pieces of the self."

The perceived weaknesses in the relationship may stem from Webster's decision to fashion her work as an epistolary college novel. In effect, because she chooses to focus on Judy, subordinating the romance to Judy's coming-of-age, she reduces Jervis to the figure in the shadows. It is true that in the novel Jervis might seem to have fostered an imbalance of power in his relationship with Judy. Because he hasn't told her that he is both "Daddy-Long-Legs" and Jervis Pendleton, he has had access to Judy's thoughts and discussion about their relationship without sharing his own with her. Certainly Jervis is all too human. He forbids her to spend her summer vacation with the McBrides (after all, her roommate's brother, a Princeton student, might be a rival for her affections), and he criticizes much of the fiction she writes during vacation (though he does encourage her to publish the best material—significantly, the "little sketch laid in college" [193]). After this point in the novel, however, Judy's relationship with her mentor is much more an equal one. She is awarded a scholarship for her final two years of college, based on her excellence in English, and at first "Mr. John Smith" directs her, by way of his secretary, not to accept it. Judy stands up to him, declaring, "I never knew a man so obstinate and stubborn and unreasonable, and tenacious, and bull-doggish, and unable-to-see-other-people's-points-of-view as you" (200), and she delivers her own ultimatum: "I refuse, sir, to give up the scholarship; and if you make any more fuss, I won't accept the monthly allowance either, but will wear myself into a nervous wreck tutoring stupid Freshmen" (201). When Jervis tries to convince her to travel to Europe after her junior year, she refuses. She reports, "He said I was a silly, foolish, irrational, quixotic, idiotic, stubborn child (those are a few of his abusive adjectives; the rest escape me) and that I didn't know what was good for me; I ought to let older people judge" (239)—but she holds her ground, and she spends the summer as she has chosen to, tutoring two young women. Judy fights for her independence, writing of Jervis, "I *must* show him that he can't dictate to me" (244, emphasis in original). Her financial independence, both as a tutor and, later, as a successful writer, enables her to meet Jervis on a more equal footing.

The notes Webster made on characterization as she prepared to write the stage play of *Daddy-Long-Legs* affirm Judy's authoritative role in the relationship. Whereas Jervis is described as "crabbed pessimistic suspicious blasé, cynical," Judy is full of "[b]uoyant youthfulness. Freedom, optimism, promise." Elsewhere, in a draft for the play, Jervis tells Miss Pritchard, Judy's advocate, "I never let her know who I was because I didn't want her to like me through gratitude or any feeling of indebtedness—also the kind of love that Daddy Long Legs inspired was a touch too paternal."[19] Finally, though Jervis initially determined to send Judy to college in order for her to become a writer, and though Judy actually publishes a novel (in addition to winning literary contests throughout her college career), she is not limited to a sense of herself solely as a writer. Her interest in social work and socialism, evident throughout the novel, suggests that Judy will become more active as a philanthropist than as a writer. In this area, the lovers meet on equal ground. Though Jervis, because of his wealth, is able to support a variety of charities including the John Grier Home, it is Judy, because of her experience and her position as a connected learner, who will best be able to envision ways of enacting and improving their reforms. Karen Rosenberg suggests that Jervis is the reason that Judy is interested in social work—"small wonder, then, that Jerusha signs up for a course in Charity and Reform" (24)—however, it is far more likely that Judy's own life experience is her impetus. It is even possible that Jervis has learned something from Judy about social work, reform, and common humanity. Even prior to her involvement with Jervis, Judy describes her beliefs about how an asylum should and should not be organized—and how people should and should not be dealt with. In relation to this subject, Alkalay-Gut writes perceptively of the change in the balance in power between Jervis and Judy:

> [C]ertainly an underlying basis for the relationship of the two
> lovers is political: Pendleton's initial intervention in Judy's edu-
> cation results from the socialism that labels him a "black sheep."
> But although at the beginning of their relationship he teaches

her about socialism and her individual potential, the capitalis-
tic/philanthropic basis of his socialism that causes him to remove
the individual from his environment rather than correcting the
general situation itself . . . suggests that he has something more
to learn about politics and people. This he learns from Judy in
their confrontations as she grows to understand and explain the
precise nature of the damage imposed by a charitable institution
lacking in humanity and individuality and as she comes to refuse
to accept even overwhelming gifts while reiterating the need for
responsible freedom. (97)

Though in this post-Freudian age the term "Daddy" for a lover
understandably makes readers uneasy, there are additional reasons
why Jervis might indeed be a worthy partner for Judy. First, they
share a sense of humor—Mrs. Lippett describes Jervis's sense of humor at the very beginning of the novel as "immoderate"; she notes
that the (whimsical) perspective on the asylum displayed in Judy's
essay has struck the trustee as humorous (13). And Judy comments,
"He and I always think the same things are funny, and that is such a
lot; it's dreadful when two people's sense of humor are antagonistic.
I don't believe there's any bridging that gulf!" (291).[20] Second, from
the earliest stages of her friendship with Jervis, Judy has considered
him a "kindred spirit": during her first summer at Lock Willow, she
describes Jervis as "someone who speaks my language" (181). Representative of their equality is their term of address for each other once
Judy learns that "Daddy" and Jervis are one and the same. She reports
that on her arrival at his New York home, Jervis refers to her as "dear
little Judy" (302); she responds in kind by continuing to refer to him,
in her salutation and in her letter, as "Master Jervie." In the context
of male-female relationships in Webster's fiction, particularly *Daddy-
Long-Legs* and its sequel, *Dear Enemy,* Judy and Jervis's relationship,
built on complementary personalities and profound mutual interests,
is indeed a positive one.

That Webster's novel was highly successful, no one can doubt. Not
only has it sold millions of copies, but it has been produced on stage
(becoming the most popular play of the early twentieth century)[21]
and transformed into four American films between 1919 and 1955.[22]
With its message that women not only could but should attend college, *Daddy-Long-Legs* is an important cultural marker. The effect of its
message is, however, contested. Marchalonis, for instance, asserts that

"[b]ecause of its enormous popularity, the message it carried about women in college was widespread. Judy Abbott's situation was unique, but the story presents the college as a magical place, the green world in which she and others might mature and find identity . . . ; the college has changed her potentially limited, wasted life to something rich, secure, and positive" (62–63). In contrast, Inness maintains that "the readers of women's college novels are shown that little of the empowerment they experience while students can be retained after leaving college" (109). Writing of *Daddy-Long-Legs* in particular, Inness argues that "college novels reassured their early twentieth-century readers that women's college life would not interfere with a woman's progression to marriage and domesticity. Moreover, the women's college was represented as even facilitating a desirable marriage" (165 n.1). Judy Abbott's marriage, however, does not alter her most important power base—her sense of herself as a constructed knower. Combined with her ongoing interest in reform, Judy's self-awareness and confidence will enable her to act not merely as a wife but as a worker after the close of her college career. Particularly in *Daddy-Long-Legs* and *Dear Enemy*, marriage does not negate the possibility of reform; instead, it facilitates personal and social transformation.

It is perhaps ironic that *Daddy-Long-Legs*, with its emphatic campaign on behalf of women's colleges and women's rights, should have been serialized in *The Ladies' Home Journal*. Though the editor of the *Journal*, Edward W. Bok, engaged in a bidding war with other popular magazines for Webster's manuscript (eventually paying the princely sum of $1,500 for it), and though he counted Webster among his most successful authors, he was quite conservative with regard to women's issues. Bok's biographer, Salme Harju Steinberg, strives to make a case for Bok's impartiality regarding women's issues—or at least his willingness to allow both sides space to make their arguments on issues such as suffrage. Nonetheless, he abhorred women's clubs and consistently argued that a woman's place was in the home. Throughout the first decade of the twentieth century, his magazine published articles questioning whether women should even attend college.[23] Marchalonis describes the *Journal*'s pattern of "determined trivializing" of women's issues (176); Bok wrote approvingly of the woman for whom "her home is her empire and in that she is supreme" (quoted in Steinberg 47). Even Steinberg writes that "[I]n a period when much talk centered on women's widening horizons, Bok wrote to one of his contributors, 'My idea, you know, is rather to keep women [*sic*] in the home especially as there are enough writers who are trying to take her out of it" (66). The resolution of *Daddy-Long-Legs*, in which Judy agrees to marry Jervis, must have seemed, to Bok, to reinforce the status quo—but in accepting the story, he nonetheless introduced some profound arguments in favor of the college life to his middle-class audience.

Daddy-Long-Legs is the only popular epistolary novel from the turn of the century that remains in print. It is also the most well known and enduring of all the novels about "college girls." It would be a mistake to discount the appeal of its romance; the engagement of Judy to Jervis in the final letter of the novel contributes a sense of completion to the work. Its longevity and continued ability to attract both recreational readers and literary scholars need to be studied from more diverse perspectives, however. Its participation in both the epistolary and the college novel traditions adds layers of literary and historical relevance to the novel that have not been often enough acknowledged. In particular, the heroine's emerging voice (as opposed to her benefactor's silence) should be recognized as a significant aspect of the novel. Surveying the closings of her letters, we recognize the energy, diversity, and attraction of this young woman. Whether she is chagrined ("Yours in sackcloth" [63]); playful ("yours most graciously, Ophelia, Queen of Denmark" [135]); exultant ("Yours ever, Jerusha Abbott, Author of, 'When the Sophomores Won the Game.' For sale at all news stands, price ten cents" [195]); determined ("Yours, With a Mind, Completely and Irrevocably and World-Without-End Made-up. Jerusha Abbott" [202]); or sentimental ("Yours, forever and ever" [304]), she lifts a vividly drawn, compelling voice. Thoroughly "loquacious," Judy is also profoundly interesting.

Notes

1. Hart mistakenly includes *Dear Enemy*, the sequel to *Daddy-Long-Legs*, as an "orphan" tale (213); although the protagonist of *Dear Enemy*, Sally McBride, is employed as the matron at an orphan asylum, she is not herself an orphan. Perry Nodelman doesn't specifically discuss *Daddy-Long-Legs*, but his essay "Progressive Utopia" provides a useful overview of the early-twentieth-century orphan-protagonist genre.

2. See, e.g., Janice M. Alberghene's "Will the Real Young Adult Novel Please Stand Up?," Karen Alkalay-Gut's "'If Mark Twain Had a Sister'"; Anne Bower's chapter on *Daddy-Long-Legs* in *Epistolary Responses*; and Karen Rosenberg's "Daddy's Girl." As Bower writes, the novel version of *Daddy-Long-Legs* "features an epistolary heroine devoted to writing as a scene of discovery—a powerful, protected, personal site of agency" (96).

3. Cadogan and Craig write that the epistolary form is "a literary form which better writers than Jean Webster have found cumbersome" (105).

4. Paralleling Webster's initial serialization of her novel, individual letters from *The Familiar Letters of Peppermint Perkins* were originally published in the Boston *Saturday Evening Gazette.*

5. The Simpsons' reference to Webster's earlier epistolary work is probably made in connection with the unfinished drafts of *Carnival House,* set in Italy. A later version of this story, *The Pigs of Palestrina,* remained unpublished at Webster's death.

6. Among these critics, see Alberghene, "Daddies' Girls," and Cadogan and Craig, who write, "Jarvis [*sic*] Pendleton, who, we are told early in the book, 'does not care for girls,' can have only one motive for undertaking to pay for Judy's education. Having failed, like Adam Ladd [of *Rebecca of Sunnybrook Farm*], to find a girl who suits his 'somewhat fastidious and exacting tastes' he has determined to fashion one for himself, by a process of fairly remote control" (107).

7. As Shirley Marchalonis notes in *College Girls,* the vast majority of authors of novels about young women attending college in the late nineteenth and early twentieth centuries referred to their subjects as "girls." I retain the term, according to her convincing rationale: "'girl' as used in these texts denotes a stage in female development, movement from child to girl to woman, and the term in context is not one of belittlement, but a definition of an age and status group: young and unmarried, characterized by innocence, unworldliness, virginity, and youthful freshness" (7). Although Marchalonis comments more extensively on *Daddy-Long-Legs* than on many of her other subjects, her decision to develop her study as a broad survey of college fiction for women limits the depth of her analysis. She identifies the potential for personal development inherent in the college setting, in addition to the romantic aspect of the novel, as the strengths of Webster's work; she doesn't, however, comment specifically on the evolution of Judy's voice in *Daddy-Long-Legs.*

8. For thorough discussions of the culture of women's colleges and the effect of higher education for women on the American public, see Helen Lefkowitz Horowitz, *Alma Mater,* and Barbara Miller Solomon, *In the Company of Educated Women,* as well as Sherrie A. Inness, *Intimate Communities.*

9. Numerous sources provide information about women's colleges and race suicide. See, e.g., G. Stanley Hall and Theodore L. Smith, "Marriage and Fecundity of College Men and Women" or Charles Franklin Emerick, "College Women and Race Suicide," as well as Julia Ward Howe's *Sex and Education.* For a more substantial late-twentieth-century overview, see Carroll Smith-Rosenberg, *Disorderly Conduct..*

10. For studies of fiction about college students in America, see John O. Lyons, *The College Novel in America,* which contains one chapter on women's college stories; Caroline Zilboorg's "Women Before World War I"; and Marchalonis's recent and most comprehensive study.

11. Though Zilboorg does not discuss *Daddy-Long-Legs,* I would argue that Webster's novel, though to some extent a romance, fits many of the characteristics of her second category. According to Zilboorg, "most of the female figures in these novels have long before college sensed their real 'difference' from others" (33); they "frequently have an exclusive relationship with their fathers" (34); also, the female protagonist "confronts independently of her family and familiar community a sense of her identity as a self-reliant woman with a rare intellect and rare academic achievements" (34).

12. *Daddy-Long-Legs* is an autobiographical coming-of-age novel, though not in the way that Webster's biographers suggest. They focus on the romantic aspect of the novel, writing that Webster "knew more about the characters than anyone else because, though no orphan herself, she was Judy Abbott in imagination and was recapitulating her own experiences, writing in the Berkshires, secretly engaged to her own rich man" (Simpson and Simpson 8). I would argue that the novel is based less on Webster's own epistolary romance than on her experiences at college. Though *Daddy-Long-Legs* is perhaps the best known and most enduring of Webster's works, it is not her first

experiment with college fiction. *When Patty Went to College* (1903), a collection of short stories based on her own experiences at Vassar College (1897–1901), was the third such publication about Vassar by an alumna to appear between 1899 and 1903. Julia August Schwartz ('96) published *Vassar Studies* in May 1899; Grace Gallagher ('97), a former editor of the *Vassar Miscellany,* published *Vassar Stories* in December of the same year. Webster reviewed these works in her column on college life in the *Poughkeepsie Sunday Courier* (Simpson and Simpson 63). Her own work, dedicated "to 234 Main [Webster's dorm suite], and all the good times we had there," was highly praised at its publication. Though Webster published other works, including a murder mystery in the tradition of Anna Katherine Green (*The Four Pools Mystery*), a romantic comedy (*Jerry Junior*), and a political novel about the economic plight of Italian peasants (*The Wheat Princess*), it is her fiction about the college experience that has been most enduring.

13. Though critics such as Inness and Martha Banta persist in identifying Judy as a "Vassar girl," the college is not identified in Webster's novel, in part, I would argue, because Webster is writing generically and metaphorically about women's college experiences.

14. Buck arrived at Vassar with a Ph.D. from Michigan in 1897, the same year that Webster began her studies. Simpson and Simpson explain that freshman and sophomore students studied expository writing and argumentation, respectively; Webster herself wrote in her column in the *Poughkeepsie Sunday Courier* that "[I]f any mortal should ever escape from the freshman class without knowing how to write readily and fluently in every style, it will be due entirely to her own utter and irrevocable stupidity and not to the fault of the English Department. . . . She is put through a course of English gymnastics which tends to bring out every atom of native ability that she possesses, and she emerges at the end of the year astonished at her own literary prowess" (quoted in Simpson and Simpson 50–51). Buck was, because of her particular research interest in the psychology of the writer, an especially significant influence on Webster. As JoAnn Campbell writes in "Women's Work, Worthy Work: Composition Instruction at Vassar College, 1897–1922," Buck especially maintained that in order to facilitate the development of the writer, "familiar forms of writing such as letters, narration, and description should be used" (36). Gerald P. Mulderig concurs, writing that "Buck's textbooks illustrate her desire to revitalize composition instruction by emphasizing the psychological processes that underlie writing" (99). Finally, in her essay " 'In an Atmosphere of Peril': College Women and Their Writing," Vickie Ricks argues that the curriculum in English in general at Vassar was "particularly aimed at self-realization" (74). It is apt that Judy achieves such distinctive self-realization in Webster's novel.

15. Bashkirtseff's journal was popular enough that two separate (and competitive) editions were published. The first, an abridgment translated by Mary J. Serrano, was published by Cassel in 1889. In 1890, Rand, McNally published a second edition, newly translated and advertised as the "only complete English Edition" by A. D. Hall and G. B. Heckel. In their introduction they write, "mutilated translations of the journal have been published, but the translators of this edition have not found it in their hearts to resist the mute pleadings of that stilled voice. . . ." (8).

16. For a useful analysis of the methodology employed in *Women's Ways of Knowing,* as well as an assessment of its place in current scholarship on gender and psychology, see Bernice Lott, "Dual Natures or Learned Behavior," as well as Rachel T. Hare-Mustin and Jeanne Marecek's "Gender and the Meaning of Difference" in the same volume. Incidentally, like the women interviewed by Belenky and her colleagues, Judy does not progress in a strictly linear fashion from silence to constructed knowledge. She may move from a period of connected knowing back into received knowledge in the middle of the novel; nonetheless, once she achieves constructed knowledge, she does not regress to the earlier stages.

17. Another significant aspect of Judy's "letters as journal" is the mode of illus-

tration, which serves to establish verisimilitude. Culley writes that "all the material aspects of a diary create important impressions" (14), and the illustrations certainly convey character and tone throughout the novel. Schiwy concurs, noting that "the paper on which it is written, possible enclosures, fluctuations in handwriting, sketches, diagrams, and anything else that reveals the journal writer's personality and experience" (16) provide a "tangible" link between writer and reader. Judy's choice, in various letters, of italics, bold print, and other variations all convey tone and meaning, as do her variant salutations and closings. The difference between a letter addressed to "Mr. John Smith" and one addressed to "My very dearest Master-Jervie-Daddy-Long-Legs-Pendleton-Smith" is essential to the work as a whole. As Altman asserts, "[t]he ritual of opening and closing a letter imposes upon the writer a gesture of self-definition vis-à-vis the addressee" (146).

18. I am indebted to John Seelye and Elizabeth Keyser for their interest in *Daddy-Long-Legs* as a literary descendant of *Jane Eyre*. Both novels feature orphans sent away to school, powerful male mentors who must, in some way, be physically diminished before the conclusion of the novel, and strong, articulate, compassionate heroines.

19. All quotations from notes and drafts are courtesy of the Jean Webster McKinney Collection, Special Collections, Lockwood Library, Vassar College.

20. Webster provides examples of marriages that fail in part because the couples lack a common sense of humor in *Daddy-Long-Legs* and *Dear Enemy*. In the latter, Sally McBride writes to Judy of the divorce of one of their classmates, Helen Brooks. Chief among the reasons for the dissolution of the marriage is the couple's lack of a common sense of humor. Sally writes, "But as they began to get acquainted, they didn't like the same books or jokes or people or amusements. He was expansive and social and hilarious, and she wasn't. . . . And she, on her side, was awfully unresponsive and irritating,—she realized it fully,—she got to the point where she wouldn't laugh at his jokes" (277).

21. Writing in the *Chicago Herald* on 4 May 1916, Richard Henry Little claimed that Webster's play was "in danger of rivaling . . . 'Uncle Tom's Cabin.'" The West Coast road company (the third to simultaneously tour different regions of the country) smashed every attendance record previously set. Between the continued book sales and the success of the stage play, Webster was, as reported by the *Sacramento Bee* (8 April 1916), "the highest paid woman writer in the United States."

22. After Ruth Chatterton became famous for playing Judy on stage, Mary Pickford starred in and produced a silent film version in 1919; Janet Gaynor starred in the 1931 "talkie" remake; Shirley Temple starred in an uncredited version of the story in *Curly Top* (1935); and Leslie Caron and Fred Astaire starred in the 1955 film of the same title (although the plot bears little resemblance to Webster's novel). Bower assesses each of the films (plus a 1984 Japanese cartoon version) in her *Epistolary Responses*.

23. See, e.g., An American Mother, "Is College the Best Thing for Our Girls?" According to Marchalonis, Bok "firmly and consistently held that higher education could be tolerated unless it were to interfere with woman's destined role as wife and mother" (39).

Works Cited

Alberghene, Janice M. "Daddies' Girls." *ChLA Quarterly* 12, no. 2 (summer 1987): 75–78.
——— . "Will the Real Young Adult Novel Please Stand Up?" *ChLA Quarterly* 10, no. 3 (fall 1985): 135–36.
Alkalay-Gut, Karen. "'If Mark Twain Had a Sister': Gender-Specific Values and Structure in Daddy Long-Legs." *Journal of American Culture* 16, no. 4 (winter 1993): 91–99.
Altman, Janet Gurkin. *Epistolarity: Approaches to a Form.* Columbus: Ohio State University Press, 1982.

American Mother, An. "Is College the Best Thing for Our Girls?" *Ladies' Home Journal* 17 (June 1900): 15.

Banta, Martha. *Imaging American Women: Idea and Ideals in Cultural History.* New York: Columbia University Press, 1987.

Bashkirtseff, Marie. *The Journal of a Young Artist 1860–1884.* Trans. Mary J. Serrano. New York: Cassell, 1889.

Belenky, Mary F., Blythe Clinchy, Nancy Goldberger, and Jill Tarule. *Women's Ways of Knowing: The Development of Self, Voice, and Mind.* New York: Basic, 1986.

Bower, Anne. *Epistolary Responses: The Letter in 20th-Century American Fiction and Criticism.* Tuscaloosa: University of Alabama Press, 1997.

Buck, Gertrude, and Elisabeth Woodbridge. *A Course in Expository Writing.* New York: Henry Holt, 1899.

Cadogan, Mary, and Patricia Craig. *You're a Brick, Angela! A New Look at Girls' Fiction from 1839 to 1975.* London: Victor Gollancz, 1976.

Campbell, JoAnn. "Women's Work, Worthy Work: Composition Instruction at Vassar College, 1897–1922." In *Constructing Rhetorical Education.* Ed. Marie Secor and Davida Charney. Carbondale: Southern Illinois University Press, 1992. Pp. 26–42.

Clarke, Edward H. *Sex in Education.* Reprinted in *Sex and Education: A Reply to Dr. E. H. Clarke's "Sex in Education."* Ed. Julia Ward Howe. Boston: Roberts, 1874; New York: Arno, 1972.

Culley, Margo, ed. *A Day at a Time: The Diary Literature of American Women from 1764 to the Present.* New York: Feminist Press-City University of New York, 1985.

Emerick, Charles Franklin. "College Women and Race Suicide." *Political Science Quarterly* 24 (June 1909).

Goldsmith, Elizabeth C. "Introduction." In *Writing the Female Voice: Essays on Epistolary Literature.* Boston: Northeastern University Press, 1989. Pp. vii–xiii.

Hall, A. D., and G. B. Heckel, eds. *The Journal of Marie Bashkirtseff.* New York: Rand, McNally, 1890.

Hall, G. Stanley, and Theodore L. Smith. "Marriage and Fecundity of College Men and Women." *The Pedagogical Seminary* 10 (September 1903).

Hare-Mustin, Rachel T., and Jeanne Marecek. "Gender and the Meaning of Difference." In *Making a Difference: Psychology and the Construction of Gender.* New Haven: Yale University Press, 1990. Pp. 22–64.

Hart, James D. *The Popular Book: A History of America's Literary Taste.* Berkeley: University of California Press, 1963.

Horowitz, Helen Lefkowitz. *Alma Mater: Design and Experience in the Women's Colleges from Their Nineteenth-Century Beginnings to the 1930s.* Amherst: University of Massachusetts Press, 1993.

Howe, Julia Ward. 1874. *Sex and Education: A Reply to Dr. E. H. Clarke's "Sex in Education."* New York: Arno, 1972.

Inness, Sherrie A. *Intimate Communities: Representation and Social Transformation in Women's College Fiction, 1895–1910.* Bowling Green, Ohio: Bowling Green State University Popular Press, 1995.

Kauffman, Linda. "Special Delivery: Twenty-first-Century Epistolarity in *The Handmaid's Tale.*" In *Writing the Female Voice: Essays on Epistolary Literature.* Ed. Elizabeth C. Goldsmith. Boston: Northeastern University Press, 1989. Pp. 221–44.

Little, Richard Henry. "The Theatres." *Chicago Herald,* 4 May 1916.

Lott, Bernice. "Dual Natures or Learned Behavior: The Challenge to Feminist Psychology." In *Making a Difference: Psychology and the Construction of Gender.* New Haven: Yale University Press, 1990. Pp. 65–101.

Lyons, John O. *The College Novel in America.* Carbondale: Southern Illinois University Press, 1962.

Marchalonis, Shirley. *College Girls: A Century in Fiction.* New Brunswick, N.J.: Rutgers University Press, 1995.

Mitchell, S. Weir. "When the College Is Harmful to a Girl." *Ladies' Home Journal* (June 1900): 14.

Mulderig, Gerald P. "Gertrude Buck's Rhetorical Theory and Modern Composition Teaching." *Rhetorical Society Quarterly* 14, nos. 3–4 (1984): 95–104.

Nodelman, Perry. "Progressive Utopia: Or, How to Grow Up Without Growing Up." In *Such a Simple Little Tale: Critical Responses to L. M. Montgomery's* Anne of Green Gables. Ed. Mavis Reimer. Metuchen, N.J.: Children's Literature Association-Scarecrow, 1992. Pp. 29–38.

Review of *Daddy-Long-Legs. Sacramento Bee,* 8 April 1916.

Ricks, Vickie. " 'In an Atmosphere of Peril': College Women and Their Writing." In *Nineteenth-Century Women Learn to Write.* Ed. Catherine Hobbs. Charlottesville: University Press of Virgina, 1995. Pp. 59–83.

Rosenberg, Karen. "Daddy's Girl." *The Women's Review of Books* 10 (July 1993): 23–24.

Schiwy, Marlene A. "Taking Things Personally: Women, Journal Writing, and Self-Creation." *NWSA Journal* 6 (1994): 234–54.

Simpson, Alan, and Mary Simpson, with Ralph Connor. *Jean Webster, Storyteller.* Tymor, 1984.

Singer, Godfrey Frank. 1933. *The Epistolary Novel: Its Origin, Development, Decline, and Residuary Influence.* New York: Russell and Russell, 1963.

Smith-Rosenberg, Carroll. *Disorderly Conduct: Visions of Gender in Victorian America.* New York: Knopf, 1985.

Solomon, Barbara Miller. *In the Company of Educated Women: A History of Women and Higher Education in America.* New Haven: Yale University Press, 1985.

Steinberg, Salme Harju. *Reformer in the Marketplace: Edward W. Bok and the* Ladies' Home Journal. Baton Rouge: Louisiana State University Press, 1979.

Webster, Jean. 1912. *Daddy-Long-Legs.* New York: Grosset and Dunlap, 1931.

———. *Dear Enemy.* New York: Century, 1915.

———. *When Patty Went to College.* 1903. New York: Grosset and Dunlap, 1906.

Zilboorg, Caroline. "Women Before World War I: An Exploration of Their Awakening in the College Novel." *Great Lakes Review* 7 (summer 1981): 29–38.

Pollyanna and the Not So Glad Game

Alice Mills

> *Pity would be no more*
> *If we did not make somebody poor;*
> *And Mercy no more could be*
> *If all were as happy as we.*
> —William Blake, "The Human Abstract"

When Eleanor Porter's *Pollyanna* was issued by the Boston publisher L. C. Page in 1913, Porter was already a successful author, with the best-selling *Miss Billie* to her credit. But *Pollyanna* was more than a best-seller; it was a publishing phenomenon. For two years *Pollyanna* stayed on the American best-seller list, to be joined in 1915 by its sequel, *Pollyanna Grows Up*, also published by Page.[1] In both books, Porter sets up and solves mysteries of identity and relationships. *Pollyanna* is the story of an orphan reluctantly taken in by the bitter spinster Aunt Polly and of the child's transformation of her aunt and everyone else who comes close to her by means of her Glad Game. *Pollyanna Grows Up* deals with the mysterious origins of Pollyanna's friends Jamie and Jimmy alongside Pollyanna's own maturation and falling in love, together with more examples of the Glad Game at work transforming the unhappy and the unwell.

After Porter's death, her publishers commissioned other writers to carry on Pollyanna's story in twelve more "Glad Books," to marriage and beyond, to her family's travels and the adventures of her children from babyhood to marriage. The sequels' titles indicate the general drift of most of their plots from Porter's original. Harriet Lummis Smith began with Pollyanna's marriage, in *Pollyanna of the Orange Blossoms*, and then started to move Pollyanna across America for fresh interest in *Pollyanna's Jewels*, *Pollyanna's Debt of Honor*, and *Pollyanna's Western Adventure*. Elizabeth Borton kept changing the locale in her contributions to the series, *Pollyanna in Hollywood*, *Pollyanna's Castle in Mexico*, *Pollyanna's Door to Happiness*, and *Pollyanna's Golden Horseshoe*.

I wish to acknowledge the help of Marcia Pope with the clarification and organization of this paper's argument.
Children's Literature 27, ed. Elizabeth Lennox Keyser (Yale University Press, © 1999 Hollins University).

Margaret Piper Chalmers contributed only one book, *Pollyanna's Pro-tegée,* before the publishers turned to a fourth author, Virginia May Moffitt, for the twelfth and thirteenth volumes in the series, *Pollyanna at Six Star Ranch* and *Pollyanna of Magic Valley.* For the final, tired Glad Book, Elizabeth Borton tried her hand at a spy story in *Pollyanna and the Secret Mission.* By 1950 Porter's two volumes and the other Glad Books had sold two million copies.[2] The Glad Books by other writers are almost forgotten now, but *Pollyanna* and *Pollyanna Grows Up* are still readily available.

Although all the Glad Books pay homage to Pollyanna's powers of positive thinking, it is the treatment of the Glad Game—Polly-anna's strategy for happiness—that distinguishes Porter's two-volume story of Pollyanna from all of its sequels. Without the game, *Pollyanna* would be little more than an insipid variant on the stories of Anne of Green Gables, Rebecca of Sunnybrook Farm, or Porter's own Miss Billie: the story, that is, of a poor girl transforming the lives of all the unhappy people among whom she comes to live, winning hearts with her unspoiled innocence, and finally marrying happily. The Glad Game distinguishes Pollyanna from these other spontaneously happy heroines,[3] for it is a specific technique learned from her father and taught to all she helps.

After her mother's death, Pollyanna's missionary father is sent a barrel of charity goods for himself and his daughter. The child hopes to find a doll, but the only item in the barrel suitable for a child is a pair of small crutches. At the height of Pollyanna's disappointment, the girl later recalls, her father taught her to find something to be glad about:

> "Oh, yes; the game was to just find something about everything to be glad about—no matter what 'twas," rejoined Pollyanna ear-nestly. "And we began right then—on the crutches."

> "Well, goodness me! I can't see anythin' ter be glad about—gettin' a pair of crutches when you wanted a doll!"

> Pollyanna clapped her hands.

> "There is—there is," she crowed. "But *I* couldn't see it either, Nancy, at first," she added with quick honesty. "Father had to tell it to me."

> "Well, then, suppose *you* tell *me,*" almost snapped Nancy.

"Goosey! Why, just be glad because you *don't—need—'em!*" (*Pollyanna* 38)

This strategy for gladness is Pollyanna's only inheritance from her father, who dies and leaves her an orphan shortly before the start of the first book. It becomes critical to her sense of who she is, how she should behave, and how she might console others in trouble.

The original game is described retrospectively in each of the books except Chalmers's *Pollyanna's Protegée*. In Borton's *Pollyanna's Door to Happiness*, for instance, Pollyanna explains it this way:

"Why, I used to play the Glad Game," she began. "It went like this. No matter what happened that was sad or unexpected, one needn't ever be sad or cry. Because if you looked and studied enough, you could find something to be glad about. My father was a poor missionary, and at Christmas I used to look forward to the missionary box from the church . . . oh with such longings and dreams. One year I wanted a doll . . . dreadfully. But there was no doll in the missionary barrel. There was only one thing for a little girl. It was a crutch. I've no idea how it came to be sent. But I was glad I didn't have to *use* the crutch. And then . . . oh, millions of times, I've played the Glad Game. It has always been the key to contentment, and the door to happiness, for me. . . ." (34)

In this book, as in the rest of the Glad Book sequels, it is the technique of thinking positive thoughts that is significant, and the reliving of Pollyanna's childhood is not entailed each time the game is played. Borton does not consider it important, for instance, to mention that it was her father and not Pollyanna herself who invented the game. In *Pollyanna* and *Pollyanna Grows Up*, however, the Glad Game is emphatically Pollyanna's paternal inheritance, not so much an intellectual technique as a scene from her earlier childhood lived out again and again either by Pollyanna herself or by those whom she instructs. In a psychoanalytic reading, this compulsively relived childhood episode is Pollyanna's version of the Freudian primal scene, and it dominates her life, as far as Porter takes the story.[4]

In *Pollyanna* and *Pollyanna Grows Up* the original Glad Game is relived three times. In the first book, Pollyanna's new neighbor, the sad and lonely John Pendleton, falls and breaks a leg; as he graduates from bed to crutches to recovery, he learns to play the Glad Game and find new happiness:

> "I thought you didn't like to have folk round," she said.
>
> He made a wry face.
>
> "Oh, but that was before you taught me to play that wonderful game of yours. *Now* I'm glad to be waited on, hand and foot! Never mind, I'll be on my own two feet yet, one of these days. Then I'll see who steps around," he finished, picking up one of the crutches at his side and shaking it playfully at the little girl. (139)

Pollyanna herself is later knocked down by a car, and her lower back is injured. She is expected to remain paralyzed from the hips down for the rest of her life, but a doctor provides a miraculous cure. *Pollyanna* ends as its heroine begins to walk again. At this point Pollyanna may well be a little girl in need of a crutch. The child who once found gladness in not needing a crutch becomes the child who finds gladness simply in being able to walk.

In *Pollyanna Grows Up*, the crutch episode is revisited explicitly when Pollyanna meets Jamie, a boy injured in two falls, who is confined to a wheelchair. In the worst times of his troubles, he had compiled a Jolly Book: "Everythin' that had anythin' about it that I liked I'd put down in the book. Then I'd just show how many 'joys' I had. . . . Well, I didn't expect to get many, but—do you know?—I got a lot. There was somethin' about 'most everythin' that I liked a *little,* so in it had to go. . . ." (68). Pollyanna instantly appropriates the Jolly Book as her own game, played unknowingly by the boy before he met her. By the book's end Jamie is able to walk with the help of crutches, though he never makes a full recovery. Jamie has more trouble than Pollyanna in finding a source of gladness in his crutches. He compares himself unfavorably with Pollyanna and her able-bodied friends Sadie and Jimmy. Thus Jamie might be said to play a Sad Game with his disability.

Superficially, Jamie's Jolly Book and Pollyanna's Glad Game can be regarded as demonstrations of a reframing technique at which Pollyanna is an adept. "Reframing" is a method of changing the meaning of an experience by "changing the frame in which a person perceives events" (Bandler and Grinder, *Reframing* 1). One of the strategies for therapeutic intervention developed by Bandler and Grinder as part

of their neurolinguistic programming (NLP) approach to human behavior modification, as a general process it is neither novel nor un-
familiar. For example, reframing occurs when the ugly duckling of
the Hans Christian Andersen story no longer conceives his judgment
of himself in the world of ducks but moves to the world of swans.
For Rudolf the reindeer the red nose is in one context ridiculous and
in another a precious source of light. Bandler and Grinder formalize
the reframing intervention in a six-step model and an advanced six-
step model, which generalize the process to any perception of events
and any emotional response. One significant difference between their
model and Pollyanna's practice, however, is that her version of reframing has gladness as its sole outcome.

The Glad Game is thus a very limited version of reframing, a way to
recast what has been understood as bitter, painful, hopeless, or unen-
durable into something cheering. Each turn of the Game is a similar
maneuver applied to another personal or domestic complaint. Being
able to walk just a few steps, for example, is a source of misery if put
in the context of having the full use of one's limbs; reframed in the
context of being bed-ridden and unable to move one's legs at all, it
is a source of gladness. In the later Glad Books a wide variety of personal and domestic problems are reframed. In *Pollyanna* and *Pollyanna
Grows Up*, however, Pollyanna's own bout of paralysis, John Pendleton's broken leg, and Jamie's permanent disability suggest that for
Eleanor Porter there is something peculiarly attractive in the game's
primal episode, which draws the child to return to it not only by way
of retelling but also through reenactment with variations. Porter's reframing, then, is limited not only in outcome but in the type of problem to be considered .

To a psychoanalytic critic, such repetitions indicate the return of
the repressed; to a psychotherapist, they represent an unsatisfactory
therapeutic model. In order for the Glad Game to operate, there
must be a problem. Porter's iteration of the same problem—how can
one be glad about crutches?—hints at something unresolved in Pollyanna's father's first response. What is lacking in the original case, in
which the little girl longs for a doll and is offered a crutch, is any
allowance for grief, disappointment, longing, or rage. Reframing can
be a potent therapeutic device when it refocuses conscious attention
on another way of perceiving an issue, but not when it denies and
suppresses a problem. Bandler and Grinder's model also differs significantly from Pollyanna's practice in its level of coercion. For the

NLP practitioner, the client must always consent to the change in context, and all parts of the client's psyche must agree that the new outcome is preferable to the old understanding. In contrast, Pollyanna, like her father before her, expects her "clients" and herself to accept reframing almost as a moral duty. Pollyanna's father is insistent that his daughter feel nothing but gladness, even when she is left orphaned by his death:

> "Glad!" Nancy, surprised into an interruption.
>
> "Yes—that father's gone to heaven to be with mother and the rest of us, you know. He said I must be glad. (*Pollyanna* 24)

Pollyanna successfully pursues the same strategem with all those who cross her path (or almost all: a would-be seducer in *Pollyanna Grows Up* is outside her range). Pollyanna can be seen in this context as a compulsive rescuer who is endlessly though unconsciously trying to save her own child-self from the desolation that her father forbade her to experience. In Freudian terms she is using projection and denial as defense mechanisms against the return of the repressed. She forever is drawn to external manifestations of her own repressed grief and rage and, like her father, manipulates other sufferers into denying their first responses. The lost child within Pollyanna weeps still for the doll she never received and is denied each time the story is retold.

The Glad Game is a set of crutches rather than a cure. In the case of Aunt Polly, especially, transformation is only temporary and depends on outside supports for its continuation. Once she loses her husband and her money, she is back to her old bitter self.[5] Aunt Polly is not the only character, though, who relies on external help to play the Glad Game. In *Pollyanna*, the servant Nancy practices the game by reframing the doctor's life. The doctor, she says,

> "can be glad because *he* isn't like other folks—the sick ones, I mean, what he doctors," finished Nancy in triumph.
>
> It was Pollyanna's turn to frown.
>
> "Why, y-yes," she admitted. "Of course that *is* one way, but it isn't the way I said. And—someway, I don't seem to quite like the sound of it." (115)

Here Pollyanna knows that something is wrong with this argument but does not work out exactly what the difficulty is (presumably because that would have made her philosophy untenable). The problem lies in Nancy's reliance on other people's misfortunes, on feeling superior and judging others as less worthy or happy.

There is a similar difficulty with Pollyanna's own technique of reframing. She finds reason for gladness in a covert comparison with others after which she can congratulate herself on her difference. Her whole philosophy is based on this tactic. To be glad because she does not need crutches predicates a class of people who *do* need them. Porter can allow her heroine to criticize Nancy's efforts to play the Glad Game but never to apply the same moral discrimination to herself; otherwise the game would self-destruct.

Another problem with the Glad Game is revealed when Pollyanna uses her favorite technique on her Aunt Polly's cold and loveless behavior toward her. Each time Aunt Polly tries to rebuke or punish Pollyanna, the child reframes her words and actions as loving, leaving her aunt disoriented: "Certainly, as those first July days passed, Aunt Polly found occasions many times to ejaculate, 'What an extraordinary child!' and certainly the reading and sewing lessons found her at their conclusion each day somewhat dazed and wholly exhausted" (57).

Small wonder that Aunt Polly feels light-headed and fatigued, for her true feelings are being denied by Pollyanna's insistence on an ideal aunt, a procedure that if consciously chosen would be moral blackmail.[6] This is almost the mirror image of Aunt Polly's attempts to convert the child Pollyanna into a "good" little girl according to her aunt's standards. In this sense, Pollyanna is simply playing back the tactics that adults employ with her. Aunt Polly is Pollyanna's double in this respect, as the similarity in names would indicate. Eventually the flesh-and-blood woman learns to love, of course, and Pollyanna's naive trust becomes justified retrospectively—or, to put it rather differently, her unconscious manipulation succeeds. In this case, unlike Pollyanna's own first encounter with the Glad Game, the aunt is given plenty of time to apply her niece's insights to her own behavior, plenty of time to transform rather than suppress her bitterness. Even so, she slips back into her old self very easily. If she is understood as Pollyanna's double, her relapse into the old ways suggests that Pollyanna too is not totally secure in her gladness, that the Glad Game is a tactic of self-persuasion producing an inauthenticity in both the aunt-mother and the niece-daughter.

The Glad Game is not only rather too close to moral blackmail, not only dependent on self-congratulatory comparison, it is also limited in its operation. It is a fair critique of the novels that the game's range is limited largely to domestic problems, relationships, and illnesses, for there is an implicit claim that Pollyanna's technique can cure anything that ails the psyche. Yet even as early as in Porter's second book, some characters and some behaviors are beyond the game's reach. In *Pollyanna Grows Up* the young Pollyanna talks to Sadie, a distressed young woman whose heart is suddenly converted back to virtue as a result of the Glad Game. The worldly-wise reader knows, though Pollyanna does not, that it is sexual seduction that tempts Sadie. When a would-be seducer comes to the park bench where Pollyanna and Sadie are sitting, he coaxes, she refuses, but "then he sneer[s] with a hateful look in his eyes. At last he sa[ys] something very low and angry, which Pollyanna d[oes] not understand. The next moment he wheel[s] about and str[ides] away" (51), never to be seen again. Pollyanna and Sadie rejoice in the Glad Game together, but the anonymous seducer remains unregenerate and invisible in this book's list of gladnesses. Pollyanna's aunt-to-be, Mrs. Carew, eventually establishes homes for virtuous girls to supplement the houses for fallen girls of which Sadie is so painfully aware. The unreformed male seducer is invisible in this part of the story, while all the women's efforts go into saving potential female victims.

A less obvious limitation of the Glad Game is its need of an endless supply of problems. Pollyanna transforms the lives of sour bachelors and spinsters, lost children, cripples, and the bed-ridden, but it is questionable who needs the other more. Her dominant philosophy is all too dependent on problems and misery. This suggests one reason why the seducers and other evil characters remain unreformed: quite apart from Porter's limited range of characterization, Pollyanna needs a continuous supply of wicked people who cause distress to others, to whom she can then teach the game. Lois Lowry, in her 1986 afterword to *Pollyanna,* argues that there is "something charming in the book's innocence. . . . It's a never-never land, far away from the stark reality of modern problem novels. Pollyanna's world is full of problems, to be sure, but one by one they unwind and resolve themselves" (220–21). What Lowry misses here is Pollyanna's need for fresh problems to keep the Glad Game in play, a need not so very far removed from that of the charity-givers whom Sadie rebukes in the second volume. To Lowry, Pollyanna's universe is utopian, but in practice it is stuck repeating the same moves toward utopia via a transformation of dystopian characters and events. The Glad Game feeds off misery.

Porter's successors in the series apply the game to a more diverse group of characters than do the first two volumes. Pollyanna is happily and virtuously married, with ideal children, so that the figures of the lost child, the orphan, the unloved, and unloving who need to play the Glad Game are for the most part displaced from Pollyanna's immediate family to neighbors and new friends. As the series continues, the authors attempt to attract readers by the added interest of exotic (but not too faraway) settings such as Texas and Mexico. Everywhere, of course, the Glad Game prevails. At best, the ease with which Pollyanna can be transplanted suggests that the Glad Game has universal validity, at least across North and Central America; at worst it suggests a superficial attempt to keep up sales.

The fourteenth volume, *Pollyanna and the Secret Mission*, attempts to combine all the features of the earlier Glad Books with another genre, the spy story, but the combination does not enhance any of its components. The spy story is told indirectly for the most part, with Pollyanna an uncomprehending observer, so that most opportunities for suspense and excitement are foregone. More seriously for the book's success as a Glad Book, little attempt is made to apply the game to the social, economic, and political issues raised by the spy story. Toward the end, Pollyanna dutifully turns her mind to the game: "About Ron and Judy. Yes, I can be glad now. My darling need not yet know of Ron's work, since he doesn't want it that way, but she need not be so worried at this moment. Perhaps he will be allowed a small vacation. Oh, I am glad that nothing happened to Ron in all this dangerous business. I am glad of that!" (159). Pollyanna finds these reasons for gladness: her daughter Judy has not been sexually betrayed by her husband the spy; one of the female characters has escaped from a dangerous love affair; another woman has "done right" even though it cost her her life. Notably missing from her list of gladnesses are the nastier characters involved in the spy story. With nothing to be glad about in their lives, no transformation to goodness and love, they are as featureless as Sadie's seducer in *Pollyanna Grows Up*. Applied to the world of domesticity and personal problems, the game is presented as omnipotent in book after book, but in the outer world of doing, of politics and business, the authors usually do not even try to apply it.

Pollyanna and the Secret Mission is the exception among the Glad

Books. The rest of the sequels stay within the domestic and romantic confines of the genre, and, like *Pollyanna* and *Pollyanna Grows Up*, their plots range from melodrama to mild social satire. Several, although not all, of the volumes include a mystery concerning a lost boy or girl who is eventually reunited with his or her anguished family. This takes up one of Porter's themes from the first two books: that of the lost child and heir for whom a grieving adult desperately searches. (Of course this motif is not original to Porter.) Another motif (again not originated by Porter) involves a character melodramatically saved from death. In Virginia May Moffitt's *Pollyanna of Magic Valley* the two motifs are combined: Pollyanna's daughter saves an unknown girl from death under a train's wheels in the first page, and the girl's lost aunt is finally rediscovered and reunited with her grieving father. Similarly, in Harriet Lummis Smith's *Pollyanna's Debt of Honor*, a mysterious stranger saves Pollyanna's baby from being killed on the road.

A Glad Book, then, has to include Pollyanna herself and to accommodate the plots and characters introduced in previous books in the series; has to demonstrate the game, particularly by a ritual retelling of its first episode; and may include a mildly exotic setting, a mystery, a character saved from death, or all three. What it need not include, however, is the reliving of the primal episode that characterizes Porter's two books. In Smith's *Pollyanna's Western Adventure*, for instance, Luke Geist is a version of the bed-ridden Jamie, but without the crutches, a man whose miraculous cure occurs completely offstage. Nelson Kipps in *Pollyanna of Magic Valley* is another reclusive John Pendleton, but when he falls downstairs and hurts his leg the story speeds on to his full change of heart, and nothing is mentioned of crutches. Porter's successors may repeat favorite motifs, but they do not have their characters reenact stories from the previous books.

When the Glad Game is freed from this compulsive quality of reenactment, it sometimes ceases to be the Glad Game at all. In Smith's vapid *Pollyanna's Western Adventure*, for instance, we find the following:

> "You never were at my house," Mattie insisted doggedly. "There's nothing nice about it. And nobody has anything to say, and nobody ever laughs the way you do here. There's nothing nice at all—except your books."

> "Well then," smiled Pollyanna, "You can start with being glad for the books."

"Oh, yes. I'm glad of them," said Mattie quickly. She looked at her new friend with worshipful eyes. "And I'm glad of you." (96)

This conversation occurs just after the critical moment, when Pollyanna has told her primal story, but Smith's version, with its escape from a confined life through Pollyanna's friendship and gifts of books, has lost its reframing characteristic. Mattie is asked not to reassess her domestic problems but to leave them behind. Nothing here is transformed, denied, or repressed, and Pollyanna's peculiar gift of finding gladness in calamity itself does not come into operation. *Pollyanna's Western Adventure* is a Glad Book in name only, although the source of gladness in this episode is less questionable than most in the series.

A similar contrast between the formulaic and the compulsive can be drawn when the love affairs in the series are compared. As with the Glad Game—so suggestive of repression and coercion in Porter's two books and so bland and clichéd in her successors' volumes— the love affairs that provide most of the plots and puzzles of the series are suggestive in Porter's books, banal in the rest of the series. Porter's intricate tangle of orphans, missing heirs, substitute fathers, mothers, daughters, and sons are in psychoanalytic terms prime cases of potentially incestuous relationships. In their obscurely troubling love games, the Oedipus complex—that is, the little girl's longing to be her father's sexual partner and to rid herself of her rival, the mother—is played out. In the rest of the Glad Books, love affairs involve straightforward sexual attraction and relationship outside the incest taboo.

Whereas the sequels abound in formulaic love stories with a simple, simply resolved choice of partners, Porter's love stories abound in mysteries and shifting family relationships, to the point of obsessiveness. *Pollyanna* ends with one marriage, *Pollyanna Grows Up* with three, but both books involve at least three potential marriage partners and at least one mystery about the past for each marriage. Each marriage also entails a readjustment of the characters', and the reader's, understanding of how these people are related to one another.

In *Pollyanna*, Aunt Polly has a secret lover from her past. Little Pollyanna has to learn through trial and error whether he is the morose neighbor John Pendleton or the lonely Dr. Chilton. As she discovers the truth, the doctor finds happiness with his beloved Polly. This seems not unlike the situation of Dorothy in *Pollyanna's Western*

Adventure, who has to find out which of her suitors she really prefers (again with Pollyanna's help), but Porter's love story also contains the revelation that John Pendleton loved and failed to win Pollyanna's dead mother, Aunt Polly's sister. Thus at the time he invites Pollyanna to live with him, saying, "It takes a woman's hand and heart, or a child's presence, to make a home, Pollyanna, and I have not had either" (140), Pollyanna understands him to be inviting her as the daughter he might have had with his supposed lost love Aunt Polly, and she understands the "woman's hand and heart" to refer to her aunt. But he is really thinking of Pollyanna as the daughter he might have had with his actual lost love, Pollyanna's dead mother. These implied relationships are further complicated by Aunt Polly's development toward becoming a loving substitute mother for Pollyanna, taking her dead sister's place for the child though not for the man.

Jerry Griswold is one of the few literary critics to discuss Pollyanna at any length, and he finds her (as I do) to be an expert manipulator, even a blackmailer. Griswold sketches out a Freudian reading of *Pollyanna,* along with all the other children's books that he includes in his study. As Griswold comments, "*Pollyanna* is like these other books in its account of oedipal development. Like many of America's other literary orphans, Pollyanna's 'angelic' mother, the mother of infancy, dies before the story opens" (227). Griswold tracks the oedipal theme through the stages of Pollyanna's relationship with her aunt and the development of the child's friendship with John Pendleton and the doctor. He sets out a brief Freudian overview of the love affair in *Pollyanna,* the aunt's hostility toward the child, and the potential sexual rivalry between aunt-mother and niece-daughter where Dr. Chilton is concerned.

Griswold's analysis of *Pollyanna* backs away, however, from the novel's most psychoanalytically interesting section, towards the end. What in Griswold's reading is "murky confusion and revealing reduplication" (89) is better understood as variations on a basic oedipal problem in which mother and daughter, father and son, struggle for the same sexual partner. Read thus, *Pollyanna'*s "revealing reduplications" make excellent psychological sense. It is a shame that Griswold confines his psychoanalytic reading to Porter's first volume, because there is much richer material for an oedipal reading in the second book.

The interrelationships in *Pollyanna* are not developed into their full complexity until the end of *Pollyanna Grows Up.* In this book, the orphan child Jimmy, whom John Pendleton has adopted in lieu of

Pollyanna, grows up to court her and become engaged to her. Pollyanna will now become John Pendleton's daughter by marriage as well as desire. Furthermore, several characters in the second volume suspect that John and Pollyanna have enjoyed a secret romance, that they are in love and will marry. This suggests, in retrospect, an incestuous reading of his proposal to the child Pollyanna. If he asks not only for her presence but for *her* woman's hand and heart, as Jimmy believes, then Pollyanna is being asked to substitute for her dead mother in John's bed; and Jimmy, whom she actually desires for a husband and who desires her for a wife, is in danger of becoming her son.

Pollyanna Grows Up deals with this tangle by summarily discarding it. Pollyanna becomes engaged to Jimmy, John Pendleton is an uncle-father safely married to another woman, and Aunt Polly is safely and sadly widowed. These endings do not, however, outweigh the plot developments of volume two in particular, the ever-more-complex family relationships, their ever-increasing potential for incest. Both of Porter's Pollyanna books are amazingly oedipal in their fascination with crippled legs, mysterious parentage, incest, and marrying one's father. Their happy endings can be read as retreats from overdetermined intimate relations rather than as resolutions.

There is further mystery and confusion about the male orphans in Porter's two books, but not about the orphan Pollyanna's origins. At the start of the first book the reader is informed about her dead father and mother, and nothing afterwards calls this account into question. Orphans, like people on crutches, proliferate in *Pollyanna* and *Pollyanna Grows Up*. The two orphan boys, the able-bodied Jimmy and the crippled Jamie, are marked as doubles by their names as well as the mystery of their parentage. Toward the end of *Pollyanna Grows Up*, they act as doubles in Pollyanna's love life in that Jimmy believes that Jamie is his successful rival. The two orphan boys are also rivals for the place in life belonging to Mrs. Carew's lost nephew Jamie, whom she yearns for as a son. In fact, when the crippled Jamie is eventually accepted as the lost nephew, she adopts him as a son. Meanwhile, John Pendleton has adopted the real missing nephew, Jimmy, as his son.

So far all is fairly clear, but in the course of courtship most of these relationships become more confusingly overdetermined. John Pendleton now falls in love with Mrs. Carew. Pollyanna comes to think that Jimmy (her beloved, John's adopted son, Mrs. Carew's real nephew) is in love with Mrs. Carew, his real aunt-mother, who turns out to be his new step-mother when John Pendleton marries her.

Meanwhile, Jimmy believes that Pollyanna is in love with the crippled Jamie (Mrs. Carew's adopted son, not her real nephew), who turns out to be Pollyanna's new brother-in-law when Mrs. Carew marries John (adoptive father to Jimmy, who marries Pollyanna).

There are two particularly surprising elements in this oedipal farrago. Porter's second volume ends with the wrong Jamie publicly acknowledged as the nephew-son, while the right one (Jimmy) knows the truth but yields his place out of love. In a sense, both candidates receive the prize of status and wealth, one overtly and the other privately. Porter reassures the reader that Mrs. Carew loves the crippled Jamie as a son, so that this ending could be considered the best possible solution for everyone, but only if the element of deceit, in his family's withholding critical information from Jamie, is ignored.

Equally surprising is Porter's insistence on sexual partnering possibilities between parent and child. Jimmy is supposed by Pollyanna to be in love with a woman who becomes his step-mother, while Pollyanna herself is suspected of a love affair with John Pendleton, her mother's suitor, her future father-in-law. When Jimmy explains to her that John, his adoptive father, is his rival for Pollyanna's hand, she sadly argues that she must marry the older man: "Don't you see? It was Mother, long ago, that broke his heart—*my mother*. And all these years he's lived a lonely, unloved life in consequence. If now he should come to me and ask me to make that up to him, I'd *have* to do it, Jimmy. I'd *have* to. I couldn't *refuse!* Don't you see?" (*Pollyanna Grows Up* 199). Pollyanna's remarkable willingness to take the blame for John's reaction to her mother's behavior is symptomatic either of a rescuing pattern that is compulsive to the point of being ludicrous or of an oedipal drama like Jimmy's supposed courtship of his father's beloved, Mrs. Carew. The incestuous implications of these relationships are just manageable when the partnerings remain in the realm of jealous fantasy, but when Pollyanna puts into words her obligation to live out her mother's unlived life, to please her substitute father, the whole Glad Game begins to look like a desperate oedipal ploy to gain the father's love.

Although Porter's successors all include a love story in their Glad Books, only one, Harriet Lummis Smith, takes up the oedipal mysteries and cripplings from the first two volumes. *Pollyanna's Jewels* rounds out the mystery of the crippled Jamie's parentage with full disclosure. Despite all the secrecy that Pollyanna, Jimmy, John Pendleton, Aunt Polly, Sadie, and Mrs. Carew have sustained, Jamie finds out one night at the dinner table that it is Jimmy, not he, who is the true nephew by blood. Quite reasonably, it might seem, Jamie feels distraught, betrayed, and out of place: " 'If you don't mind,' he said, 'I'd rather be by myself for a little. The fact is I married you under false pretences. Our child is the descendant, not of one of the leading families of America, but of a nameless waif. Please give me a little time to think this out' " (228). John Pendleton responds to the crisis by reframing the family's behavior from conspiracy to sacrifice: "But Jim, here, was willing to relinquish his rights to spare Jamie's feelings. I don't see why, when we've all been ready to make every sacrifice, he should act as if we'd been in a conspiracy against him" (229). Jamie is quite correct when he accuses the others of conspiracy. He has indeed been both conspired against and treated as an untrustworthy child. What has been sacrificed by Jimmy is social status; Jamie has lost dignity and been denied the truth. Pollyanna wants him to surrender still more than has already been taken from him: " 'If I had an idea of trying to comfort anyone,' explained Pollyanna, choosing her words carefully, 'it would be Aunt Ruth [Mrs. Carew]. I'm sure there's nothing that hurts like ingratitude. . . . Jimmy was willing to be regarded as a waif, whose heritage was an unknown quantity. If anybody had made such a sacrifice for me, I think I should feel a little bit grateful' " (231–33). Like her father in the long-ago primal Glad Game, she cannot tolerate Jamie's negative reaction, which she characterizes as selfish ingratitude. She is explicitly described as behaving toward Jamie like a mother scolding her small boy—casting Jamie into the very role of irresponsible child that she is supposedly helping him to grow out of. The whole extended family, then, has conspired against and continues to behave in such a way as to infantilize the unfortunate Jamie. For many of his subsequent appearances in the Glad Books he is sulky, resentful, and prone to play the Sad Game once more.

Apart from Jamie's moral blackmail, Porter style, in *Pollyanna's Jewels,* the love stories in the sequels to Porter's works do not rise above the perfunctory and formulaic. At the books' simplest, a man and a woman are attracted sexually and the story line ends with their friendship, engagement, or marriage. There are usually problems that call for the Glad Game in the process. The basic romance formula usually followed by these authors complicates the love story by placing two or three suitors or several girls in rivalry for the same person. *Pollyanna's Western Adventure* offers a straightforward example of this type of love story: for much of the novel Jerry and two other men are rivals for

Dorothy's affections, and toward the end Dorothy, Minnie, and Ange the nurse vie for Jerry's attention. There is no doubt in this love story about the identity of any of the characters, and there are no disclosures about hidden parentage or unexpected family relationships. All is very much as it seems.

So too is the treatment of the lost child motif in the Glad Books that were written after Porter's death. A mystery is set up, but it is completely solved and has no uncomfortable ramifications. Examples of lostness, literal and metaphoric, abound throughout the Glad Books (Pollyanna lost in Boston, Sadie on the edge of a sexual fall, Judith's husband possibly committing suicide, and so on), and they range from the momentary (a girl snatched from the path of a train, a baby from the wheels of a car) to the temporary (a child missing for an afternoon, a baby kidnapped for some weeks) to the very long term (a missing daughter kidnapped by bandits and believed to be long dead). These examples almost all concern a mystery as well as a risk (who is the boy who claims to be the lost daughter's son? who is the mystery woman who rescues baby Ruth? where is baby David?). For most of the Glad Books such mysteries are fairly mechanical plot devices with a guaranteed happy ending. Everything is resolved, and there is no interference between the lost child motif and the love story.

In comparison with the later books in the series, Porter's works shine out as original,[7] for it is the weaker, more conventional aspects of her work that her imitators repeat. Apart from Smith's unpleasant finale to the mystery of Jamie's identity, the sequel writers generally soften the moral blackmail of Porter's Pollyanna. Always they avoid the incestuous potential of sexual liaisons among their characters; always they avoid the compulsively detailed iterations of the primal Glad Game that Pollyanna and those around her play out in the pages of *Pollyanna* and *Pollyanna Grows Up*. In avoiding these characteristics, the books are at best mediocre, at worst hack work.

Porter is never a hack. Rather, she offers a set of fascinating case studies in the psychology of the child victim and the child victim turned manipulator. There is little Jamie, the infantilized cripple, the bad lost child who can never escape his mother's admonitions to stay little, take the blame, and hold on to his crutches. There is little Pollyanna, the good lost child who can never escape her father's admonitions to please him, to be glad that she does not need crutches. There are all the child and adult players of the Glad Game whose psyches are manipulated by expert moral blackmail and who do not always stay glad. There are the families who dance their not-quite-incestuous patterns around Pòllyanna at two critical stages in her development: the little girl not allowed to grieve for her dead father, the young woman moving into sexual experience. Beneath all that happens to her in Porter's stories, a little girl is compulsively reliving her abusive past and forcing those around her to relive it with her. It is not surprising that Porter's successors avoided such dangerous ground.

Porter's Pollyanna is both victim and expert manipulator, under the guise of the innocently loving child. She and almost all the other players of the Glad Game in the two books report that they feel much better for it. Feeling better has a hidden cost, though, that is hinted at by the books' repetitions. The first episode can never be walked away from. It is no accident, psychologically, that Pollyanna is surrounded by sad and angry people, cripples and crutch-wielders. In some sense she is attracting them so that she can deal with her own repressed pain as best she can, which is never completely. If Pollyanna were ever to wake up to what she is doing, in Porter's books, she might become a tragic figure, finally feeling the pain of that long-ago denial that her father demanded from her, finally able to renounce the crutches that have crippled her. And after that, if only Porter had been able to imagine it, Pollyanna might have been truly able to be glad.

Notes

1. See I. Hart's "The One Hundred Leading Authors of Best Sellers in Fiction from 1895 to 1944," p. 288.

2. This is according to J. Hart's *The Popular Book*, p. 213.

3. See MacLeod's *American Childhood*, pp. 22–23.

4. My reading of the *Pollyanna* series is informed by my practice as a psychotherapist, in which I have found a Freudian framework useful in treating clients who compulsively repeat early childhood experiences. As in this paper, I use in such therapy Jungian understandings of the lost child and Bandler and Grinder's neurolinguistic concept of reframing.

5. Allentuck's comment that "because Pollyanna treats her like an integrated individual, she is able to integrate herself" (448) ignores this later development in order to argue for *Pollyanna*'s healthy optimism.

6. Jerry Griswold also interprets Pollyanna's tactics as highly manipulative to the point of blackmail.

7. This is not to claim that they are better written.

Works Cited

Allentuck, Marcia E. "*Pollyanna* by Eleanor H. Porter." *Georgia Review* 14 (1960): 447–49.

Bandler, Richard, and John Grinder. *Reframing: Neuro-Linguistic Programming and the Transformation of Meaning.* Moab, Utah: Real People, 1982.

Borton, Elizabeth. *Pollyanna and the Secret Mission.* 1951. London: George G. Harrap, 1952.

———. *Pollyanna in Hollywood.* Boston: L. C. Page, 1931.

———. *Pollyanna's Castle in Mexico.* Boston: L. C. Page, 1934.

———. *Pollyanna's Door to Happiness.* 1936. Sydney: Angus and Robertson, 1939.

———. *Pollyanna's Golden Horseshoe.* Boston: L. C. Page, 1939.

Chalmers, Margaret Piper. *Pollyanna's Protegée.* Boston: L. C. Page, 1944.

Griswold, Jerry. *Audacious Kids: Coming of Age in America's Classic Children's Books.* New York: Oxford University Press, 1992.

Hart, Irving Harlow. "The One Hundred Leading Authors of Best Sellers in Fiction from 1895 to 1944." *Publishers Weekly* 148 (January 19, 1946): 285–90.

Hart, James D. *The Popular Book: A History of America's Literary Taste.* New York: Oxford University Press, 1950.

MacLeod, Anne S. *American Childhood: Essays on Children's Literature of the Nineteenth and Twentieth Centuries.* Athens: University of Georgia Press, 1994.

Moffitt, Virginia May. *Pollyanna at Six Star Ranch.* Boston: L. C. Page, 1947.

———. *Pollyanna of Magic Valley.* 1949. London: George G. Harrap, 1950.

Porter, Eleanor H. *Pollyanna.* 1913. Afterword Lois Lowry. New York: Dell, 1986.

———. *Pollyanna Grows Up.* 1915. New York: Dell, 1988.

Smith, Harriet Lummis. *Pollyanna of the Orange Blossoms.* Boston: L. C. Page, 1924.

———. *Pollyanna's Debt of Honor.* Boston: L. C. Page, 1927.

———. *Pollyanna's Jewels.* London: George G. Harrap, 1925.

———. *Pollyanna's Western Adventure.* 1929. Sydney: Angus and Robertson, 1941.

Lacan with Runt Pigs

Karen Coats

When Fern Arable realizes that her father is headed out to the barn to kill a runt pig, she is immediately engulfed in identificatory existential angst: "But it's unfair," cries Fern. "The pig couldn't help being born small, could it? If *I* had been very small at birth, would you have killed me?" (*Charlotte's Web* 3). In a flash of horror and insight, she articulates the truth of Lacan's assertion that all humans (and some pigs) are born prematurely,[1] and she understands that it is the task of an "other" to save their lives and bring them into the human community as subjects. In fact, reading *Charlotte's Web* through Lacan's theory of subjectivity (and reading Lacan's theory through *Charlotte's Web*) enables us to come to an understanding of just how implicated the Other (as other people, as our own unconscious, as language itself) is in the formation of our own identities. "Through the effects of speech," Lacan says, "the subject always realizes himself more in the Other, but he is already pursuing there more than half of himself" (*Four Fundamental Concepts* 188). When John Arable makes his daughter a mother, he initiates a process of subject formation that shows clearly how each of the characters in the book is already more than half in the Other; Fern, Wilbur, Charlotte, and ultimately the child reader all emerge as effects of their encounters with others and of their encounters with language. In this essay, then, I explore one possible way of opening a text through a Lacanian poetics, with the result (I hope) that both the text and the theory are made richer thereby.

Written in 1952 by E. B. White, *Charlotte's Web* is a homely, comforting story about friendship. It is often, as noted by Perry Nodelman, the first "chapter" book adults choose to read to children; it has all the elements that make a story feel right for the very young—a main character with whom the child can identify, a wise and loving mother figure, villains that aren't too frightening, and a triumphant story line, all woven together with gentle humor and carefully crafted language that emphasize the glories of the natural world. More than that, the story is empowering for the young child; it offers a vision of what most

Children's Literature 27, ed. Elizabeth Lennox Keyser (Yale University Press, © 1999 Hollins University).

parents want for their children (and themselves) in that it can be read as a "consoling fantasy in which a small Everyman survives and triumphs over the pathos of being alone" (Griffith 111). Not only does Wilbur triumph over his fundamental isolation, but he also triumphs over the terror of his being-toward-death. He is saved not once, but twice, by women who act as mothers to him and who use language to intervene in his destiny and to turn him into something that, by any objective standard, he should not be. In order to save Wilbur, first Fern and then Charlotte have to convince Mr. Arable and Farmer Zuckerman that Wilbur is worth saving, that he is more than simply a runt pig, good for nothing and a lot of trouble besides. The way they do this is by speaking for him, by connecting him to the world of language; in a sense, they do what the Lacanian (m)Other[2] does— together, they provide the conditions for him to have a "voice," at the expense of their own erasure.

The story of Fern, Wilbur, and Charlotte, then, is one of love, death, and the role of language in the formation and transformation of the self. Approaching it from the perspective of Lacan's theory of the subject allows us to situate it in terms of its own preoccupations, for Lacan's theory, like White's tale, is engaged in existentialist concerns regarding the relations between language, meaning, and being.[3] This is not to say that Lacanian theory is existentialist. Rather, it is *informed by* existentialism, but also by structuralism; the two are at some points radically irreconcilable. For instance, Laurence Gagnon's Heideggerian reading of *Charlotte's Web* centers on what he calls the characters' "various personal struggles to live authentically" (Gagnon 61). Wilbur and Charlotte "find themselves thrown into existence together, inescapably confronted with the task of truly becoming what they can be—even unto death" (63). At the heart of this type of reading of the human, there is an interior sort of "unique identity proper to oneself" (62) that must be found and cultivated. The words that appear in Charlotte's web regarding Wilbur are read by Gagnon as temptations for the pig to live inauthentically—to be what Gagnon calls a "people-self," one defined by what others have to say about him rather than what he somehow *is*, essentially. The only word that Gagnon finds appropriate to Wilbur's true self is the word *humble*: "Only with the last, prophetic message is there a genuineness in Wilbur's attitude—he has finally become more of himself, a humble pig" (65). But what Gagnon's strictly existential reading doesn't take into account is the role of language in the creation of that self. Lacan's particular blend of structuralism and existentialism dismantles the notion of an "authentic" self, relocating it as the subject of language; in fact, for Lacan, *the subject is the effect of language,* a concept that infuses all of his theory and that I shall explain further in what follows. But for Gagnon, the power of language is descriptive rather than constitutive; Wilbur is under threat of inauthenticity because "[a]s a young pig, he does not have an especially strong personality" (65), and hence cannot ward off identifications that Gagnon sees as inappropriate or inaccurate. But if we see the subject as the end product of those identifications, as structured by them rather than merely corresponding to them or not, we see that the notion of the subject as an interiority seeking words that suit it is not tenable.

Certainly, the subject comes to invest its world with its own meanings, with what could be called in existentialist thought its own idiosyncratic "calls of concern" (Gagnon 66). Despite the fact that Fern and Charlotte speak for him, and in many ways call him into being, Wilbur must develop his own projects; he must find ways to articulate his own desires. Ultimately, as Gagnon points out, he must approach his life, and his death, differently from Charlotte or Fern. But nonetheless there are laws that regulate those meanings, structures that contain and constrain the production of (meaning in) the subject. Those structures are not organic or idiosyncratic to the individual, as a sort of innate ego. Instead, they are located in language, a public order in which we always already find ourselves. The identifications that Gagnon condemns as temptations toward inauthenticity are in fact the necessary linguistic positings of the subject by the Other. As I noted earlier, this Other should be understood in its multivalent dimensions: the term denotes the others that surround us as parents, siblings, teachers, and so on, as well as the societal structures, formal and informal, that provide the racial, cultural, and gender markers through which we define ourselves. Wilbur teaches us that in order to come into being as any sort of self whatsoever, one must first be recognized by an Other in language, which implicates the Other, and the Other's words, in the construction of the self. In fact, White's story is exemplary of the ways in which language constitutes subjectivity in its structural dimension. It also offers us a way to look at the substantive aspects of a specifically modernist subjectivity. A Lacanian poetics is one that explores how "literature operates a magnetic pull on the reader because it is an allegory of the psyche's fundamental structure" (Ragland-Sullivan 381). In the case of *Charlotte's Web,* the pull is so strong that its allegorical dimensions with respect to subjectivity beg to be explored.

Fern Enjoys Her Symptom

The first two chapters of *Charlotte's Web* are not really Charlotte's story at all, nor are they Wilbur's. They belong to an eight-year-old girl named Fern. She is the "cause" of the story, so to speak, in that it is her dramatic reaction to her father's intended action that brings Wilbur into existence in the first place. Without Fern, the runt pig is of no importance whatsoever. Interestingly enough, as a pig, he is not especially important to her either. He is simply a symbol with whom she narcissistically identifies. Her father exercises absolute authority over his pigs, just as he exercises absolute authority over his daughter. When he threatens the life of a small pig, Fern, a small girl, is compelled to challenge his authority. She does so in the way that is most threatening to the symbolic male power structure — she loses control and grabs her father's, um, ax.[4] It is not so much that she cares about the life of this particular pig as it is her desire to assert her place with respect to the law. She immediately questions the fairness of her father's decision. If the law that exercises power over small pigs and small girls tends toward capricious whims rather than logic and justice, then she is in a very vulnerable position indeed. After all, though she may get his attention by grabbing the ax, she has no real power to stay her father's hand; the phallus does not belong to her. Instead, she uses her only weapon, language, to advance a reasonable (to her mind, anyway) argument on the pig's behalf. Fern's speech act is an anticipatory gesture in the following way: Fern argues the merits of the sanctity of life in the manner of a defense attorney before a judge, calling to mind the ultimate expression of the power of the law. But at only eight years of age, she is not yet in a position for such a speech act to be effective on her word alone. Her arguments do not count as compelling unless an authority figure, one whose power is legitimated by the societal Other, is willing to allow them to count. Hence her father responds more to the fact of her speech act than to its content; that is, because she bothers to make such an impassioned argument, he allows it to carry the day, despite the fact that he disagrees with her.

Although admonishing her to control herself, Mr. Arable nevertheless reasserts his control over her by giving her more than she asks for. He turns her into something more than an object of his and his wife's affection. It is a loving gesture but one implicated in power nonetheless. John Arable is acting at this moment as the primordial Freudian father, exercising complete control over who may acquire the phallus in his wee tribe. Significantly, Arable's son Avery, "heavily armed" with pretend versions of his father's weapon ("an air rifle in one hand, a wooden dagger in the other" *Charlotte's Web* 4), is excluded from his father's bequeathal of phallic authority. He is then and remains throughout the story (until the end, where he acts as Wilbur's fool) a threat to Wilbur's well-being, and Arable is not about to let him assume a role that he is not yet ready for. Fern, on the other hand, has shown her readiness by attempting a speech act that the Other finds compelling—the reasoned argument. Hence her father grants her a male "child" to take care of—a sort of phallus on loan—in order to show her the responsibility that lies behind the privilege of wielding the ax.[5]

Fern has received her father's mandate (authorization) to mother the pig. In the confrontation between Fern's desire and the law, Wilbur is precipitated as an object. He is a narcissistic object-choice, according to Freud, who first defined this type of object-choice in his discussion of homosexuals but later integrated it into the stages of development of the ego. The narcissistic object "is chosen on the model of the little child or adolescent that the subject once was, while the subject identifies with the mother who used to take care of him" (Laplanche and Pontalis 259). The pig is connected to Fern through the characteristics of smallness, dependency, and their positions under her father's authority. Her father encourages the narcissistic connection, and hence helps to foster Fern's psychic development, by emphasizing her role as mother: "I'll let you start it on a bottle, like a baby" (*Charlotte's Web* 3). Since narcissism constitutes the "central imaginary relation of interhuman relationships" (Lacan, Seminar III, 92), the constitution of Wilbur as an object is crucial to the constitution of Fern as a subject. Together, they form an Imaginary dyad, with Fern (presumably) replicating her own mother's desire when she herself was a narcissistic object for her mother. Hence the mother's desire is the first cause in the inauguration of the subject. But no less critical is the replication of that desire in the subject herself. For it is only when one stands on the side of the mother, so to speak, that one is able to pass through to the other side of the Lacanian mirror stage.

The mirror stage is probably the most well-known concept in Lacanian thought. The story goes as follows: At some point very early in the child's life, he looks into a mirror and apprehends the fact that his body is a distinct and coherent entity unto itself, that there are boundaries between what constitutes himself and what constitutes Other. Of course, this image is just that—an image, and an idealized image at that. The image has control of its body; the baby does not. The image is autonomous; the baby is "still sunk in his motor inca-pacity and nursling dependence" (*Ecrits* 2). Thereafter, however, the baby will be in a position to know himself, but only in a fictional way, because the Imaginary register of ideal images has come into being and has determined the only way in which we can know anything— through alienation (knowing oneself through an external image), duality (the result of a deep ambivalence caused by the alienation be-tween the subject and its ideal image), and identification (the attempt to dissolve self into an ideal image and say "this is me"). The baby has entered the world of signifying transactions, where image, or repre-sentation, has displaced being; the subsequent and inevitable entry into language represents a further displacement or alienation, a fur-ther aphanisis, or fading, of the Real in favor of the Symbolic, by way of the Imaginary.[6]

Of course, one would be disingenuous or naive in suggesting that these transactions are not mediated—the apprehension of the image by the baby is probably never spontaneous, because it is almost always interpreted for the baby by someone else, usually the mother, who tells the baby what he is looking at. And until the baby can make the conceptual distinction of what "I" means and then identify him-self with that "I," the baby is not a full subject. Interestingly enough, children tend to learn the personal pronouns in the order *mine, me*, and then *I*, suggesting a grammatical progression from knowing what bounds them to recognizing their object status to finally assuming a subject position. Because the mother mediates the entire experience, because the child encounters the shifters (*I* and *me*) that will come to stand for himself first in her voice, it would seem inevitable that the mother, as one of the idealized images in the child's Imaginary, will always stand alongside any Symbolic representation the child makes for himself. And indeed this is the case—the Imaginary acts as a sup-port for the Symbolic. If for some reason a child does not make that initial Imaginary mirror-stage identification, then it is impossible to enter into the Symbolic network of relations, with its substitutionary logic of the signifier. If on the other hand the Imaginary fusional rela-tionship remains primary, the child's relation to the Symbolic is compromised in ways that can result in neurosis or psychosis. This is what worries Fern's mother with regard to Wilbur. When Fern's teacher asks her what the capital of Pennsylvania is, she is so locked in her dream of mothering that she says "Wilbur," which in a sense is appropriate, because Wilbur has filled up her entire psychic geography. This is a potentially dangerous situation for Fern, but also for Wilbur. But as it turns out, Fern's mother's fears are unfounded because the necessary intervention of the third term has already begun to have its effect.

The "third term" in Lacanian theory is the position of the Law, or the Name-of-the-Father, as that which breaks the dyadic logic of the mother-child connection. Shoshana Felman explains: "The triangular structure, crucial to Lacan's conception, is not the simple psychological triangle of love and rivalry, but a socio-symbolic structural positioning of the child in a complex constellation of alliance (family, elementary social cell) in which the combination of desire and a Law prohibiting desire is regulated, through a linguistic structure of exchange, into a repetitive process of replacement—of substitution—of symbolic objects (substitutes) of desire" (*Adventure of Insight* 104). Just as Fern's father mandates the mothering relationship between Fern and Wilbur, so he also mandates its termination. What breaks the dyadic relation of the Imaginary is the intervention of the Name-of-the-Father. The Name-of-the-Father inaugurates a chain of substitutions that come to signify—replace or bar—the mother's desire. The Lacanian analyst Bruce Fink points out that it doesn't matter whether you read the mother's desire as the child's desire for the mother, the mother's desire for the child, or the whole thing in its totality. The point is that it is dangerous to the child and the mother because it is built on an impossibility. In the dyad, there is an illusion of totality. But with the triangle—child, mother, father—comes a hole in the middle that continually needs not filling up but covering over as the child seeks to regain the unity with the mother that was always already lost. The substitution of signifiers for that desire inaugurates the subject as a *desiring being*, which is what is considered normal and healthy in late capitalism.

Thus the Name-of-the-Father (alternately called the paternal metaphor, the phallus) separates the subject from the mother's desire by means of a sort of redundant prohibition—redundant because it prohibits that which doesn't really exist—that eventually normalizes the subject's desire.[7] Fern's father requires Fern to sell Wilbur, thus effecting the initial separation. Seeing how much that separation will hurt

Fern, her mother intervenes, suggesting that she sell him to an uncle who lives nearby. Farmer Zuckerman, her uncle and hence once removed from her father, puts Wilbur in a pen with the following prohibition: "Mr. Zuckerman did not allow her to take Wilbur out, and he did not allow her to get into the pigpen" (15–16). Still, he allows her to visit every day, which she does, causing her mother to worry that the prohibitions are not working to channel Fern's desire in a normal direction. She consults Fern's doctor (whose illustration by Garth Williams bears an uncanny resemblance to Freud), who reassures her that the substitution will eventually take hold in the form of a boy, namely Henry Fussy. Of course by the end of the book it does, and Fern voluntarily separates herself from the moment of Wilbur's triumph in order to ride the Ferris wheel with Henry. Presumably, since Fern is only eight, Henry is merely the first in a line of signifiers for Fern's desire, indicating that she has been successfully integrated as a full member of the Symbolic.

But we must not forget that it is the psychic work performed through Wilbur that makes this happen. As the representational nexus of Fern's narcissism, her desire, and her relation to the Law, he cannot simply be sold and forgotten, no matter what a Symbolic authority says. Instead he is repressed. The lovely imagery that White provides is of Wilbur being put in the cellar of a barn where he becomes a Real pig, rather than an Imaginary baby. Repressed representations function in just that way. They take on the status of the Real for the subject. The Real is one of the most difficult concepts to grasp in Lacan, much debated and little understood. It helps, I find, to consider the Real in two veins—a presymbolic Real and postsymbolic Real-of-the-subject. The presymbolic Real is the subject's absolute Other. It is unsymbolizable and hence has no effect whatsoever on the subject[8] as such. The American philosopher C. S. Peirce addresses the problem in this way:

> "But what," some listener . . . may say, "are we not to occupy ourselves at all with earthquakes[,] droughts[,] and pestilence?" To which I reply, if those earthquakes, droughts, and pestilences are subject to *laws*, those laws being of the nature of signs, then, no doubt being signs of those laws they are thereby made worthy of human attention; but if they be mere arbitrary brute interruptions of our course of life, let us wrap our cloaks about us, and endure them as we may; for they cannot injure us, though they may strike us down. (Peirce 235)

Inasmuch as Fern is a *subject,* she worries about the contingency of existence and impending death. Fern is forced into expressing these fears in language when she sees her father with the ax. At that point, her father allows her language to stay Wilbur's execution, preserving, for a time, her illusion of the wholeness of the world and her place in it. But immediately the work of repression begins when she realizes that her words alone are inadequate to save Wilbur's life. By taking on the project of saving the life of a runt pig, paradoxically, Fern has entered into an economy where death becomes a possibility for her through her narcissistic connection with Wilbur. For what *can* injure us, what does have effects, is the postsymbolic Real, that is, the repressed representations that create our material conditions.

In order for something to exist in the Real-of-the-subject, it must somehow be conceived of as having slipped the boundaries of symbolization. What we can conceive of symbolically is what makes up our reality, but implicit in that conception is the idea that since we have conceived it, and since we know that signifiers slide endlessly and substitute one for another in an endless chain, there must be some "outside" of signification where the sliding stops. Joan Copjec says that it is the very duplicity of language that points to an outside which is the Real; hence the Real is an effect of language's inability to be self-identical (56). Bruce Fink phrases the same idea another way, positing "a real after the letter which is characterized by impasses and impossibilities due to the relations among the elements of the symbolic order itself . . . , that is, which is generated by the symbolic" (27). We have already seen how Wilbur-as-baby was generated by Fern's encounter with the law; when he is excluded as a baby by that same law, he has nowhere to go, structurally speaking, but into that register of the Real which is postsymbolic. Repressed representations, in that they are unavailable to us, form independent relations among themselves and create material effects in our realities, take on the status of this postsymbolic Real, just as Wilbur becomes a pig in the midst of other animals in Zuckerman's cellar–Fern's unconscious.

The story of Charlotte, the talking animals, and Wilbur's dilemma, then, can be read on one level as Fern's symptom. Despite the fact that both Fern's father and her uncle have introduced a bar of separation between Fern and her Imaginary Other, she still has work to do in order to effect her own separation from him. In fact she does not separate from Wilbur until Charlotte is certain that Wilbur is safe. When Wilbur's special award is announced, Charlotte "was sure at last that she had saved Wilbur's life, and she felt peaceful and contented"

(153). Immediately, Fern asks for some money so that she can be off in search of Henry Fussy. Rather than join in the general excitement surrounding her pig, she insists on being allowed to leave, having no interest at all in sharing in the accolades of her surrogate child. Since we know the end of the story—that Fern is free to separate from Wilbur at his moment of triumph—we can retroactively posit that when she sells Wilbur, she still fears for his life. And since we have seen how interconnected his life is with her coming into being as a subject, we can also posit that the entire story of Charlotte and her web is Fern's attempt to save herself. As long as she (and Wilbur) are not full subjects, they are under threat. The Imaginary is a wonderful place to visit, but the child-subject mustn't continue to live there. At the same time, the sense of loss that would be generated by the death of Wilbur as Fern's Imaginary other would be too traumatic. Fern is at an impasse until Wilbur can be brought out of both an Imaginary relation and a Real that cannot be symbolized into a network of sig- nifiers. Until that happens, or more precisely, until Fern is sure of Wilbur's place in the Symbolic network, she is unable to break the Imaginary dyad that is holding them both in place. As a result, she unaccountably (to her mother at least) "hears" the voices of all the barnyard animals as they go about their business.

As repressed representations of Fern's unconscious, the animals in the barn cellar aren't hard to recognize—Templeton as almost pure id, Charlotte as wise and protective (but also bloodthirsty) superego, and all the others, which we could speculate may have been tried- and-discarded attempts to produce an acceptable ego, but the sheep were too snobbish, the geese too garrulous, the cows too dull. They have all come to coexist comfortably, and all have advice for Wilbur that he must weigh and ponder, accept or reject, as he performs the ego's role as negotiator. In his role as ego, Wilbur gets it right. He gives just enough food and attention to Templeton so that Templeton serves him and not the other way around, and he does all he can to live up to the high calling of the words Charlotte chooses to describe him and make him valuable in the world.

But more than that, Charlotte's web-words bring Wilbur into the network of signifiers in the Symbolic and free Fern from her fixation. Fixation indicates a trauma. In Fern's case, I think that we can safely posit that the trauma of realizing that her father would kill a harm- less creature in cold blood was the cause of her being unable to get over Wilbur, especially in light of her identification with him. Fern's connection to Wilbur and her subsequent symptom of believing that the animals talk send her mother scurrying to the doctor, who says in effect that eventually Fern will find a substitute that will relieve her of her fixation. But in order to do that, the fixated object needs to be drawn into the dialectical movement of the signifier. Fern's father, her uncle, and Henry Fussy set the stage for this process to occur by excluding Fern's maternal desire and introducing a hole in the structure of Fern's relationship to Wilbur. But it is finally Charlotte who realizes that words are the way to unlock Wilbur from his position as Real object in Fern's unconscious (and as such unsymbolizable) and constitute him as a substitutable entity (that is, bring him into the Symbolic). Paradoxically, the words that "kill" Wilbur in the Real save his life symbolically for Fern. The words, by signifying Wilbur, free him from the kind of "authenticity" or Realness that he has come to embody for Fern and that ultimately is a fantasy of the Imaginary. The words in Charlotte's web become "a Real manifestation of an Imaginary use of Symbolic-order language, whose 'first cause' is [Fern's] unconscious" (Ragland-Sullivan 405).

Some Pig

Thus far we have looked at Wilbur as a part of Fern—her ego, or in Lacanian terms her *moi*. But more can be learned about the construction of subjectivity by looking at Wilbur as a subject in his own right. Structurally speaking, Wilbur's emergence as a subject is fairly straightforward. The Lacanian subject is alienated from its own desire from its very inception. It is not Wilbur's desire that brings him into existence, but Fern's. None of us asks to be born; parental desire, in whatever form it may take, causes a child's presence in the world. And that desire continues to function in the child's life, creating the space in which the child will come to exist as a subject within language. Inasmuch as the child-subject is caused by the desire of an Other, he or she is always already alienated. In fact, such alienation is the necessary condition for any subjectivity whatsoever. If Fern's desire had not been mobilized in Wilbur's direction, there would have been no Wilbur.

But Wilbur, like all subjects, doesn't immediately jump from nothingness into subjectivity. As I have pointed out, the first two chapters of the book don't belong to Wilbur, even though he is there. But he is there as something to be loved, fed, talked about, and ultimately sold. His being is not at all a surety. In fact, it is almost assuredly the case that unless something happens, he will remain ontologically questionable, just filling a place in the world until he is fat enough to fill a place, so to speak, in the Other. Alienation (understood in terms of Wilbur's existence as Fern's desire) has opened a space for him, but it is an empty space in terms of subjectivity. Wilbur has a "thereness" but not a "whoness." Gagnon says that Wilbur didn't have a "strong personality"; as a Lacanian subject, he has no predetermined personality at all. Fink points out that this empty space, this lack, is the "first guise" of the subject. "To qualify something as empty is to use a spatial metaphor implying that it could alternately be full," says Fink (52); that is, a runt pig now occupies a place that has been set aside in the Symbolic order for Wilbur to come to be as a full subject.

Fern chooses the proper name Wilbur as a signifier for the pig because it is "the most beautiful name she could think of" (*Charlotte's Web* 7). Already we can see alienation working—this name, connected in Fern's mind to absolute beauty, designates what her mother has called a "runt," her father has dismissed as a "weakling," and her brother has disparaged as a "miserable thing . . . no bigger than a white rat." Wilbur as Fern's desire has completely annulled Wilbur as runt pig and has alienated him into the Symbolic order. Being has therefore been ruled out for Wilbur (thankfully so, because as a mere being, he would have been killed), and he has come into *existence*. But he is not a subject yet. Alienation involves what Lacan calls a *vel*, a choice between the subject and the Other (compare *Four Fundamental Concepts* 210–13). If we think of Fern and her father together as the Other and Wilbur as the potential subject, we see that initially Wilbur is the excluded term; that is, as we have seen, they are in complete charge of the inauguration of Wilbur's existence as anything at all.

The next step in the constitution of the subject is separation, "a situation in which both the subject and the Other are excluded" (Fink 53). It starts with the recognition of a lack in the Other. Up until Fern sells Wilbur, he has lived under the illusion of the two of them as one, that Fern is the whole world. He follows her around, and when she is away he simply waits for her to come again so that he can follow her some more. She is his source of food, love, fun, happiness, and life itself. Under her care he has come to love the world. In one sense, we could say that the place he has been holding in the Symbolic is the space of her lack—he has covered over that lack and has produced the illusion of Fern as whole. Fern is "enchanted" by Wilbur, and

Wilbur adores Fern. Williams's illustrations emphasize this relationship; the gaze of Wilbur at Fern and of Fern at Wilbur locks out the
rest of the world. But when Fern is forced to sell Wilbur, to separate
from him, her position as a barred subject within the Symbolic order
is made plain. Here again, both the text and the illustration emphasize the separation of the two. Fern is shown on the other side of a
fence (which is on the opposite page as well), and Wilbur does not
even appear to notice her, being too engrossed in his food. Fern has
been revealed as lacking, which is the same as saying that Fern has
been revealed as a desiring being, not at all coextensive with Wilbur.
Although her status is much more privileged with regard to the Symbolic than his, she nonetheless suffers from a lack of power with respect to its structures of authority, which have shut her off from direct
contact with Wilbur and have forced her exclusion from his development. He has been turned over to the forces of the paternal metaphor in order to fill out his place in the Symbolic apart from Fern.

The intervention of the third term, the paternal metaphor, as discussed in the previous section, coincides with and is the necessary
condition for Wilbur's emergence into language. As long as Fern was
able to speak for Wilbur, he had no need (and indeed no ability) to
speak for himself. Fern's loss (read here as the loss of Fern to Wilbur
as well as the loss of Wilbur to Fern) is thus potentially Wilbur's gain.
For Fern, the injunction to sell Wilbur institutes the Name-of-the-
Father, which bars the desire of the mother. For Wilbur, it is the rule
established by Homer Zuckerman that bars him from Fern and re-
leases (or forces) him into the assumption of his place in language
as a signifier. And although that signifier may well start out as something like "pork chops" for the Zuckermans, it is a signifier nonetheless, and hence open to contingency, substitution, displacement, and
all the other operations of the signifier in the Symbolic order.

Significantly, Wilbur's entry into language is preceded in the story
by a rather long introduction to the barn in which he finds himself.
Nodelman points out that "the basic structural pattern in *Charlotte's
Web* is the list" (116). The lists encompass everything in the book; what
the characters see, what they do, where they are, what they eat, what
they plan—are all given to the reader in long, detailed lists. Nodelman asserts that the lists "not only evoke the qualities of barns but
also imply the glorious wholeness of existence" (118). But the lists are
noticeably absent in the first two chapters of the book. According to
Nodelman, this indicates that the first two chapters are doing some-

thing different from the rest of the book. In my reading of Wilbur's development as a subject, this isn't the case at all.

Nodelman notices that the first two chapters offer a vision of a "prelapsarian world, a paradise of innocence" (117). He suggests further that this paradise is a space of naive wish-fulfillment. What better way to describe the mythologized place of the *infans,* the infant before he enters into the registers of the Imaginary and the Symbolic? In this prelapsarian world, before the infant has "fallen" into language, he knows nothing of his own alienation. Here the child in his prelinguistic state is un-self-differentiated, an " 'hommelette'—a little man and also like a broken egg spreading without hindrance in all directions" (Coward and Ellis 101). The child has no impression of otherness. He assimilates everything, experiencing what Lacan called "plenitude" and Freud called the "oceanic self." Lists in such a world would make no sense, precisely because lists imply differentiation, an acknowledgment of things that are not oneself and the placement of those things within a structure. Prior to its entry into language, the subject has to learn what constitutes its own body and what constitutes Other. It must be expelled from its place in the mother, structurally speaking, which creates a hole in both. And though that expulsion is registered as a loss in the Lacanian economy, it also represents a gain—specifically, the gain of a place from which to speak.

The prelapsarian world of the infant is characterized by two registers: the presymbolic Real and the Imaginary. The presymbolic Real might be thought of as perceptual information without a subject to organize it. Ragland-Sullivan explains: "More primordial than the *je* (the social, speaking self), the Other is created by imprinting the outside world in networks of meaning made up of images, sounds, and effects. Such concrete elements, symbolized as mental representations, have the power to constitute the *source* of meaning only because the biological and psychic infant perceives reality directly from its birth. No ego is needed to accomplish such perception . . ." (383). Certainly Wilbur is a perceiving being. The two lists that do appear in the first two chapters (which Nodelman remarks are only perceived as lists retroactively, in light of what comes after—a nice parallel to the retroactive way any sort of analysis is projected onto this stage of infant development) are "evocations of sensuous detail" (Nodelman 118) that seem coextensive with the baby pig. Kitchen smells are described right after the pig is brought in, and there is a description of the kind of mud Wilbur likes: "warm and moist and delightfully sticky and oozy" (*Charlotte's Web* 11). These perceptions begin to get organized when the baby develops the capacity for mirror-stage iden- tifications. The unity that the baby projects onto the image and iden- tifies with himself provides the necessary fiction that holds the world together. But interestingly enough, as we have seen in the case of Wilbur, the subject himself is not the guarantor of the world's cohe- sion; rather, it is the Other. Wilbur's world is initially put together, and held together, through Fern. Over the course of the book, there are other "ego ideal" representations that Wilbur tries to substitute for Fern, with the ultimate result that "through the identificatory and mimetic processes of introjection and projection, the *moi* is consti- tuted from the Other" (Ragland-Sullivan 383). We don't have a single instant when Wilbur apprehends himself in any kind of mirror. This is just as well, because it clears up a common misunderstanding that the phenomenon of the mirror-stage is an all-at-once, one-time event that takes place between a presubject and herself. It is, instead, a pro- cess, and it may not involve a mirror at all, but is rather the ability to identify oneself with an Other and *as* an Other, that is, the ability to place oneself into the play of signification.

As I said earlier, separation is "a situation in which both the subject and the Other are excluded" (Fink 53). But excluded in favor of what? In favor of the Symbolic order. Chapter 2 ends with Fern being forced to separate from Wilbur; Chapter 3 begins with an extensive descrip- tion of the barn, the new world they both must enter in order to stay together—the Symbolic. We know it is representative of the Symbolic because everything in it is distinct, separate, and located in terms of a structure—smells, seasons, housings for the different animals, and tools are all represented as collections. We also know it is part of the Symbolic because of its link to the Name-of-the-Father: "And the whole thing was owned by Fern's uncle, Mr. Homer L. Zuckerman" (14). It exists as an order apart from Wilbur in which he must never- theless find his place. Hence White accomplishes temporally in his narrative what exists structurally for the subject—the existence of the Symbolic prior to and independent of any conscious ordering of it by any subject. White presents the barn and its environs as a wondrous place indeed, but Wilbur is not yet ready for it. The first two chap- ters that are rightfully Wilbur's are called "Escape" and "Loneliness," indicating how overwhelming and marked with loss the entry into the Symbolic is for the young child, because what is excluded is the mother. Without Fern, Wilbur is not quite sure who he is or what to do with himself. His first reaction is to try to escape his predicament, but the cacophony of voices telling him what to do is too much for him, and he succumbs to the "old pail trick," concluding that whatever is out there in the wide world (the "beyond" of the Symbolic) is much more terrifying than what he has to deal with in the barn. Next he tries to fit in through assimilation—he becomes a maker of lists himself. He plans out his whole day, hour by hour, but then it rains. He is undone. "Friendless, dejected, and hungry, he threw himself down in the manure and sobbed" (31). It is clearly a time of crisis for Wilbur, a time when he must come to be something or other. He is faced with a choice—he can stay in the place assigned for him as an object of Zuckerman's demand, or he can come to be in the place of Fern and Charlotte's desire.

There are four privileged objects in Lacan that relate the subject to the Other—the breast, the feces, the gaze, and the voice (*Television* 85–87). The breast and the feces are on the side of demand, that is, they represent the time of the subject when he does not clearly differentiate himself as a desiring being apart from the Other. It should be noted that time here is structural as well as chronological, in that the subject often "retreats" to a relation of demand once desire has been established. To remain in this position always is for Lacan the definition of obsessional neurosis; the subject is locked in the position of always wondering what the Other wants of him and has no sense of what he may want apart from the Other. But basic appetites are taken care of in this position, and people can live this way in a sort of infantilized position that ultimately leads to their complete consumption by the Other. This is the offer Zuckerman makes to Wilbur. He feeds him warm, wonderful slops and gives him a nice manure pile to sleep in. But it is a trap, and to accept it blithely will lead to Wilbur's annihilation. It is better for him to enter the world of desire, where the privileged objects are the gaze (provided by Fern, who sits "quietly during the long afternoons, thinking and listening and watching Wilbur" [15]) and, of course, the voice: "You can imagine Wilbur's surprise when, out of the darkness, came a small voice he had never heard before. It sounded rather thin, but pleasant. 'Do you want a friend, Wilbur?' it said. 'I'll be a friend to you. I've watched you all day and I like you'" (31). Hence Charlotte begins Wilbur's substantive development as a subject. Separated from his "mother," empty in his own being, he needs some other structuring relationship to give his life meaning and to help him achieve a place outside of Zuckerman's demand. Fern can't do this for him, for many reasons. Structurally speaking, as we have already noted, she must be excluded in her maternal function. The danger is, according to Lacan, that the mother's desire is like a crocodile; you never know when the jaws might clamp shut, so you insert a stone roller, the phallus, in her mouth to prevent her from clamping down on you (*Seminar XVII* 129). If we think of Fern as a human, who presumably eats the bacon her mother fixes for breakfast (*Charlotte's Web* 3), we see that the metaphor is not an idle one in this case. But in addition, in her position in the Symbolic, Fern is ultimately ineffectual. Certainly she wins her argument with her father to save Wilbur's life initially, but White makes it clear that it is her father's love, and not the force of her argument, that wins the case. Wilbur needs a spokesperson whose relation to the Other as language is a bit less tenuous. Fern only had the phallic authority loaned to her by her father; Charlotte, through her connection to language and her ability to spin her own web, possesses her own version of the phallus. In this sense, she can be read as a phallic mother for Wilbur. A phallic mother is believed by the child to possess the phallus (*Feminine Sexuality* 76). This is an important fantasy because through it and its subsequent debunking the child locates desire—a desire either to have what she feels she lacks (in the case of a girl) or to keep what he believes can be taken away (in the case of a boy). Wilbur certainly believes Charlotte to have the phallus, and she perpetuates that belief in her descriptions of her long and complicated legs. Hence Wilbur strives to be like Charlotte, to identify with her as an ideal maternal image.[9] He is never placed in a position to be disabused of his notion that Charlotte has a phallus; if anything, the impression is strengthened by her bloodthirsty tales of conquest. Unlike Fern, who is shown to be powerless, Charlotte's power is preserved even under the threat of Avery. This is the power of fantasy—be it White's, Fern's, Wilbur's, or the child reader's—that Charlotte is every bit as wonderful and as powerful as we think she is, as indeed we need her to be. She can provide the signifiers that cover Wilbur's lack of being and firmly implant him as a subject in his own right in the Symbolic order.

In doing this she is continuing the work that Fern began when she treated Wilbur as what Nodelman calls a "'pretend' human being." In the barn, Nodelman says of Wilbur, "he *is* a person, so it was silly indeed to treat him like a pretend person" (125). Like Gagnon, Nodelman posits a "true" Wilbur to whom Fern and Charlotte must respond. But this is not the case in a Lacanian frame. The individual personality of the subject, the qualities that fill out the structures of his subjectivity, owe their very existence to the Other's language. Hence the substantive conditions of subjectivity are time-bound and culture-specific, rather than atemporal and universal. Wilbur's concerns are largely modernist in composition. He is engulfed in existential angst regarding his death, his loneliness (his essential isolation), and the banality of his existence. He seeks intimacy, a person whom he can trust. He wants to know how to live. Such questions imply many things about the subject in modernity. They imply the sense of a certain emptiness at the core of one's being. They imply a desire for unity and connectedness as a hedge against personal disintegration. And they imply a sense of choice in the way we deal with our angst. White's "solutions" to Wilbur's problems also imply something about the modernist subject. Wilbur finds someone he can trust, and trust her he does. Charlotte proves to him that his trust was well founded. She understands something about modernity herself. She understands the faith people have in the printed word. She understands that it is not enough to find personal meaning; in order to survive, you must prove yourself in ways that the world finds profitable. She understands the connection between the public self and the private one, and she understands the role and power of language in creating that self.

In a limited way, Fern understands this too. Fern's treating Wilbur as a pretend person is not silly; it is the necessary precondition for his becoming a person. Similarly, Charlotte does not search for words that will describe the Wilbur that she somehow "finds." Rather, she chooses words, weaves them into her web, and expects Wilbur to embody or, in other words, to perform them. It works wonderfully. When Charlotte decides to write the word "terrific" in her web, Wilbur at first objects:

> "But Charlotte," said Wilbur, "I'm *not* terrific."
>
> "That doesn't make a particle of difference," replied Charlotte. "Not a particle. People believe almost anything they see in print." (89)

When the web is finished and people come to look at it, Wilbur really feels terrific, and Zuckerman confirms it: "'There isn't a pig in the whole state that is as terrific as our pig'" (96). What's more, Zuckerman improves Wilbur's circumstances in such a way that he waxes radiant. He becomes "a pig any man would be proud of" (114). Hence, in a very real way, Wilbur emerges as the effect of Charlotte's words. Thus it can be seen how a subject may be called an effect of language.

Charlotte saves Wilbur's life through the performance of speech acts; indeed, it could be said that she brings the Wilbur that comes to be known to the outside world into existence through speech acts. But what is significant is that these speech acts are not publicly attributed to Charlotte. When Mr. Zuckerman explains the "miracle" that signifies to him that they have no ordinary pig to Mrs. Zuckerman, she replies, " 'Well . . . it seems to me you're a little off. It seems to me we have no ordinary *spider*' " (80). But Zuckerman insists that the words in the web are a sign from God, completely referential with regard to Wilbur, and have nothing whatever to do with a spider. Zuckerman is here represented as actively repressing the possibility of a performative subjectivity, as well as the role of the Other in that performance. Considering his role as the Name-of-the-Father, this move on his part is uniquely appropriate in that it is part of his function to delimit the possibilities of being. A performative subjectivity implies endless possibilities, constrained only by the unpredictable desire of the mother, who channels the desire of the subject in the first place. Hence the production of subjectivity is to some degree out of his control. But Wilbur had two fine, strong, modernist mothers, who offer no challenge to the authoritative role of Zuckerman, even as they subvert the natural order of things regarding the fate of runt pigs.

But as Lucy Rollins points out in her essay "The Reproduction of Mothering in *Charlotte's Web*," Charlotte is not a typical mother. She neither feeds nor touches Wilbur. In fact, one might say that she is not maternal. Yet she is female. She is an embodiment of what Lacan would call a person with a feminine structure. For Lacan, the categories of male and female are marked by structural distinctions with relation to the Symbolic order.[10] The male subject is one who is completely subjected to or immersed in the Symbolic. The female subject, on the other hand, has, so to speak, one foot in the Symbolic but one foot somewhere else. As a result, a male cannot encounter a true female, only his fantasized constructions of "woman." Fern's father behaves as a male when he wants to kill the runt pig. It makes sense in the Symbolic order to get rid of things that have no purpose and might cause trouble. Zuckerman falls into this category as well. As we have seen, he misrecognizes the words in the web as belonging to

Wilbur and not Charlotte. Interestingly enough, *Mrs.* Zuckerman is
the one who points out his error, but he, working from within his own
fantasy, rejects her insight. Charlotte, as a female subject, knows how
the Symbolic order operates but is herself only partially subjected to
it. This way, she can function within its structures, but she can also
function outside its structures as well. She can behave as something
other than a common spider. A writer, for instance, and a friend.

As for Wilbur, he becomes fully actualized as a subject when he
becomes the "mother" of Charlotte's babies. In so doing, he "tra-
verses the fundamental fantasy": "The traversing of fantasy involves
the subject's assumption of a new position with respect to the Other
as language and the Other as desire. A move is made to invest or inhabit that which brought him or her into existence as split subject, to
become that which *caused* him or her" (Fink 62, emphasis in original).
The initial trauma that "caused" Wilbur's existence was the fear of his
imminent death. By taking responsibility for Charlotte's children, he
enters into a new position with respect to death. He doesn't exactly
take responsibility for Charlotte's death, but he inserts himself into
it as her heir. Not only does he inherit her egg sac, but he inherits
her desire to help others and to be a true friend. The very satisfying
closure of the novel indicates a certain completeness in Wilbur's development that the traversing of the fundamental fantasy suggests.

The Child Reader of Charlotte's Web

Clearly, *Charlotte's Web* serves a Lacanian poetics well in its allegorical
representation of the development of subjectivity. But what remains
to be discussed is whether such a poetics might have a transactional
(or in our language performative) component as well. That is, although a Lacanian poetics figures the text as a metaphor for the
subject, it may also be the case that it is not merely metaphorical. I
have argued that language has effects, and that among these effects
is the development of subjectivity itself, through the individual's assumption of the position ascribed to the subject in language (just as
Wilbur became what Charlotte said he was). I have also argued that
this process is ongoing, though it is most active in childhood, when
the libidinal attachments of the subject are finding their preferred
channels. Hence a Lacanian poetics specific to children's literature
should take into account the relative lack of reification in the substance attaching to the structures of subjectivity. Perhaps even those

very structures are less stable than traditional psychoanalysis suggests (see note 7); that the triangular structure of the oedipal configuration has held sway for so long does not necessarily mean that it will continue to do so in a less textually monolithic, more imagistically multivalent society. At any rate, a child in a literate society has a radically text-based subjectivity; print manifestations of the Other, as well as of authority and the law, are everywhere for the child, so it is quite natural for her to identify with them through Imaginary fusion. Moreover, there is enough residual faith in the authority of the printed word for the text itself to be in the position of the "subject presumed to know"—that is, the place of transferential love (see *Four Fundamental Concepts*, chapter 18). At first blush this sounds odd, but how often do we consult books for the "last word" on a subject or for instructions on how to do things properly?[11] As Charlotte says, "people believe almost anything they see in print." Western culture has built its religious traditions, its academic traditions, its popular culture all on the basis of the book. It should come as no surprise to think that we would construct our identities through the book as well.

The rhetoric White uses in the first two chapters is an invitation to the reader to do just that. Nodelman points out that White provides just enough detail to evoke a recognizable world and sets up a situation that will be recognizable and enjoyable for the young reader: "It is enjoyable because it describes a pleasurable fulfillment of common wishes: to have a real live doll to play with, to get your own way with your parents and feel the satisfaction of saving another creature's life in the bargain, always to be happy" (Nodelman 122). But these wishes could be said to be generated in the reader by the text itself. All is dependent on the successful interpellation of the reader in an initial identification. Whereas the young reader might not immediately make an interspecies identification with a small pig waking up in a barn, he or she is invited to identify with a curious young girl. Nothing is given in the opening lines that would distance the reader from the scene—no physical description of Fern or her mother or their setting. Further, the book opens with Fern asking a question, placing her in the same position as the reader—a position of ignorance of what is about to happen. Once the reader has made the initial Imaginary fusion that covers his or her constitutive lack, Fern's concerns can become the reader's concerns in a process so seamless as to seem the other way around. She inaugurates the identificatory relationship with the pig through the characterization of him as "very small and weak." Through both Fern and Wilbur, the reader's angst over her being-toward-death is created and relieved. Hence the reader is placed in a position to learn that the way to save your life is through the successful performance of speech acts.

The recent movie *Babe* (based on the book by Dick King-Smith) produces a similar set of concerns and addresses them in similar ways. A young pig is separated from his mother, enters language—his first words in the film are in fact "bye, mom"—and is adopted by a wise and loving surrogate of a different species. The cast is a bit different—the threatening authoritative male is not the human male but the dog Rex, who supervises the activities of all the animals in the barnyard. Nonetheless, in the story that follows, the pig's life is saved through the intervention of the new mother who gives the pig a new identity; he becomes a sheep-pig. Unlike the dogs, who bite, chase, and growl, he uses his words to herd the sheep. In the most crucial moment of the pig's existential angst, when he is ready to die because he has learned that pigs have no purpose but to be eaten, the farmer revives the pig by singing, "If I had words to make a day for you, I'd give you a morning, golden and true. I would make this day last for all time, then fill the night deep in moonshine." Words to make a day . . . words to craft an identity . . . words to save a life. The subject is constituted, again and again, in and through language.

Notes

1. "You are aware that one can say that the human being is born with fetalized traits, that is to say deriving from premature birth" (Lacan, *Seminar I* 210).

2. For Lacan, the mother is "the first Other [the child] has to deal with" (*Four Fundamental Concepts* 218). As we shall see, however, at the point when the child enters language, some essential bit of the mother gets cut off from the subject's conscious awareness.

3. Ashraf H. A. Rushdy, in his "'The Miracle of the Web': Community, Desire, and Narrativity in *Charlotte's Web*," evokes Lacanian theory with respect to what he calls a "'reflective model' of interpellation," using Lacan's famous essay on the mirror stage in the service of Rushdy's own model of text as reflective of society. Focusing his attention on a reading of the metaphor of the mirror, Rushdy evokes Lacan's work mostly to dismiss it, stating that "Lacan, in the end, can represent only the model of desire as reflection" (41). In this essay, I seek, among other things, to reopen a discussion of Lacan's whole theory of desire, synthesized from a reading of many of his works, with respect to *Charlotte's Web*.

4. This is a psychoanalytic reading. I aim to explore many of the less generally understood concepts of Lacanian thought, but I will nevertheless assume a familiarity on the part of the reader with certain overdetermined "truths" of psychoanalysis. Among these, phallic symbols loom large.

5. Freud makes the argument that a male child is a surrogate penis: "Not until the

emergence of the wish for a penis does the doll-baby become a baby from the girl's father, and thereafter the aim of the most powerful feminine wish" ("Femininity" 128). Obviously, Freud is not talking about the actual organ here but more or less the power it symbolizes.

6. A few very simplified definitions: The Imaginary is the realm of ideal images that a subject chooses to identify with and strives to embody. It is in the Imaginary that we experience a sense of personal coherence. The Symbolic, on the other hand, is the more public order of language, society, and culture. Here is where irony is experienced, because the culturally nuanced and languaged representations we find there do not match our Imaginary images. As a result, we may experience the feeling of playing a role rather than having an identity. The Real will be explained in greater detail below.

7. "Normalization of the subject's desire" refers to the rejection of the mother as a proper object of desire. The girl first replaces her with the father and then substitutes for him other, unrelated males, and the boy substitutes unrelated females, according to requirements of the incest taboo. Lacan's appropriation of the oedipal structure of desire (taken over from Freud and Levi-Strauss) that sets up the incest taboo as the foundation of culture is often targeted by interpreters as his reinscription of this myth as an unavoidable or universal structure. Lacan himself, however, insists on its contingency within the sociohistorical organization of Western cultures and societies. "The apparent necessity of the phallic function turns out to be merely contingent" (*Seminar XX* 87), he says, indicating the possibility that subjective organization around the oedipal triangle is cultural, not universal. Both Dr. Dorian and Fern's mother wish that Fern's desire would fit into the categories of what is considered normal in their society.

8. I mean here the subject as we have been discussing it, not the human organism. What matters to the life of the subject are the things for which we have language. Certainly humans as organisms can be injured or touched by things they cannot symbolize.

9. In her compelling reading of mothering in *Charlotte's Web*, Lucy Rollins points out the ambiguities regarding Wilbur's persistence as a sort of eternal child. Perhaps the fact that he is never forced to lose faith in Charlotte's status as phallic mother contributes to his continuing in a childlike state, because, as Lacan points out, the child's realization that the mother is "castrated" is what precipitates phallic-stage development and symptom formation (*Feminine Sexuality* 76–77).

10. Lacan has articulated his views of masculinity and femininity in various places throughout the last decade of his writing. The fullest explanations can be found in *Seminar XX.*

11. Note that White himself coauthored the text that has helped for so long to teach us how to use language to construct ourselves and our students as articulate scholars— *The Elements of Style.*

Works Cited

Babe. Based on the book by Dick King-Smith. Screenplay by George Miller and Chris Noonan. Dir. Chris Noonan. Universal, 1995.

Copjec, Joan. *Read My Desire: Lacan Against the Historicists.* Cambridge: MIT Press, 1994.

Coward, Rosalind, and John Ellis. *Language and Materialism.* London: Routledge, 1977.

Felman, Shoshana. *Jacques Lacan and the Adventure of Insight: Psychoanalysis in Contemporary Culture.* Cambridge: Harvard University Press, 1987.

———. *The Literary Speech Act: Don Juan with J. L. Austin, or Seduction in Two Languages.* Trans. Catherine Porter. Ithaca: Cornell University Press, 1983.

Fink, Bruce. *The Lacanian Subject: Between Language and Jouissance.* Princeton: Princeton University Press, 1995.

Freud, Sigmund. "Femininity." *New Introductory Lectures on Psychoanalysis.* SE 22. Ed. James Strachey. New York: Norton, 1966.

Gagnon, Laurence. "Webs of Concern: *The Little Prince* and *Charlotte's Web.*" *Children's Literature* 2 (1973): 61–66.

Griffith, John. "*Charlotte's Web:* A Lonely Fantasy of Love." *Children's Literature* 8 (1979): 111–17.

Heidegger, Martin. *Being and Time.* Trans. John Macquarrie and Edward Robinson. San Francisco: Harper and Row, 1962.

Lacan, Jacques. *Ecrits: A Selection.* Trans. Alan Sheridan. New York: Norton, 1977.

———. *Feminine Sexuality.* Ed. Juliet Mitchell and Jacqueline Rose. Trans. Jacqueline Rose. New York: Norton, 1982.

———. *The Four Fundamental Concepts of Psychoanalysis.* Trans. Alan Sheridan. New York: Norton, 1978.

———. *Seminar I: Freud's Papers on Technique* 1953–54. Trans. John Forrester. New York: Norton, 1988.

———. *Seminar III: The Psychoses* 1955–56. Trans. Russell Grigg. New York: Norton, 1993.

———. *Seminar XVII: L'envers de la psychanalyse* 1969–70. Trans. Russell Grigg. New York: Norton, forthcoming.

———. *Seminar XX: Encore* 1972–73. Trans. Bruce Fink. New York: Norton, 1998.

———. *Television.* Trans. Denis Hollier, Rosalind Krauss, and Annette Michelson. New York: Norton, 1990.

Laplanche, Jean, and Jean-Baptiste Pontalis. *The Language of Psychoanalysis.* Trans. Donald Nicholson-Smith. New York: Norton, 1973.

Nodelman, Perry. "Text as Teacher: The Beginning of *Charlotte's Web.*" *Children's Literature* 13 (1985): 109–27.

Peirce, C. S. *Collected Papers.* Vol. 6. Ed. Charles Hartshorne and Paul Weiss. Cambridge: Harvard University Press, 1931.

Ragland-Sullivan, Ellie. "The Magnetism Between Reader and Text: Prolegomena to a Lacanian Poetics." *Poetics 13* (1984): 381–406.

Rollins, Lucy. "The Reproduction of Mothering in *Charlotte's Web.*" *Children's Literature* 18 (1990): 42–52.

Rushdy, Ashraf H. A. "'The Miracle of the Web': Community, Desire, and Narrativity in *Charlotte's Web.*" *The Lion and the Unicorn* 15 (1991): 35–60.

Strunk, William, Jr., and E. B. White. *The Elements of Style* 3d ed. Boston: Allyn and Bacon, 1979.

White, E. B. *Charlotte's Web.* New York: Harper and Row, 1952.

Narrative Resolution: Photography in Adolescent Literature

Roberta Seelinger Trites

Introduction

Martha Banta's *Imaging American Women* is an exhaustive treatise on the power of the image to affect cultural consciousness in which she demonstrates that "images of American women were *created* as ideas, not *found*" between 1876 and 1918 (xxxi, emphasis Banta's). My focus is neither on cultural history during the Progressive era nor on images of women; rather, I wish to concentrate on an assumption implicit in Banta's argument: creating an image has a two-fold empowering ability because the power of both the creator and of the image itself shifts in the process of calling the image to other people's attention. This process of empowerment seems to have a particularly dramatic effect when the image is created through photography, in part because photography provides even the artistically challenged (like me) the power of creating an image, in part because photographs convey an illusion of mimesis, in part because of "the photograph's perceived transparency and universal comprehensibility" (Hirsch 51), in part because the captured image carries with it the illusion of having stopped time momentarily.

Banta explicitly acknowledges the camera as a tool of empowerment in a series of pictures she supplies for the reader. The photos are of her mother, Irma Purman, taken while she was coming of age by the photographer Merle Smith. The final picture in the book is of Irma Purman holding a camera:

But what is nice about this photograph is that—although it is only one of the scores of occasions she faced a camera once she had been classified as the Town Beauty by the age of sixteen—

I dedicate this paper to the memory of Gayle Moody, who first brought women photographers as a literary motif to my attention. And I thank Elizabeth Keyser and Lois Kuznets for their helpful suggestions at the early stage of this project and Michael Cadden for the time he so generously dedicated to helping me revise it.
Children's Literature 27, ed. Elizabeth Lennox Keyser (Yale University Press, © 1999 Hollins University).

she at last, at the age of twenty-four, picks up her own camera
and aims it directly at the man with the camera. . . . Reciprocal energy is released through this double image of perception
and thought, action and counteraction. It is a small statement
she makes here, and a quiet one, but her steady gaze says clearly
enough, "Look, I can do it too!" (700)

In Banta's economy, her mother's possession of a camera symbolizes
her maturity; while Purman was an adolescent, she was the object of
photography, but now that she is an adult, she can be a photographing subject. The "reciprocal energy" Banta describes in this photograph is a significant function of the camera because the process of
photography calls into question the agency of both the photographer
and the photographed image.

For that matter, the same self-conscious image of agency occurs
in the opening credits of *Arthur,* the popular PBS program for preschoolers based on Marc Brown's books. While Ziggy Marly sings a
snappy song about empowerment that begins, "Every day / When
you're walking down the street / Everybody that you meet / Has an
original point of view," Arthur drives his family crazy taking pictures
of them. They finally retaliate; as he tries to take a group picture of
his parents, his grandparents, and his sisters, they all pull cameras
out of their pockets and snap pictures of him. The camera empowers
Arthur, and it also affords his family a way to communicate to him;
all of them gain something by communicating through the language
of photographs.

The metaphor of the camera bestowing on the photographer a
sense of empowerment based on the communicative abilities of
photographs occurs often in literature. Margaret Atwood's *Bodily
Harm* (1982), Marilyn French's *Her Mother's Daughter* (1987), Ann Beat-
tie's *Picturing Will* (1989), Jamaica Kincaid's *Lucy* (1990), and Amy
Tan's *The Hundred Secret Senses* (1995), for example, are novels that depict women developing their own sense of personal power through
photography. Since women's literature shares with adolescent literature a concern for people who initially feel disempowered but grow
into an increased awareness of what exactly agency entails, it seems
natural that the metaphor of the camera recurs as often in adolescent
literature as it does in women's literature. Four novels about adolescents or preadolescents that demonstrate the protagonist employing
photography as a metaphorical representation for achieving agency

include Lois Lowry's *A Summer to Die* (1977), Patricia MacLachlan's *Journey* (1991), Francesca Lia Block's *Witch Baby* (1991), and Trudy Krisher's *Spite Fences* (1994).[1]

The intricacy of the photography metaphor also allows these authors to explore the nature of subjectivity as constructed by language while simultaneously foregrounding death as an issue of both theme and narrative structure. In other words, the protagonist's increased awareness of the subject-object relation occurs in conjunction with her or his maturing into some sort of acceptance of the grief that accompanies death and loss. Moreover, the parallel lines of the character's understanding of subjectivity and of death pass through a series of points created by the repetition of various photographs. Viewing these pictures from differing vantage points increases each character's perspicacity. The protagonist must experience this series of photographic repetitions in order to achieve resolution in both the photographic and the narrative sense: she or he must perceive herself or himself clearly in order to achieve the emotional resolution that seems at times almost de rigueur in the genre.[2] Thus, photography affects both content and form in *A Summer to Die, Journey, Witch Baby,* and *Spite Fences.*

Photography and Language

In *Camera Lucida,* an extended essay on photography, Roland Barthes discusses how the fluid relation between subject and object becomes an issue in the art of photography when a camera negotiates the space between them.[3] The photographer has agency and the photograph does not, for it is an artifact, but the camera is an object that transforms images of people—acting subjects—into objects, in the process giving them a new significance they might not have previously held. As Banta notes, the concept of "camera vision" reflects the tendency of the wandering human eye to focus on one object; the act of focusing singles out the object, giving it importance (26). Indeed, the earliest portrait photos "transformed subject into object, and even, one might say, into a museum object: in order to take the first portraits (around 1840) the subject had to assume long poses under a glass roof in bright sunlight; to become an object made one suffer as much as a surgical operation" (Barthes 13). The camera and the act of photography demonstrate that the relation between subject and object is often continuous rather than discrete; separating the actor from the acted on is not always easy. As Marianne Hirsch puts it, "we both look and are looked at . . . the subject is installed in the social through that double, mutual, perceptual relationship which makes every spectator also a spectacle" (103). In a photograph, "the looking subject is always already *in* the image, shaping it with his or her own reflection or projection" (Hirsch 103, emphasis Hirsch's). The photograph is therefore a unique artifact in the way that it is capable of capturing at once images of the individual's subjectivity and objectivity. In this dual role, then, photography shares one similarity with language: both depend on the subject-object relation and the fluid relationship between them to function.

Photography bears another similarity to language in the way it forces us to consider the relation between signifier and signified. Whereas Saussure has taught us to separate the signifier from the signified in linguistic constructions, Barthes points out that photographs are a type of signifier immediately indistinguishable from the signified.[4] Is the picture itself a signifier, representing some other object, or is it signified, itself an artifact communicating directly to the viewer? Hirsch defines it this way: "The referent is both present (implied in the photograph) and absent (it has been there but is not here now)" (5). Hirsch even uses photography as the metaphor whereby she explains signification in language, connecting the process to the fluidity of social power:

> The triangular field in which signifier, signified, and interpreting subject interact in the process of symbolization is much like the triangular field of the photograph, in which the photographer, the object, and the viewer interrelate through imaginary projections they more or less share. Power, in this structure of play, is not unidimensional or unidirectional: it circulates in multiple ways within the process of taking, developing, assembling, and reading pictures and within the social space and the historical moment in which photography operates. (176)

Barthes's description of the photograph synthesizes the dichotomy between signifier and signified that Hirsch is describing: the photograph is to the viewer, at least initially, signifier and signified, just as it can contain the paradoxical image of a communicating subject that has become an object (5).

It is perhaps for this reason—because of the unique way that cameras allow adolescents to blend subject and object, to integrate signifier and signified—that adolescent novels employ camera metaphors as a way to explore agency as a linguistic construct that empowers the adolescent. The four novels I am discussing also provide characters with some of the tendencies Susan Sontag identifies for photography: in their ubiquity and passivity, photographs can become a source of aggression (7), and cameras can create a sense of vicariousness (10) that may also sanction the photographer's nonintervention in painful issues (11). For characters who take pictures instead of becoming involved, photography can become a source of complicity, a way to approve tacitly that which she or he might not otherwise be able to change (12). What holds true for Sontag holds true in each of these four novels: the photographic act and the character's capacity to view the photograph matter more than the photograph itself.[5]

Deborah Bowen identifies Sontag's definition of photography as differing epistemologically from Barthes's approach to photography: Sontag views pictures as a means to an end, as a way of coming to some sort of understanding; Barthes celebrates photos as an end in themselves; he values what the photograph reveals far more than he values what the photographer or viewer has learned in taking or observing the picture. As Bowen puts it, Sontag privileges "function" and Barthes "form" (21). Not surprisingly, given the moral impulse that shapes so much preadolescent and adolescent fiction, most adolescent novels that employ photographic metaphors value the function of taking pictures over the form of the final product: pictures are important not so much in and of themselves but for how they affect the adolescent, especially as repeated artifacts that allow the character to witness the same scene during several different points in her or his development. As a result, the process of photography engages the fictional adolescent's agency in a way that enables the character to embrace her or his subjectivity.

A Summer to Die

Lois Lowry's *A Summer to Die* is a clearcut example of this tendency. Most of the story is about Meg's reactions to her sister Molly as Molly dies of leukemia. Meg's camera is crucial to her acceptance of Molly's death; before she realizes that her sister has a fatal disease, Meg cares more about her camera than almost anything (9, 67). She says, "All those times when I feel awkward and inept—all those times are made up for when I have my camera, when I can look through the viewfinder and feel that I can control the focus and the light and the composition, when I can capture what I see, in a way that no one else is seeing it" (29). These final clauses identify Meg's photography as a crucial aspect of her exploration of subjectivity and objectivity: she wants to claim for herself what she sees, to own it, hold it captive, as she would any object; but most important, she wants to prove that her perceptions are different from everyone else's. She explores her subjectivity by manipulating photographic objects. Meg's insistence on manipulating the subject and object sets up the text's awareness that language is predicated on perceptions of subjectivity and objectivity; Meg's experiments seem like metaphorical experiments with language as well, especially in the way that Meg is concerned with how the pictures she takes communicate something to other people.

Meg even recognizes that her imagistic interpretations of those she has photographed must have an effect on their sense of their own subjectivity: "It must be a funny feeling, I think, to see your own face like that, caught by someone else, with all your feelings showing in it" (48). As Barthes says, "In front of the lens, I am . . . the one I think I am, the one I want others to think I am, the one the photographer thinks I am, and the one he makes use of to exhibit his art" (13). In identifying four positions on a continuum from subject to object that the photographed person holds, Barthes outlines the nuances a photograph can contain. Meg intuitively understands them when she says, "I care about the expressions on people's faces, the way the light falls onto them, and the way the shadows are in soft patterns and contrast" (113). She cares most about the two object positions Barthes identifies: how she perceives people and how she can transform their images into art. To Meg, her art is a matter of engaging her agency to transform other people into objects *as a way to communicate to them.* Her camera is her language; the resulting pictures are her specific speech acts.[6]

Meg acknowledges consciously the importance of processing her pictures herself. She recognizes how to use processing as a way to "compensate for all sorts of things, how to build up contrast, how to reduce it" (80). It is the process of achieving a final product that has the resolution of her choosing, not necessarily the end product itself, that empowers Meg. In other words, Meg recognizes that the photographic process entails more than just *granting* agency to the person taking the picture; agency can be *achieved* in the photographic process, as agency can also be achieved within the process of constructing ourselves of language. As Catherine Belsey notes, the subject is constructed by language and by the exterior forces that language exerts on the individual (46–50), for—as Lacan puts it—the unconscious mind is constructed like a language system (149).[7] In this sense, Meg's photographic equipment also serves as a metaphor for the unconscious mind: within the equipment lie the structures necessary to discern—and to blend—the differences between subject and object.

Despite the intricacy with which Lowry imbues Meg's use of photography, the greatest flaw in this book is how easy the camera makes birth and death experiences for Meg. In that, the book fulfills Sontag's definition of photographer as voyeur and nonparticipant. And in this case, the voyeurism deprives Meg of agency and, therefore, of some degree of maturity. For example, a friend of Meg's delivers a baby as quickly and painlessly as a character in a soap opera. Meg has been asked to photograph the birth, and she deals with her panic in this situation by hiding behind her camera: "I lifted my camera and photographed Maria smiling. The instant I had the camera in my hands, things felt comfortable. The light was good; the settings fell into place as I manipulated them; everything was okay" (128). Meg and the reader are both deprived of any sense of the necessary pain surrounding childbirth. Moreover, Meg's sister Molly dies offstage so that Meg does not have to witness the pain of death firsthand, either. Apparently, although her parents think she is old enough to watch someone being born, she is not old enough to watch someone die.

Significantly, however, Meg reconciles herself to her grief over her sister's death by gazing at a photograph of herself taken by a friend.

It was a large photograph, against a white mount, framed in a narrow black frame, and it was not just the coincidence of a stranger who happened to look like me; it was my face. It was taken at an angle; the wind was blowing my hair, and I was looking off in the distance somewhere, far beyond the meticulously trimmed edges of the photograph or the rigid confines of its frame. The outline of my neck and chin and half-turned cheek was sharp against the blurred and subtle shapes of pine trees in the background. . . . There was something of Molly in my face. It startled me, seeing it. The line that defined my face, the line that separated the darkness of the trees from the light that curved into my forehead and cheek was the same line that had once identified Molly by its shape. The way I held my shoulders was the

way she had held hers. It was a transient thing, I knew, but when
Will had held the camera and released the shutter for one five-
hundredth of a second, he had captured it and made permanent
whatever of Molly was in me. I was grateful, and glad. (150–51)

The emotional climax of the book occurs when Meg for the first time
views herself as an object in a photograph. As John Stephens notes,
Meg "breaks into a new way of seeing and a new subject position"
after this experience (286). But she can only achieve the resulting
emotional equanimity when she has experienced both the subject
and the object positions afforded by photography, after she has been
both photographing subject and photographed object.

Journey

MacLachlan's *Journey* provides another excellent example of how the
camera metaphor operates.[8] Journey is a young boy who is grieving
his mother's desertion of him; after having had a tantrum in which
she has ripped up all the family photographs, she has abandoned her
children, leaving them at her parents' home. Journey grieves the loss
of his mother and the destruction of the photographs because he
understands the basic premise of Marianne Hirsch's study of family
photographs: "Family pictures depend on . . . a narrative act of adoption that transforms rectangular pieces of cardboard into telling details connecting lives and stories across continents and generations"
(xii). Journey's grandfather wants to replace the photographs, so he
begins taking pictures almost obsessively. Early in the narrative, Journey expresses rage at his grandfather for photographing him so in-
cessantly. Being the object of his grandfather's photographic gaze
reinforces the eleven-year-old's sense of his own powerlessness; his
anger demonstrates his frustrated sense that he occupies only the object position.

But eventually Journey begins to use the camera to take pictures
of himself. As he does so, he gains for the first time an awareness
of occupying the subject position—that is, a position of action, of
agency.[9] This need to recognize one's own agency is a central pattern
of (pre)adolescent literature; we achieve adulthood more comfortably if we recognize that we have some control over the various subject positions we occupy than if we feel entirely like objects, pawns,
in other people's movements. But conversely, maturity also depends

on our ability to maintain, when necessary, an object position, for we are all objects of the cultural forces that constantly shape us. Again, the relation between subject and object is a fluid one, but gaining an increased understanding of one's power as an acting subject is inevitable during maturation.

Sontag focuses on the cultural power photography gives the photographing subject: "To photograph is to appropriate the thing photographed. It means putting oneself into a certain relation to the world that feels like knowledge—and, therefore, power" (4). Journey experiences this sense of power in taking pictures of himself and his family with the camera on a timer. Even when a friend offers to take one of these group portraits, Journey insists that he wants to be the one to focus the camera and set the timer: "*I* want to take this picture" (60, emphasis MacLachlan's). In sitting for one of his own photographs, Journey simultaneously occupies both the subject and the object position in a process that Barthes considers unique to photography (13), so the boy's split subjectivity is fused. For Journey, the major crisis of his adolescence is resolved as he recognizes that he is both subject and object, not just behind the camera but in his entire life.

Understanding the process of photography is an important one for Journey. He learns that sometimes photographs "show us the truth" (56) and "sometimes . . . the truth is somewhere behind the pictures. Not in them" (57). This duality plays an important part in Journey's increased understanding of his own life; just as he learns that photographs enable him to be both subject and object, he learns that photographs can both clarify and obscure truth. For a boy who has tended to interpret things one-dimensionally, this ability to see two sides of things represents a major step toward maturity.

Witch Baby

Francesca Lia Block's *Witch Baby* also ties issues of subjectivity and objectivity to issues of maturity by means of photography metaphors. A postmodern fairy tale like its predecessor *Weetzie Bat* (1989), *Witch Baby* is the story of the eponymous character, who asks, "What time are we upon and where do I belong?" (3, 9, 15). Suffering from the same sense of fragmentation that Sharon Wilson identifies as common in the Margaret Atwood novels that deal with photography (31), Witch Baby understands neither her paternity nor her culture, postmodern Los Angeles. As she seeks to better understand them both, she grows to recognize her subjectivity. Witch Baby is confused about her identity because her parents have not been honest with her. She was abandoned as an infant at the home of Weetzie Bat and her significant other, whose name is My Secret Agent Lover Man; Weetzie and My Secret have not told her that he is her biological father. Much of Witch Baby's identity is defined by her jealousy of Weetzie's biological daughter, Cherokee. Witch Baby has dark, tangled hair and slanting purple eyes; she is mysterious and—like Journey—very angry.

When it comes to photography, however, Witch Baby is almost the exact opposite of Journey and more like Meg in that she takes pictures from the outset of the narrative, but she is never the object of any photo. "Witch Baby had taken photographs of everyone in her almost-family. . . . Because she had taken all the pictures herself, there was no witch child with dark tangled hair and tilted purple eyes" in her collection of pictures pasted on the family clock (3). She sees but feels herself to be unseen; she lives in the shadow of her vibrant sister, Cherokee.

When a boy on whom Witch Baby has a crush hears her play the drums, she is pleased by his attention: "It was as if she were being seen by someone for the first time" (23). But she grieves because My Secret Agent Lover Man does not recognize how similar they are in worrying about the pain in the world around them. Witch Baby even tapes three articles or news photos to her wall each night that detail something wrong with the world; one of these articles, about a group of Native Americans who have died of radiation poisoning, inspires My Secret to make a movie. Later, Witch Baby is again pleased when another friend, Coyote, sees how similar she is to him and to My Secret in that they share a concern for world issues. She thinks of Coyote, "But he recognizes that I am like him and My Secret doesn't see" (31). Again, feeling that she is unseen causes Witch Baby pain.

Throughout the story Witch Baby continues to snap pictures of her family and their life together, of homeless people on the street, of people dying of AIDS, of the beach, of the redwood forest. She continues to ask herself and other people where she belongs. Eventually she learns that My Secret Agent Lover Man is her father. She runs away to seek her biological mother, Vixanne Wigg, and is disillusioned when she discovers that Vixanne is the leader of a Jayne Mansfield cult that does nothing but watch Mansfield movies, eat sugar, and deny that evil exists in the world. Trying to communicate that these attempts to escape from pain are futile, Witch Baby leaves behind her a series of photographs she has taken of homeless people and victims of AIDS; she hopes that her mother "will look at them and see" (93). At this juncture in the novel, Witch Baby clearly perceives her photography as a form of language, for these pictures are signifiers of both world angst and Witch Baby's feelings. Only through photographs can she communicate to Vixanne what she cares about most.

Witch Baby finally returns home, where her father recognizes how alike they are and where the other members of her family also voice their appreciation of her. The family's final tribute to Witch Baby is to pose for a family portrait, but this time with the camera on a timer so that Witch Baby can be included. Witch Baby looks around at the people in this family portrait and recognizes their pain and their grief: some fear AIDS, others have lost their beloved; some suffer from discrimination, others mourn "for the sky and sea, animals and vegetables, that were full of toxins" (102). Yet she finally understands that "her own sadness was only a small piece of the puzzle of pain that made up the globe. But she was a part of the globe—she had her place" (102–3). Witch Baby has gained a sense of identity, but she cannot fully claim the subject position until she recognizes that the people around her accept her in both the object and the subject position. Her transformation seems to be almost the exact opposite of Journey's: Witch Baby needs to understand herself as object before she can place herself within the matrix of her own subject-positions. Either way, however, it is the process of photography that has led these characters to their transcendent understanding of their own agency.

Spite Fences

Spite Fences, by Trudy Krisher, employs photography metaphors in a narrative that explores racial tension. Thirteen-year-old Maggie Pugh uses her camera as a way to look at life in small-town Georgia in 1960. Throughout the narrative, when she wants to evaluate a situation, she thinks of it in terms of a freeze-frame, telling herself, "*Aim. Click. . . . Advance the film. Trip the shutter. . . . Focus. Click*" (2). Maggie, who is white, receives the camera as a gift from a black friend named Zeke after she starts teaching him to read because she thinks he does not know how to read the word *white* on a restroom door. Because he has used the restroom, he is arrested and beaten and later brutalized by a mob that urinates on him and masturbates over his unconscious body. Maggie, hidden from the mob in a tree, has witnessed the near-lynching of her friend and ultimately agrees to serve as a witness in court so that his case can be prosecuted. Her words thus have the power to change the course of her hometown's history.

While Maggie learns to respect the Civil Rights Movement as it un-folds around her, she must also learn how to handle the effects of racism on white people, specifically on her mother and on their spite-ful neighbors. Maggie's mother beats her after seeing photographs of Maggie with some of her black friends. The next-door neighbor has already tried to rape her. In an ugly altercation between the two families Maggie's camera gets broken, and she is devastated. She rec-ognizes that because of the evil of racism "everything" in her home-town is as "smashed and broken to bits" as her camera is (171). But when her best girlfriend gives her a new single-lens camera, she says she feels, "for the first time in my whole life, like I'd finally been *born*" (195).

For Maggie, the perspective the camera provides her is more than a matter of feeling a sense of agency—it is a matter of expressing truth. Thus, as the text unravels, Maggie identifies occupying the subject position as seeing and speaking the truth. Early in the text, Zeke has told her, "Never be afraid of the truth" (12). When he gives Maggie her first camera, he tells her, "I got you this camera, Maggie, to help you with the truth. So you'll first trust your eyes to see it and then trust your own voice to tell it" (102). In order for Maggie to quit being a victim of racism, classism, physical abuse, and sexual assault, she needs to learn to be honest and to be vocal. And she uses pho-tography as her voice to express the truth as she sees it. She demon-strates how language and photography are related for her when she describes her memories of Zeke's brutalization: "They were images inside me that I wanted to forget, but they were things, in truth, that I needed to remember. They were the undeveloped pictures in the camera of my mind" (182).

When the African American people of Maggie's community stage a lunch counter sit-in that white supremacists turn into a riot, Maggie takes pictures that capture the horror of the violence. She tells her-self, "*Trip the shutter, Maggie. You know what you're seeing here. You've got to get it down*" (271). The rioters assault one of her closest friends, and she says, "What filled my lens was more than the blood gush-ing from my sweet friend. It was the red color of the fence, the red color of the earth on which I stood. It was red, the color of my life this summer. . . . Red: it was the color of [my hometown]" (272). The photographs Maggie takes that day win a contest and are published in *Life* magazine as part of a series on racial violence during the Civil Rights Movement. Maggie's mother can't forgive her for befriending people of another race, so at the text's end, Maggie and her mother are estranged. Maggie accepts the necessity of their emotional distance, however, for she recognizes that her mother will never respect her daughter's agency. But because Maggie has found a life's work that foregrounds her subjectivity in ways that she values, and because she has found friends who respect that subjectivity, Maggie has grown into a self-acceptance that indicates her maturity.

Maggie, like Meg, Journey, and Witch Baby, has used photography as a physical expression of the primacy of her interiority. Operating the camera represents her internal process of claiming the subject position. More than any of the other novels, *Spite Fences* celebrates photography as a means of expressing truth. But the photographs all four characters take ultimately represent truth for each of them. And a truth that each of these novels shares is that without the camera—that is, without her or his individual artistic representation of language and, it follows, without some form of language itself—the character would remain a victim, stranded in the object position of some other camera's gaze.

Death and Photography

Significantly, another topic that these four novels share is a concern with death. *A Summer to Die* identifies the topic in the title; Meg experiences and eventually reconciles herself to her sister's death. In *Journey,* death is perhaps more metaphorical than in the other novels: Journey experiences his mother's abandonment of him as a death. Indeed, his sister refers to their mother's ritualistic destruction of the family photographs as a "murder"; Journey agrees that the box of shredded pictures looks like "a killing" (49). Journey must work through the same sort of separation from and acceptance of his mother's actions that Meg has undergone with her sister's death; his grief seems at times even more poignant than Meg's. Witch Baby's anxieties can almost all be traced back to a strong sense of grief for the death of living things: she fears the destruction of the environment and what the AIDS pandemic does to people; she fears serial killers and what will happen to the missing children pictured on milk cartons; she fears "nuclear accidents, violence, poverty and disease" (8), and she mourns for "families dying of radiation, old people in rest homes listening for sirens, ragged men and women wandering barefoot through the city, becoming ghosts because no one wanted to see them" (92). Maggie, like Journey, experiences the metaphorical death of her relationship with her mother, but even more important, she experiences the near-death of her friend Zeke. Her fear of the violence her friend has suffered is the greatest emotional transformation of her life because it is the first time she has confronted anyone's mortality. The experience is a chilling one.

Roland Barthes, perhaps, would think it no small coincidence that death permeates these novels, which are ostensibly about photography; *Camera Lucida* is, after all, his elegy for his mother. Photographs have as their subtext the death of the person photographed; they are both memory and memorial. Barthes has argued not only for the subject-object duality in photography but also for its conflation of life and death. He calls the photograph "that very subtle moment when, to tell the truth, I am neither subject nor object but a subject who feels he is becoming an object: I then experience a micro-version of death . . . : I am truly becoming a specter" (14).[10] Barthes calls the photographer a type of embalmer (14) and the photograph a "flat Death" (92); the separation between life and death "is reduced to a simple click, the one separating the initial pose from the final print" (92). Indeed, Journey describes the one picture he has of his father in terms that indicate that the man is effectively dead to his son: "I carried that picture around, trying to remember him, trying to place the picture so that the eyes would look into mine. But they never did. His face was like carved stone, not flesh and blood" (4). Every photograph of a person captures in a lifeless position someone who is either dead or will die eventually; in "every photograph is this catastrophe" (Barthes 96). In this, Barthes defines death as the ultimate position of objectivity, for in death the body is completely without agency.

Barthes cites Edgar Morin's observation that the "crisis of death," that is, the beginning of a time when our society became more obsessively negative about death, began in the mid-nineteenth century at about the same time that photography became a cultural institution (92). It was only shortly after this that developmental psychologists codified adolescence as a stage of life. The very fact that Freud and his followers felt so compelled to compartmentalize the passing stages of our lives marks a cultural view of life as an inexorable march to death. In other words, both photography and developmental psychology confirmed the process of fixing things in time for a culture that was increasingly teleologically oriented.

It seems only natural, then, that people living a stage of their lives that marks them one step closer to a progression toward death would fix on photography as a way of understanding the relation between life and death. Indeed, adolescence is often the stage of life associated with the individual's first serious grappling with death as an inevitability. Photographs seem to mark a way of slowing the process down for the adolescent and preadolescent characters in these novels. If they can capture truth on film, creating a series of miniature death images for themselves in transforming the subjects around them into objects, perhaps death will not have as much power over them. If they can make time stand still, perhaps they can in some sense defeat death. Even more important, all four characters actually experience the death–object position of the camera's gaze and survive to tell their stories. Indeed, their experiences as objects prove essential to their growth.

Photography allows these characters to explore a paradox crucial to their need to understand death: is the camera stopping time or acknowledging its passage? Journey's grandfather explicitly states that "a picture stops a little piece of time, good or bad, and saves it," but Journey wants to have photographs precisely because he knows that time passes inevitably, so he wants artifacts to help him acknowledge this passing: "I sure would like things to look back on" (66). For the grandfather, pictures are memorial; for Journey, they are memory itself. In the illusion of permanence that they afford the photographer, photographs even seem to transcend death, for they can survive long after the photographer and the subject are dead.

Photography and Narrative Structure

Basing his argument on Roland Barthes's observation that narrative progression is also an inevitable action, Peter Brooks demonstrates yet another teleological factor at work here (Barthes, *S/Z* 37, quoted in Brooks, "Freud's Masterplot" 282). Brooks defines the narrative structure of the novel as an avoidance of death. The length of the narrative is designed to circumvent its own death, which is represented by the novel's ending (Brooks, "Freud's Masterplot" 282–83).[11] Narratives avoid their own endings specifically by creating a series of repetitions;

any syntagmatically related series of events allows characters to work toward greater understanding while simultaneously avoiding the narrative's own and the reading subject's demise, which will occur when the characters achieve understanding and the narrative ends (Brooks, "Freud's Masterplot" 285–96; Brooks, *Reading for the Plot* 97–109).[12]

In the novels under investigation here, photographic images serve strikingly to provide each protagonist with repetitions that move the character closer to the narrative's end while simultaneously delaying that movement. For example, Meg in *A Summer to Die* takes a series of pictures of her friend Will (28–29), then views them again when she develops them (45), when she shows them to her mother (46), when she shows them to her sister (49), when she shows them to Will himself (66–67), and when she shows them to her friends Ben and Maria (97). She does not completely understand the implications of her own photography, however, until she sees a different image: herself repeated as an object of Will's photography. Only when the repetition occurs with variation is true resolution in both senses of the term possible: Meg sees herself as a clear, highly resolved image and thus resolves her own crisis by no longer avoiding the implications of her sister's death.

Journey, Witch Baby, and Maggie use photographic repetitions similarly. Journey experiences first himself and then his grandfather in a series of repeated pictures, the most evocative of which is the shred of one picture that contains only a baby's hand; Journey returns to look at that image four times in the novel (49, 50, 59, 82). The boy finally accepts his parents for what they are when he sees a variation of this photograph: his grandfather prints another copy of the full picture from a negative so that Journey can see himself as a baby with his parents. In looking at this photograph, Journey finally understands that although the baby's hand is his, his parents are not as involved with him as he had always imagined they were when he was looking at only the fragment of the picture. The image repeated with variation reveals to him that it is his grandfather, not his parents, who has nurtured him from infancy.

Witch Baby also experiences her sense of alienation in a repeated series of family photographs, most notably the pictures she has taken of family members and pasted to the face of the clock. The pictures on the clock are described four times in the narrative; that the family's images are affixed to a clock signifies Witch Baby's awareness of the passing of time and of how pictures can transcend that passage (3, 52–53, 82, 100–1). She repeatedly returns to these images until she achieves the variation necessary for resolution by including herself in the final picture, the one she glues at the pinnacle of the clockface over the number twelve (100–1).

For Maggie, the most important repetition is her capturing of the violence waged against peaceful protesters, not only when the pictures are developed but also when they are printed in *Life* magazine. Only when she sees the images replicated in a public forum is she able to assure herself that she has accomplished something meaningful in improving race relations in her hometown. Perhaps her actions have averted other people's needless deaths; in any event, she seems better positioned to accept, as Witch Baby does, the inevitability that much of life is ugly and painful.

For all of these characters, then, either one photograph or a series of related photographs provides a recursive way of working through conflict toward resolution.[13] Photographs slow down each narrative's progression toward its own demise, but they also allow each character to resolve her or his crisis. For Meg, Witch Baby, and Maggie, these emotional resolutions involve some sort of acceptance of death; for Journey, the resolution is more an acceptance of the death of a dream, his illusion of unity with his parents. But in each case, photography functions both thematically, implicating the character in related investigations of agency and grief, and structurally, underscoring the impetus of the narrative toward its own death.

Conclusion

Deborah Bowen links death, narrative structure, and photography when she calls photographic imagery "a metaphor for the life-giving and death-dealing enterprise of writing fictions" (22). Photographs paradoxically "offer assurances of identity and clarity; at the same time they undermine the very attempt to control experience by demonstrating that to freeze time and space is to render them obsolete" (Bowen 22). For Barthes, photography is an ontological matter because the "photograph mechanically repeats what could never be repeated existentially" (4). The camera gives these characters the power to transform subject and object. This, in turn, seems to transmute the effects of death by giving them a tangible means of exploring the lin-

guistic imperatives of sentience as they return as often as necessary
to the images that provide them with the opportunity of occupying
both the subject and the object position.

In demonstrating how photography serves several functions in adolescent and preadolescent literature, critical theory about cameras
and photographs provides us with a new way of reading some works
of adolescent literature. On the most basic level, novels that include
photography demonstrate characters experiencing both subjectivity
and objectivity. In that sense, then, photography becomes an extended metaphor for language, constructed as it is entirely in terms
of the character's (and the reader's) understanding of subjectivity and
objectivity. Photographs also serve as a metaphor for death, allowing
the adolescent to reconcile herself or himself to life as a teleological process. In the process of developing this metaphor, photography
also serves metonymically in the text by providing a series of stop-
action images that serve as the delaying device necessary to the narrative's resolution. The character must experience and re-experience
these images in order to achieve the growth that is so fundamental to
the genre. The use of photography in adolescent literature is therefore at once thematic and structural. In employing photography as a
metaphor, Lowry, MacLachlan, Block, and Krisher demonstrate how
inevitably linked agency, language, and death are to the actual narrative structure of many novels written for eleven- to fifteen-year-olds.
Ultimately, this thematic and structural focus provides the adolescent
reader with an image of empowered adolescents struggling to understand agency, language, and death—and succeeding.

I would like to conclude by describing a short story about an adolescent empowered by a camera. Because of its brevity, the story lacks
the narrative sophistication of the novels under discussion here, but
it nevertheless captures very clearly the essence of how photography provides narrative resolution in fiction about adolescence. Maeve
Binchy's "The Ten Snaps of Christmas" is about Orla, a fourteen-year-
old Irish girl who receives an Instamatic camera and a roll of film
for Christmas. While her mother is looking at the first picture Orla
has taken, a snapshot of her family, the woman thinks, "They looked
oddly dead" (26). Orla uses others of her ten snaps to take pictures
of her father fondling the French au pair, of her grandmother guz-
zling brandy straight from the decanter, of her mother dropping the
Christmas turkey on the kitchen floor, of a family friend stealing silver bric-a-brac from their dining room, of her brothers smoking. One

of her brothers knows a shooting has taken place, in more than one sense of the word; he tells Orla, "We'll be killed" (30). Her parents have given her the camera because they hope somehow to raise her self-esteem, and the gift certainly does that and more, for the camera empowers her as she has never before been empowered. The story ends when after reexamining all of her snapshots "she went down to her Christmas lunch with her head held high. She knew somehow she would be a person of importance this year. A person not be taken lightly anymore" (31). Orla is similar to Marc Brown's Arthur in that she has learned the importance of photography as a tool for communication. Even more important, just as Meg, Witch Baby, Journey, and Maggie have, Orla has learned how not to be ignored anymore: by engaging her agency. Her story, as brief as it is, conflates narrative repetition with language that evokes death, providing a capsule version of the rich conjoining of theme and structure that adolescent novels involving photography create. "The Ten Snaps of Christmas," like *A Summer to Die, Journey, Witch Baby,* and *Spite Fences,* achieves narrative resolution through the lens of an adolescent's camera.

Notes

1. I am defining a preadolescent novel here as one which has a fairly basic reading level but in which the protagonist hovers on the brink of adolescence and experiences conflicts more common to adolescent than children's literature: death, sexuality, violence, abandonment. *A Summer to Die* and *Journey* both fit into this genre, which does not so much participate in the traditions of adolescent literature as it anticipates them; Paul Fleischman's *The Borning Room* (1991) is another example.

2. In aiding protagonists to explore their agency and achieve resolution, cameras and photographs provide literary characters with a number of emotional experiences. Sharon R. Wilson notes that Margaret Atwood uses photography for four purposes: to give characters " 'neutral' recorders of experience"; to demonstrate "a character's sense of fragmentation"; to provide that character with "proof" of her own existence; and to provide "lenses which distill and focus experience, facilitating a self-discovery which transcends mere 'self-surveillance'" (31–32). The four novels I discuss herein employ these four patterns to varying degrees, but the pattern of photography as a catalyst for transcendence is the most noteworthy.

3. Within this essay, I share an interest with Barthes and Hirsch in photographs of people rather than of landscapes or inanimate objects.

4. Barthes writes, "A specific photograph, in effect, is never distinguished from its referent (from what it represents), or at least it is not *immediately* or *generally* distinguished from its referent (as is the case for every other image, encumbered—from the start, and because of its status—by the way in which the object is simulated): it is not impossible to perceive the photographic signifier . . . but it requires a secondary action of knowledge or of reflection" (5, emphasis Barthes's).

5. MacLachlan demonstrates her awareness of Sontag's theories by employing a quotation from Sontag's *On Photography* as an epigraph.

6. Or, in other terms, her camera is *langue,* her pictures *parole.*

7. For a lucid explanation of Lacanian theory as it applies to photography, see Hirsch (101–3).

8. For a lengthier discussion of this metaphor, see Roberta Seelinger Trites, "Claiming the Treasures: Patricia MacLachlan's Organic Postmodernism."

9. The Hallmark Hall of Fame production of *Journey* flattens Journey's growth considerably in that the grandfather retains control of the camera throughout the narrative. Journey gets to take only a few pictures, so the central metaphor for his increased sense of his own agency—his ability to take pictures—is greatly diminished.

10. Photography as elegy is a major leitmotif in Hirsch's *Family Frames.* Not only does Hirsch cite this quotation from Barthes (Hirsch 175), but she also quotes Marguerite Duras's statement that "the fixed, flat, easily available countenance of a dead person or an infant in a photograph is only one image as against the million images that exist in the mind. And the sequence made up by the million images will never alter. It's a confirmation of death" (Hirsch 200) and Susan Sontag's statements that "all photographs are *memento mori*" and that "this link between photography and death haunts all photos of people" (Hirsch 17, 19). According to Hirsch, "The referent [of a photograph] haunts the picture like a ghost: it is a revenant, a return of the lost and dead other" (5), and the photographic still is a "deathlike fixing of one moment in time" (24).

11. Julia Kristeva, in fact, links all linguistic constructions, linear as they are, with death: "It might also be added that this linear time is that of language considered as the enunciation of sentences (noun + verb; topic-comment; beginning-ending), and that this time rests on its own stumbling block, which is also the stumbling block of that enunciation—death" (17).

12. Brooks bases his theory on Freud's essay "Beyond the Pleasure Principle," demonstrating how "if beginning is desire, and is ultimately desire for the end, between lies a process" that Brooks links to plot production. He maintains that "the sense of the beginning, then, is determined by the sense of an ending," for "all narration is obituary in that life acquires definable meaning only at, and through, death" ("Freud's Masterplot" 283–84). In the revised version of this essay that appears as a chapter in *Reading for the Plot,* Brooks embellishes this statement: "All narrative may be in essence obituary in that . . . the retrospective knowledge that it seeks, the knowledge that comes after, stands on the far side of the end, in human terms on the far side of death" (95). For a trenchant critique of what is masculinist in Brooks's argument, see Susan Winnett's "Coming Unstrung."

13. As Brooks says of similar narrative repetitions in *Great Expectations,* "repetition and return have spoken of the death instinct, the drive to return to the quiescence of the inorganic, of the nontextual. Yet the repetitions . . . both prolonging the detour and more effectively preparing the final discharge, have created that delay necessary to incorporate the past within the present and to let us understand end in relation to beginning" (*Reading for the Plot* 139).

Works Cited

Banta, Martha. *Imaging American Women: Idea and Ideals in Cultural History.* New York: Columbia University Press, 1987.

Barthes, Roland. *Camera Lucida: Reflections on Photography.* Trans. Richard Howard. New York: Hill and Wang, 1981.

Belsey, Catherine. "Constructing the Subject: Deconstructing the Text." In *Feminist Criticism and Social Change.* Ed. J. Newton and D. Rosenfelt. London: Methuen, 1985. Pp. 45–64.

Benveniste, Emile. "Subjectivity in Language." Reprinted in *Critical Theory Since 1965.*

Ed. Hazard Adams and Leroy Searle. Gainesville: University of Florida Press, 1986. Pp. 728–32.

Binchy, Maeve. "The Ten Snaps of Christmas." In *This Year Will Be Different*. New York: Dell, 1996. Pp. 19–31.

Block, Francesca Lia. *Witch Baby*. New York: Harper, 1991.

Bowen, Deborah. "In Camera: The Developed Photographs of Margaret Laurence and Alice Munro." *Studies in Canadian Literature* 13 (1988): 20–33.

Brooks, Peter. "Freud's Masterplot." *Yale French Studies* 55–56 (1977): 280–300.

———. *Reading for the Plot: Design and Intention in Narrative*. New York: Knopf, 1984.

Hirsch, Marianne. *Family Frames: Photography, Narrative, and Postmemory*. Cambridge: Harvard University Press, 1997.

Krisher, Trudy. *Spite Fences*. New York: Delacorte, 1994.

Kristeva, Julia. "Women's Time." *Signs* 7 (1981): 13–35.

Lacan, Jacques. *The Four Fundamental Concepts of Psycho-Analysis*. Ed. Jacques-Alain Miller. Trans. Alan Sheridan. New York: Norton, 1978.

Lowry, Lois. *A Summer to Die*. Boston: Houghton, 1977.

MacLachlan, Patricia. *Journey*. New York: Delacorte, 1991.

Sontag, Susan. *On Photography*. New York: Farrar, 1973.

Stephens, John. *Language and Ideology in Children's Fiction*. New York: Longman, 1992.

Trites, Roberta Seelinger. "Claiming the Treasures: Patricia MacLachlan's Organic Postmodernism." *Children's Literature Association Quarterly* 18 (1993): 23–28.

Wilson, Sharon R. "Camera Images in Margaret Atwood's Novels." In *Margaret Atwood: Reflection and Reality*. Ed. Beatrice Mendez-Egle and James M. Haule. Edinburg: Pan American University, 1987. Pp. 29–57.

Winnett, Susan. "Coming Unstrung: Women, Men, Narrative, and Principles of Pleasure." *PMLA* 105 (1990): 505–18.

Dada Knows Best: Growing up "Surreal" with Dr. Seuss

Philip Nel

Placing Dr. Seuss—the pen name of Theodor Seuss Geisel—in the company of Dadaists and Surrealists may seem a curious idea to some. Geisel (1904–1991) is best known as the author of roughly forty-seven children's books, but dada and surrealism are best known as part of a philosophical-artistic movement in twentieth-century art—the historical avant-garde. Although their images were later embraced by advertisers,[1] most surrealists and dadaists maintained an oppositional role with respect to mass culture; indeed, most were sympathetic with socialists and communists. Seuss, on the other hand, was a very successful capitalist and very much a part of American mass culture. He became nationally known for his "Quick, Henry, the Flit!" advertising campaigns for Flit bug spray in the 1920s and 1930s, he founded the immediately profitable Beginner Books division of Random House in 1958, and by the time of his death "Dr. Seuss" was a multimillion-dollar industry. But although he profited from mass culture, Geisel did not endorse all of its attendant values. For example, *The Lorax* advocates environmental conservation, *The Sneetches* criticizes anti-Semitism, and the *Butter Battle Book* agitates against nuclear proliferation not because addressing these topics would sell more books but because Seuss wished to provoke his readers into rethinking the dominant beliefs of their society.

Highlighting the connection between Dr. Seuss and the twentieth-century avant-garde calls our attention to his role as a cultural critic. It is this essay's contention that Geisel's work draws on what Andreas Huyssen has called "the original iconoclastic and subversive thrust of the historical avant-garde" (*After the Great Divide* 3), a movement initiated by the dadaists in the second decade of the twentieth century. The term *historical avant-garde* is, in Peter Bürger's words, an attempt to "re-integrate art into the life process" in order to engender in the audience a "critical cognition of reality" (50). Aware that "reality" is itself shaped by ideology, Seuss is a successful example of an artist

Children's Literature 27, ed. Elizabeth Lennox Keyser (Yale University Press, © 1999 Hollins University).

who—in the tradition of the historical avant-garde—tried to shake his audience out of their habits of thought and cause them to rethink their assumptions.

We need to be reminded of this aspect of Seuss because recent "Seuss" works—books patterned on those of Seuss but written by others—have transformed him from a subversive force into a moralist who supports the status quo. Seuss's tales have always contained morals, but they have delivered these morals by raising questions and by provoking their readers. Recent books patterned on Seuss have done exactly the opposite. For example, take the first offspring of Nickelodeon's "Wubbulous World of Dr. Seuss," a work called *The Song of the Zubble-Wump* (1996). Originally an episode of the show and now a book, this new story uses Seuss's characters and some ersatz Seussian rhymes to tell an overtly moralistic story unlike any the original Doctor ever wrote. In fact, Seuss's first published children's book, *To Think That I Saw It on Mulberry Street,* rejected by twenty-seven publishers before Vanguard Press took it on in 1937, was rejected precisely because editors thought it lacked "moral or message" and contained nothing that would help in "transforming children into good citizens" (Geisel, quoted in Morgan and Morgan 81). *The Song of the Zubble-Wump,* however, seems intent on turning Seuss into William Bennett; as a result, morals and messages take center stage. The once-iconoclastic Cat in the Hat arrives to deliver a line about the gift of life, an overtly religious reference that Geisel would never have permitted.[2] The Cat in the Hat rescues a Zubble-Wump egg from the Grinch and solemnly tells us, "That egg is a miracle." The Cat also delivers a lecture to the Grinch and to a little girl–muppet named Megan, who has broken the egg while trying to wrest it from the Grinch. This in turn prompts Megan—apparently to prove that she has learned her lesson—to offer us a speech about sharing that concludes with "amen." This scene is ridiculous: the Cat is an anarchist, not a moralist.[3] His persona does become less rambunctious in the later books, but he is always more interested in challenging the rules than in laying down the law. Original Seuss books offer not "amens" but questions to provoke the reader.[4]

As a way of debunking this imaginatively stale, *Book of Virtues* version of Dr. Seuss, this essay revives the subversive Seuss in the following four ways. The first section looks at the stylistic similarities between Dr. Seuss's paintings and those of the twentieth-century avant-garde, arguing that Seuss shares their criticisms of the artistic establishment.

Using a comparison between the work of the Belgian surrealist René Magritte and Dr. Seuss's *The Butter Battle Book,* section two illustrates how Seuss uses ambiguity as a way of challenging his audience; that is, lack of resolution in Seuss's work interpellates readers into an active critical role and invites them to take up the more rebellious sentiments of the narrative. The third section locates Seuss in the tradition of English surrealists such as Herbert Read, who looked, as Seuss did, to Edward Lear and Lewis Carroll as literary antecedents. Drawing on nonsense literature's close association with the avant-garde, Seuss's work reveals the "rational" adult world as unsound and encourages his readers to do the same. The concluding section examines the effects of the recent merchandising frenzy (of which *Zubble-Wump* is a part) in light of postmodernity: some critics contend that capitalist culture has co-opted the avant-garde, but Seuss's work demonstrates the possibilities of ideology critique in a "postmodern" era.[5] While the new Seuss book—which was written by Jim Henson Productions— exemplifies pastiche in a Jamesonian sense, a recent Seuss exhibit in New York used pastiche to critical ends and offered some hope for the survival of Seuss's avant-garde edge in the mass market.

"The Joyous Leaping of Uncanned Salmon": A Dadaist at Heart

One might say that the avant-garde moved in just down the street from Theodor Seuss Geisel: in late 1936, just before Seuss's first "children's book," *To Think That I Saw It on Mulberry Street,* was published, the Museum of Modern Art launched *Fantastic Art, Dada, and Surrealism,* the first major American exhibition of surrealist art. It stayed at MoMA into 1937, after which it toured the country. For those who did not visit *Fantastic Art* during its national tour, the American media did its best to bring the experience to them. The exhibition prompted a *New Yorker* cover and cartoons in January 1937, mentions in *The New York Times,* several stories in *Life* magazine, and newsreels from both Paramount and Universal that were shown in theaters nationwide (Marquis 173). Although the popular press seized on the entertainment value of the works, many in the artistic community took the work seriously, and, as Martica Sawin and others have shown, MoMA's *Fantastic Art* show marked the beginning of surrealism as a widely felt influence in American art.[6] In the later 1930s and early 1940s, New York would become a veritable beachhead for the European avant-garde when they fled from Hitler's armies to live in

Figure 1. Dr. Seuss: *Untitled.* © 1995, Dr. Seuss Enterprises. Reproduced by permission of Random House, Inc.

exile in America (Sawin ix–xv). Some returned after World War II, but some remained, and their presence made an impact—political and aesthetic—on American artists. As Meyer Schapiro, a neighbor and friend to many of the surrealists-in-exile, said, "It wasn't automatism that the Americans learned from the Surrealists, but how to be heroic" (Sawin ix). Although it may not be fair to argue that Dr. Seuss was influenced by the European avant-garde's heroism, it is not hard to imagine that, as a painter and cartoonist living in New York from 1928 through 1942, Seuss felt the influence of this new artistic presence. *PM,* the pro-labor New York newspaper in which Seuss published several hundred political cartoons during 1941 and 1942, ran several stories on the exiled avant-garde during this same period, including drawings by André Breton and other surrealists. And, as an artist whose lifelong interest in art produced not only original paintings but a television special on modern art,[7] it seems likely that Seuss would have been interested in visiting such widely reviewed and discussed shows.

Figure 2. Kurt Seligmann: *Life Goes On* (1942). © The MIT Press. Present whereabouts unknown. Reproduced from Martica Sawin's *Surrealism in Exile* (The MIT Press, 1995), p. 198.

When Seuss's paintings were published in *The Secret Art of Dr. Seuss* in 1995, many were struck by the echoes of cubism, surrealism, and dada in his work, influences that probably date to this period in his life. At the opening of an exhibition of his paintings in 1976, a television reporter asked Geisel, "Do you associate yourself with any of your characters?" He answered, "Yes, especially the devious ones" (Morgan and Morgan 232). It is appropriate that Dr. Seuss should speak of deviousness at an exhibition of his artwork, because his art draws on the avant-garde. Titles such as *The Rather Odd Myopic Woman Riding Piggyback on One of Helen's Many Cats* and *The Joyous Leaping of Uncanned Salmon* resemble titles of dadaist work, and some of these works are as disturbing as anything produced by the Dadaists and the Surrealists.[8] In one untitled work that explores the effects of sadism on women,[9] sadism seems to be complicit with industry and with men in military uniforms, but—like many surrealist works—the painting creates an analogy while stopping short of indicating precisely *what* the analogy means (see figure 1). That said, industry and the military seem likely targets. Indeed, the tendency of the creatures in this painting to metamorphose into other objects—often into machines—

Figure 3. Jacques Hérold, André Breton, Yves Tanguy, and Victor Brauner: *Exquisite Corpse* (1934). © 1999 Artists Rights Society (ARS), New York / ADAGP, Paris. © 1999 Estate of Yves Tanguy / Artists Rights Society (ARS), New York.

recalls Kurt Seligmann's *Life Goes On* (1942), as well as some of the *Exquisite Corpse* experiments by André Breton and his surrealist group (figures 2 and 3). Or consider the oppressively angular, geometric shapes of Seuss's *Minor Cat in a High-Yield Emerald Mine* (undated). The images in this painting share a stylistic similarity with Oscar Domínguez's *Nostalgia for Space* (1939) (figures 4 and 5).

In addition to the stylistic and titular similarities of his work with theirs, Geisel, like the Surrealists, valued the unschooled artist and held "high art" in a certain contempt (as shown by his "Escarobus" hoax, described in the following paragraph). André Breton and others sought out those whose talents had not been "corrupted" by formal artistic training (self-taught artists such as Yves Tanguy), claiming that the absence of training helps liberate the artist from bourgeois assumptions. Although such a position clearly idealizes the "untutored" as a space free of ideological constraints, Breton nonetheless has a point. Inasmuch as adherence to artistic norms indicates an acceptance of the ideological assumptions behind those norms, the self-taught artist may be more open to new experiences. As Breton writes in *Surrealism and Painting* (1928), "experience itself has been

Figure 4. Oscar Domínguez: *Nostalgia for Space* (1939). Oil on canvas, 28³/₄ × 36¹/₈" (73 × 91.8 cm). The Museum of Modern Art, New York. Gift of Peggy Guggenheim. Photograph © 1999 Museum of Modern Art, New York.

assigned limits. It inhabits a cage increasingly difficult to coax it out of" (Nadeau 80n). Echoing Breton's idea that formal training inhibits artistic development, Geisel said:

> If I'd gone to art school I'd never have been successful. In fact, I did attend one art class in high school. And at one point during the class I turned the painting I was working on upside down—I didn't exactly know what I was doing, but actually I was checking the balance: If something is wrong with the composition upside down, there's something wrong with it the other way. And the teacher said, "Theodor, real artists don't turn their paintings upside down." It's the only reason I went on—to prove that teacher wrong. (Cott 18)

And at least in the case of *Horton Hatches the Egg* (1940), Geisel's openness to unusual experience proved him right. As he recalls, "a sketch

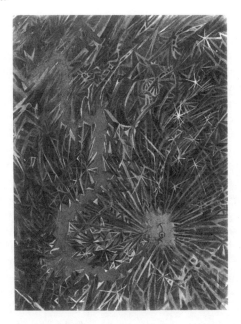

Figure 5. Dr. Seuss: *Minor Cat in a High-Yield Emerald Mine.* Copyright © 1995, Dr. Seuss Enterprises. Reproduced by permission of Random House, Inc.

of an elephant . . . happened to fall on top of a sketch of a tree." When he asked himself, "An elephant in a tree! What's he doing here?" (Hopkins 113), the story of *Horton* began.

In addition to a willingness to embrace accident, Geisel, like the dadaists, was openly skeptical of the artistic establishment. He no doubt would have been amused by Duchamp's urinal, submitted under the title of "Fountain" for the 1917 Independents Exhibition in New York, and the scandalized public's response to it. Geisel's provocations may not have been quite so public, but he did challenge accepted notions of high modernist art. For example, in apparent accord with the German dadaist Richard Huelsenbeck's claim that "art . . ., regarded from a serious point of view, is a large-scale swindle" (Motherwell 43), Geisel created a moderate-scale swindle as a way of proving exactly this point. Indeed, the story of Geisel's hoax is a classic example of his playfully antagonistic attitude toward the art establishment. In the mid-1950s, not long after moving to La Jolla, California, Edward Longstreth, a friend of Geisel's and a patron of the La Jolla Museum of Art, "launched into a condescending lecture about modern art one evening." Geisel rebelled by tricking his friend into buying some work of "the great Mexican modernist," Escarobus—a fictional painter whom Geisel invented on the spot. Geisel claimed to have five Escarobuses and let slip that he intended to sell them in order to get the money to Escarobus to help him pay his back taxes. Longstreth took the bait, and Geisel "stayed up most of the night creating the world's first Escarobus," which—as Judith and Neil Morgan describe it in their biography of Seuss—sounds like a parody of the sort of modernist work revered at the time: "[Geisel] peeled the wood off a soft pencil, scraped the lead lengthwise across art paper, dipped small hunks of bread in the vodka he was drinking, and dragged the soggy bread across the paper. Next he painted [Lady] Godivas on the smudges, bisecting and trisecting them so that it was impossible to tell that they were naked ladies" (142–43). Later that week, he sold the painting to Longstreth for five hundred dollars. Longstreth was so impressed that he offered to buy the rest.[10] As Geisel said to *New Yorker* writer E. J. Kahn several years later, "That experience made me suspect that a lot of modern art is malarkey. If I can do it myself, it can't be any good" (Kahn 53).

Geisel's hoax worked on two levels: in one sense, it fooled the self-proclaimed expert on modern art. In a larger sense, his hoax showed that standards of aesthetic quality rest more on the critic's habits of perceiving than on anything inherent in the work; that is, by creating a painting that appeared to conform to conventions of great modern art, Geisel ridiculed the notion of a category of "great modern art." Congruent with the goals of the avant-garde, Geisel mocked the notion of taste on which high art depends. In his "Escarobus" challenge, he demonstrated a principle articulated by Marcel Duchamp in an interview conducted in 1956: "Repeat the same thing long enough and it becomes taste. . . . [G]ood or bad is of no importance because it is always good for some people and bad for others. Quality is not important, it is always taste" (Duchamp 134).

Calculated Ambiguity: How Seuss and Magritte Provoke the Audience

By the time of Geisel's prank in the mid-1950s, tastes had changed and the works of surrealism and dada had been canonized as high art. Although acceptance by mainstream culture may minimize the original works' subversiveness, such acceptance does not necessarily neutralize the subversive potential of the avant-garde techniques that these works introduced. In fact, long after the works of the original historical avant-garde became museum pieces, the goals of the sur-realists and the dadaists continued to inspire generations of artists to create art that challenged the social and political mores of the day. For, in addition to the goal of challenging canons of taste, the histori-cal avant-garde wished to challenge habits of thought, to make their audience rethink its assumptions about the world. One way to achieve this effect was to create an ambiguous image—"an image that resists any explication and that simultaneously resists indifference," as René Magritte has said of his paintings (Torczyner 126). Like Magritte, Geisel consciously harnessed the power of the ambiguous as a way of provoking his readers. As he once said of his compositional tech-nique, he enjoyed approaching a book "with a situation or conflict and then [I] write myself into an impossible position so there is no [apparent] way of ending [the book]" (Morgan and Morgan 128–29).

As an illustration of the power of the ambiguous image, let us look at three works by Seuss and one by Magritte: a Seuss cartoon from 1941, a Seuss painting from 1968, Seuss's *The Butter Battle Book* (1984), and Magritte's *The Art of Living* (1967). In contrast to a similar image in Seuss's 1968 painting *Fooling Nobody,* the cartoon, "We Always Were Suckers for Ridiculous Hats" (April 1941), is not at all ambiguous (figure 6). One of the first cartoons Seuss drew for the daily New York newspaper *PM,* this cartoon uses the image of the "Ostrich Bon-net" to argue that Charles Lindbergh's isolationist stance is akin to sticking one's head in the ground. To ignore the threat of Hitler is to behave like an ostrich, Seuss tells us. A parallel image cropped up twenty-seven years later in Seuss's watercolor *Fooling Nobody,* but now the target has changed from Lindbergh to nuclear weapons. The "atom" image that appears in each eye and the year of the painting—1968—suggest that nuclear arms are a likely subject (figure 7). Unlike "Suckers for Ridiculous Hats," the *Fooling Nobody* image is ambiguous; instead of recognizing a person wearing a false head, the viewer is now unsure who is wearing whom. *Both* the "bonnet" head *and* the lower creature's head appear to be conscious. Unlike the cartoon, the painting does not present a mask that is simply hiding the face.

Fooling Nobody uses juxtaposition to pose a question that it leaves its audience to answer. As Magritte's paintings often do, Seuss's water-color places images in tension but leaves that tension unresolved. In Magritte's *The Art of Living* (1967), for example, a spherical "head"

We Always Were Suckers for Ridiculous Hats . . .

Figure 6. Dr. Seuss: "We Always Were Suckers for Ridiculous Hats" (29 April 1941).

floats like a balloon above what appears to be an empty suit of clothes. Is the "head" the "idea" of the "man" below it? Or—since the suit is empty—is the man a figment of the floating head's imagination? *The Art of Living* does not answer the questions it poses, and neither does *Fooling Nobody*. The latter employs this very sort of juxtaposition to address nuclear anxieties but encourages the anxieties to linger instead of resolving them. If the creature with the atom-shaped eyes is a projection of the lower one, then the atoms may represent the latter's nuclear anxieties; that is, the lower creature's apparent calm is—as the title suggests—fooling nobody. If, on the other hand, the lower is a projection of the "puppet" creature above, then the title is ironic, because the apparently calm demeanor of the smaller creature *is* fooling people. On the other hand, *both* beings are visible, and it's unclear who is the projection of whom or even if "projection" is the case. *Fooling Nobody* oscillates between these figures, posing but refusing to answer its provocative questions. The work forces an unresolved argument onto its audience, demanding a response that we, the viewers, must provide.

Figure 7. Dr. Seuss: *Fooling Nobody* (1968). Copyright © 1995, Dr. Seuss Enterprises. Reproduced by permission of Random House, Inc.

Seuss continued to use ambiguity as a way to address nuclear anxieties in *The Butter Battle Book*. As with *Fooling Nobody,* the book forces the task of resolution onto the audience. Like the battle between the Big-Endians (who open their eggs at the large end) and the Lilliputians (who open theirs at the small end) in Swift's *Gulliver's Travels, The Butter Battle Book* depicts an escalating arms race between Yooks, who butter their bread butter-side up, and Zooks, who butter their bread butter-side down. A Yook grandfather tells his grandson about the increasingly sophisticated weapons that Yooks and Zooks have devised to destroy each other. Their arms race culminates in the "Bitsy Big Boy Boomeroo," a bomb that "can blow all of those Zooks clear to Sala-ma-goo." But when the Yook grandfather arrives at the wall, his longtime enemy Van Itch (a Zook) is there—holding the Zooks' version of the Big Boy Boomeroo. The two stand poised on the wall that divides their nations, each holding a kind of a nuclear bomb over his opponent's side of the wall, threatening to drop it. The unresolved ending mimics a surrealist work by refusing to provide an answer and, instead, forcing the reader to deal with the tension:

"Grandpa!" I shouted. "Be careful! Oh, gee!

Who's going to drop it?

Figure 8. Dr. Seuss: final page of *The Butter Battle Book* (1984). Copyright © 1984, Theodor S. Geisel and Audrey Geisel. Reproduced by permission of Random House, Inc.

Will *you* . . . ? Or will *he* . . . ?"

"Be patient," said Grandpa. "We'll see.

"We will see . . ."

And with that, the book ends (figure 8).

But the tension continues for the reader—especially for the reader in 1984, the year of the book's publication. Although the years 1989 to 1991 saw the end of the Cold War, in the first half of the 1980s Cold War tensions rose and the threat of nuclear annihilation seemed very real. In 1984, President Ronald Reagan was investing in nuclear weapons and in the famous Strategic Defense Initiative, popularly known as "Star Wars." In the previous year, nuclear war came into American living rooms via ABC-TV's broadcast of *The Day After*, a widely watched movie that depicted America after a nuclear attack. If Seuss's goal was to draw on these anxieties in order to provoke the public, *The Butter Battle Book* succeeded by inciting much public debate. The *New York Times Book Review* offered praise but also called the book "too close to contemporary international reality for comfort." The reviewer added, "we want to protest—you can't leave us hanging like this" (Lifton 37). A self-described "concerned Christian mother" in Texas began an effort to "ban the book and halt future editions." She wrote to Random House, asking, "How dare a well-respected publishing firm" publish "the most blatant form of brainwashing I have ever encountered?" (Morgan and Morgan 254).

"An Imagination with a Long Tail," or, "On Beyond Common Sense": *The Cat in the Hat and Other Subversives*

Although the *Times* reviewer was correct in saying that *The Butter Battle Book* leaves the reader hanging, the concerned parent went too far in calling the book "brainwashing." The book's educational technique is precisely the opposite of brainwashing; instead of attempting to systematically indoctrinate its reader into a system of beliefs, *Butter Battle* delivers its anti–arms race message by questioning the logic of mutually assured destruction. Instead of preaching the virtues of peace, it uses absurdity to reveal a "commonsense" foreign policy as common but not sensible; instead of delivering clear-cut answers, it throws us back on our own imaginative resources to resolve the problem. Although not all of Seuss's works are as confrontational as *The Butter Battle Book,* many are, and they similarly confront their readers by leaving the ending open. For example, both *Yertle the Turtle* (1958) and *The Lorax* (1971) introduce an element of uncertainty at the end, encouraging the reader to take up the actively critical sentiments of each book.[11] Those who assert otherwise seem to be trying to fit Seuss into the "happy ending" that many erroneously expect from children's literature.[12] In Seuss's stories, the imagination has power, and the books often end without complete resolution in order to encourage readers to exercise that power.[13] My thesis in this section is that many of Seuss's tales emphasize the imagination and deliberately resist narrative closure for two reasons—to interpellate the reader into an active role and to encourage readers to identify with the rebellious elements of the narrative, using their imaginations as a source of strength.

The avant-garde, like Seuss, relies on the irrational or absurd in order to reveal the so-called rational world as a construct. As André Breton and others wrote in 1925, "We make no claim to change the *mores* of mankind, but we intend to show the fragility of thought, and on what shifting foundations, what caverns we have built our trembling houses" (Nadeau 240). In order to apply this idea to children's literature, think of Roland Barthes's analysis of toys in *Mythologies* (1957). If, as Barthes argues, toys "prefigure the world of adult functions" (53), preparing the child to accept the constructs of society (such as nuclear proliferation) as "natural" and "normal," then explicitly nonfunctional toys can help children to see the world as a construct, providing a basis from which to challenge it. As Geisel once argued, "If you don't get imagination as a child, you probably never will . . . because it gets knocked out of you by the time you grow up" ("Logical Insanity" 58). Nonsense literature can provide exactly this sort of toy—one that allows the child to imagine alternatives to all of the "things that the adult does not find unusual" (Barthes 53).

Seuss and the English surrealists were both drawn to the nonsensical because such literature can potentially reveal the "natural world" as ideologically determined. For example, noting that "the nonsense verse and tales of [Edward] Lear and Lewis Carroll" have been "described as mad or nonsensical" to encourage us not to take them seriously, the British surrealist Herbert Read called for "a reconsideration of such literature" so that its subversive potential may be better appreciated (Read 55–56).[14] Sixty years after his directive, Celia Catlett Anderson and Marilyn Fain Apseloff offered an analysis of nonsense tales with which Read would likely have been pleased. In *Nonsense Literature for Children,* they argue that nonsense literature has "the heretical mission of . . . teach[ing] the young that the world constructed by their elders is an artificial thing. Nonsense literature uses the spirit of playfulness to rearrange the familiar world. It thereby reveals that the rules we live by are not inevitable" (94). Geisel not only read *Alice's Adventures in Wonderland* when he was young (Bandler 2) and considered himself to be writing in the tradition of nonsense literature,[15] but, I would argue, he embraced the genre's "heretical mission," deploying nonsense to challenge the "sense" of the adult world. Calling himself "subversive as hell," Geisel explained, "I've always had a mistrust of adults" (Cott 28). In that same interview, he went on to indicate that his children's books offer a way of subversively expressing that mistrust. As he put it, "children's literature as I write it and as I see it is . . . satirizing the mores and habits of the world" (29).[16]

Seussian satirizing begins with language itself, offering a perfect occasion to critique power as well. Foucault has argued that children learn the structures of language and power simultaneously; so, while learning to speak, a child absorbs the basic knowledge of how society works. What better place to challenge knowledge-power than with a child's earliest experience with the printed word—the alphabet? Lear's many nonsense alphabets introduce this idea into children's literature, and Seuss's *On Beyond Zebra!* goes beyond mocking spelling (as Lear does) to challenging the alphabet itself. The narrator invents letters beyond *Z*, allowing both narrator and reader to discover creatures not visible to those who restrict themselves to the conventional English alphabet. In the story, increased awareness of the world depends on expanding the alphabet, suggesting that experience is confined by the structures of language. The narrator's remark, "In the places I go there are things that I see / That I never could spell if I stopped with the Z," recalls Breton's comment in *Surrealism and Painting* (1928) that "experience itself has been assigned limits" (Nadeau 80n). The narrator reveals these limits as artificially prescribed, pointing to "things beyond Z that most people don't know" and encouraging the reader to explore too. The book concludes with an unnamed letter and asks, "what do you think we should call this one, anyhow?" This open-ended question prompts the book's readers to challenge the limits imposed on experience and to imagine for themselves.

Perhaps the most famous of Seuss's open endings occurs in *The Cat in the Hat* (1957). Like Magritte's *Human Condition* paintings, *The Cat in the Hat* questions the relation between "real" and "imaginary" and by refusing to answer this question interpellates the reader into an active critical role. Magritte's *Human Condition 1* (1933) challenges the viewer to rethink the relation between experience and representations of experience (figure 9). Seuss similarly challenges the reader; at the conclusion of *The Cat in the Hat,* the narrator asks, "What would you do / If your mother asked you?" (figure 10). Should the children describe an actual experience that their mother will think they imagined, or an imagined experience that she will accept as actual? In other words, should they lie or tell the truth? Like Magritte, Seuss withholds any answer in order to provoke his audience into solving the puzzle themselves.

A brief comparison with Crockett Johnson's *A Picture for Harold's Room* (1960) shows how open-ended Seuss truly is. Johnson goes as far as Seuss in challenging the boundary between imaginary and real worlds; unlike *The Cat* or Magritte's *The Human Condition,* however, *A Picture for Harold's Room* maintains a clear boundary between the two

Figure 9. René Magritte: *The Human Condition 1* (1933). Gift of the Collectors Committee, © 1998 Board of Trustees, National Gallery of Art, Washington.

by using a frame to separate the imaginary from the real. In the story, Harold draws an unframed picture and enters it. While he stays at the horizon of his picture, he is a giant in his world; but in the process of drawing train tracks towards the front of the picture, an inattention to perspective renders him a midget—smaller than a mouse or a bird. In order to resolve his problem, he simply declares, "This is only a picture!," crosses out his picture, and announces, "I am not big or little. I am my usual size" (54–56). At the end of the story Harold draws a *framed* picture on the wall of his room, resolving the tension between the real and the imaginary worlds by providing a stable boundary between them (figure 11). There is no such frame in *The Cat in the Hat*: both the Cat and the children's mother enter and exit through the same door and are part of the same "real" world. Seuss's conclusion leaves the questions of the narrative still open for discussion after the reader closes the book. Seuss poses a genuine dilemma for a young reader, pitting the desire to be honest against the desire not to get in trouble.

Furthermore, the question at the end of the book reinforces the Cat's questioning of the existing order, which begins the moment he enters the story. As Geisel told interviewer Jonathan Cott, "*The Cat in the Hat* is a revolt against authority, but it's ameliorated by the fact that the Cat cleans up everything at the end. It's revolutionary in that

Then our mother came in
And she said to us two,
"Did you have any fun?
Tell me. What did you do?"

And Sally and I did not know
What to say.
Should we tell her
The things that went on there that day?

60

Should we tell her about it?
Now, what SHOULD we do?
Well . . .
What would you do
If your mother asked you?

61

Figure 10. Dr. Seuss: final pages of *The Cat in the Hat* (1957). ™ and copyright © 1957, 1985, Dr. Seuss Enterprises. Reproduced by permission of Random House, Inc.

it goes as far as Kerensky and then stops. It doesn't go quite as far as Lenin" (Cott 28). *The Cat* doesn't go as far as Lenin, but it did go far enough to alarm some parents and has been credited with killing the "Dick and Jane" readers. Although children would no doubt agree with Anna Quindlen that "the murder of Dick and Jane . . . was a mercy killing of the highest order" (19), their elders did not. As Geisel's biographers note, the fact that the Cat's "boisterous rampage in the absence of adults went unpunished . . . alarm[ed] some of the school establishment who felt safer with Dick and Jane and considered the Cat a 'trickster hero'" (Morgan and Morgan 171). Perhaps sharing this sentiment, schools initially resisted buying *The Cat in the Hat*.[17] Although the book may not be revolutionary in a Leninist sense, its anarchistic spirit is nonetheless close to dada. Like the dadaists before him, the Cat is a rebel whose political philosophy, such as it is, seems to be based primarily on rejecting the current order.

Evidence that Dr. Seuss endorsed the Cat's rebellious spirit can be found in the author's identification with the Cat. Not only did he make the Cat the symbol for his Beginner Books series and use the Cat as a narrator in later works such as *The Cat in the Hat Songbook* (1967) and *The Cat's Quizzer* (1976), but, just prior to writing the

"This is only a picture!" he said.

54

And he took his crayon and he crossed it out.

55

But he had no picture to hang on his wall.

63

So, before he went to bed, he drew another picture.

64

Figure 11. Crockett Johnson: pages 54–55 and 63–64 from *A Picture for Harold's Room* (1960). Copyright © 1960 by Crockett Johnson. Copyright © renewed 1988 by Ruth Krauss Johnson. Used by permission of HarperCollins Publishers.

sequel to *The Cat* in 1958, Geisel drew a picture of himself *as* the Cat in the Hat (figures 12 and 13) to accompany an article in *The Saturday Evening Post* of July 6, 1957. The caption read "Self-portrait, by Dr. Seuss." The imaginative conflation of Cat and author emphasizes Dr. Seuss's kinship with his alter ego, and suggests that the Cat shares some of his creator's values.

Although nonsense books such as *On Beyond Zebra!* do reveal experience as a construct and *The Cat in the Hat* does challenge domestic order, it is important to note that nonsense works are not ideology-proof. The surrealists tended to idealize nonsense, the unconscious, and all things irrational as neutral spaces from which to reveal and skewer social norms; however, such an idea seems a bit naïve, for these spaces are neither magically beyond ideology nor entirely defined by it. That is, although it would seem reductive to say that the irrational merely replicates ideological structures, nonsensical thinking is not ideologically immune either. If we leave behind the idea of an ideology-free space and instead think of nonsense and the illogical as providing the reader with the cognitive tools with which to build a critique of ideology, then nonsense literature becomes critically viable. For example, as *Fox in Socks* (1965) shows how the meanings of words shift according to their context, so a child could come to understand that the world's accepted truths may only be true in certain contexts. For example, the fox's stacks of bricks, chicks, blocks, and boxes have one effect when stacked on the ground and another (more painful) effect when stacked on top of the character Knox. A benign stack on one page becomes a potentially harmful stack on the next. Also, by placing common items in uncommon places, the book provides an opportunity to ask what words such as *common* and *uncommon* mean. Magritte once said of his paintings, "If the spectator finds that my paintings are a kind of defiance of 'common sense,' he realizes something obvious. I want nevertheless to add that for me the world is a defiance of common sense" (Gablik 14). Seuss's works open the door for children to ask questions of their world and explore the ways in which it often does defy common sense.

Given Seuss's challenges to common sense, the critic George Bodmer's claim that books such as these merely "reflect the anti-didactic mood of our time" and question "our ability to learn and to teach" (115) falls a bit short of the mark. The books do teach and are didactic, but, instead of delivering a lecture to their readers, Seuss's works teach by encouraging subversive thoughts and behaviors. In her book

Figure 12. Dr. Seuss: "Self-portrait" (1957). Self-portrait by Dr. Seuss by gracious consent of Dr. Seuss Enterprises, L.P.

Dr. Seuss, Ruth MacDonald claims, "Though Dr. Spock's permissive parenting has frequently been credited with spurring the youthful rebellion of the 1960s, Dr. Seuss might equally be given credit, since he demonstrates a kind of permissiveness with language" (MacDonald 169). MacDonald's connection between Seuss and the revolts of the 1960s offers us an opportunity to explore the ways in which Seuss's nonsense work both challenges and is implicated in the ideologies it critiques. As a case in point, consider *The Cat in the Hat Comes Back* (1958).

Starring the anarchic Cat in the Hat and featuring twenty-six increasingly smaller cats lettered A through Z, *The Cat in the Hat Comes Back* offers another variation on the nonsense alphabet theme. A closer look, however, suggests that the work may be an antecedent to *The Butter Battle Book* or the painting *Fooling Nobody* because the "Voom" coming from beneath the smallest cat's hat resembles atomic energy. Like the dual threats of radiation and Communist infiltration (prevalent during the 1950s, when the book was composed), a growing pink stain is pervasive and real but lingers just beyond the control of the narrator. In this sense, the stain suggests a "red menace" growing out of control, threatening the American values of home and family represented by the two children (Sally and the narrator). Living in La Jolla, California, a mere one hundred miles south

Figure 13. Dr. Seuss: The Cat in the Hat, from *The Cat in the Hat* (1957). ™ and copyright © 1957, 1985, Dr. Seuss Enterprises. Reproduced by permission of Random House, Inc.

of Hollywood, and having worked in film himself, Geisel would no doubt have been familiar with the "Hollywood Ten," alleged Communists in the film industry whom the House Committee on Un-American Activities sent to federal prison in 1947. Other incidents contributing to the climate of hysteria and fear of alleged subversives in the 1950s were, of course, the witch hunts (1950–54) led by Senator Joseph McCarthy and Congressman Richard Nixon and the widely publicized Hiss-Chambers case (1948–50), in which *Time* magazine's Whittaker Chambers accused the State Department's Alger Hiss of being a Communist spy. So, *The Cat in the Hat Comes Back*'s representation of the spreading red stain across the landscape certainly echoes the fears of the times. When, at book's end, the Voom arrives like an atomic bomb to clean away the threat of subversion, Seuss seems to be representing but not critiquing anti-Communist paranoia.

Although the pink stain and the Voom clearly locate the book in the context of the anti-Soviet mood of America in the '50s, *The Cat in the Hat Comes Back* does not endorse such paranoia. True to the radical nature he has shown in *The Cat in the Hat*, the Cat deliberately inverts the dominant logic of the day in order to challenge it. Instead of containing the symbolic "red menace," he deliberately, even merrily, spreads it everywhere. Like a dadaist, the Cat uses paradox and chance to shake Sally and the narrator out of their habitual perception of the world. What Suzi Gablik has said of Magritte's paintings applies to the Cat: he makes "a systematic attempt to disrupt any dogmatic view of the physical world" by means of the "conceptual paradox" (112). As Magritte balances a glass of water on top of an umbrella in *Hegel's Holiday* (1954), the Cat balances a fishbowl full of water (and fish) in *The Cat in the Hat* (1957). In *The Cat in the Hat Comes Back,* the Cat again employs this sort of paradoxical logic, eating cake in the bathtub and "cleaning" up the pink ink by spreading it around. (Indeed, he seems to "clean" by becoming an abstract expressionist: the Cat paints with a dress, with shoes—and little cat C spreads pink paint with a fan.) The Cat's paradoxical response to the children's growing fear of the spreading pink ink conveys an implicit criticism of anti-Communist paranoia. Their increasing anxiety prompts the Cat to keep spreading the ink and, in another paradox, spreading the ink actually leads to cleaning it up. The Cat's alphabet of increasingly smaller cats finally leads him to the Voom (under little cat Z's hat) that will clean the pink ink away.

Though the Voom has "the power of the atomic bomb" (MacDonald 129) in the swiftness with which it erases the "reds," it differs from the bomb in one very significant aspect: the characteristic of annihilation has been withdrawn from it. Whereas the Voom's historical referent is clearly an atom bomb, Seuss's depiction partakes of Magritte's "modification," in which "a property normally associated with an object is withdrawn"—as in Magritte's *The Battle of the Argonne* (1959), in which gravity is removed from a rock, allowing it to float (Gablik 129). The power of atomic destruction has been removed from the Voom: although it at first appears to have destroyed pink ink, cats and all, the Voom has in fact merely relocated them under the Cat's hat. As the Cat explains to the bewildered children immediately after the Voom has "clean[ed] up the snow" (and everything else), "That Voom blew my little cats / Back in my hat" (59, 61). He adds, gesturing to his hat, "if you ever / Have spots, now and then, I will be very happy / To come here again" (61), indicating that Voom, little cats, and all are now back under his hat and suggesting that their containment is very temporary. In response to both the Voom and the Cat's promise to return, the children's faces express a mixture of grateful surprise and worried disbelief, reinforcing the sense that peace has returned only for the moment. As he does in many of his works, Seuss ends the book without completely resolving it, requiring the audience to take an active role in providing resolution.[18]

The atomic subtext of *The Cat in the Hat Comes Back* shows that Seuss's nonsense functions in a manner similar to the historical avant-garde's use of nonsense and the irrational: the devices render the work both complicit with and critical of the world in which it is written. If children learn the structures of power as they acquire language, then deconstructing language can have a liberating effect—a potential challenge to the structures of power that language bears. Seuss's works license the imagination as a realm in which one can at least *imagine* another world—if not actually realize that world.[19] Mary Lystad has said of *The Cat in the Hat,* "The message is clear—if the world is bleak, change it, create a new world!" (201). And as Bodmer says of *The Butter Battle Book,* "If the world is to be saved, . . . it is only through leaps of imagination" (116). By providing the imaginative impetus to change the world, Dr. Seuss encourages children to subvert dominant modes of socialization. In this sense, Seuss's books go beyond the conventional definition of nonsense literature, which uses absurdity to reveal reality as a construct but less frequently indicts society at large. Whether Seuss's works have this effect on children is beyond the scope of this inquiry, but it is clear that children are drawn to the power of imagination that Seuss's books grant them. As a child once wrote in a letter to Seuss, "Dr. Seuss, you have an imagination with a long tail" (Cott 18).

Modernism, Postmodernism, and Consumerism: How Will the Lorax Survive?

At this point, the astute critic may ask: Since imagination is, as we have seen, always already implicated in the societal structures against which it may rebel, how can imaginative power ever provide an effective critique of the pervasive, even insidious, effects of late capitalist culture? After all, this reasonably skeptical person might continue, even when the historical avant-garde attempted to expose the paradoxical logic of the material world, it ultimately found itself becoming co-opted, marketed as exotic entertainment to that same world. If, instead of offending or provoking, surrealism and dada were transformed into amusement, then what hope does Dr. Seuss's work have of succeeding where the historical avant-garde failed? In order to develop an answer to these questions, let us turn to La Jolla, California, in 1971, where we find Fredric Jameson writing *Marxism and Form* and Theodor Seuss Geisel writing *The Lorax*. In the former work, Jameson argues that "the development of postindustrial monopoly capitalism has brought with it an increasing occultation of the class structure through techniques of mystification practiced by the media." He continues, "as a service economy we are henceforth so far removed from the realities of production and work on the world that we inhabit a dream world of artificial stimuli and televised experience" (xvii–xviii). In its way, *The Lorax* addresses similar concerns: it criticizes an ideology of consumption that praises material production while ignoring its material effects. To put this in the terms of the book's narrative, the Once-ler may be a material success, but his Thneed business destroys the Truffula trees and sends the wildlife into exile, leaving behind a barren, gray urban landscape. *The Lorax* also shows the media's complicity in mystifying the effects of capitalism: the Once-ler's "You need a Thneed" advertising campaign successfully convinces the buying public that these worthless pieces of knitted Truffula tufts are actually valuable, while at the same time it diverts attention from the damage done to the environment.

But where Seuss offers a moment of hope at the book's end (the last Truffula seed, thrown for us to catch, to start again), Jameson despairs. When addressing the role of the avant-garde in offering a critique of capital, Jameson argues that when surrealism was effective it worked because it interacted with a nonindustrial nature, and such a nature no longer exists. In fact, "it is the very memory of nature itself which seems to face obliteration" now (106). But while Jameson is saying that "the objects of Surrealism are gone without a trace" (104) and, anyway, "the *idea* of Surrealism is a more liberating experience than the actual texts" (101), Seuss's *Lorax* challenges Jameson's claim. Its critique of capitalism relies less on an idealized nature (though at least the *memory* of nature exists here) than on its open-ended narrative structure and the surreal disembodiment of the Once-ler himself. And, as a kind of surrealist critique of capital, I think the *Lorax* works.

That said, Jameson may yet have the last word. The recent mass commercialization of Seuss threatens to dull his critical edge, to transform "Dr. Seuss" into another Walt Disney, one of many blithe affirmations of consumer culture that dominate America's cultural landscape. In *Postmodernism* (1991), Jameson again argues that postindustrial capitalism will neutralize attempts to offer resistance. He offers the postmodernism of his title as proof: as flat, blank parody, it merely reflects the society from which it comes. In contrast to Jameson's bleak view, critics such as Linda Hutcheon, David Harvey, and Andreas Huyssen maintain the possibility of an oppositional postmodern—a postmodern that *can* offer a critique. And, at least in the versions of Harvey and Huyssen, the avant-garde has a role to play here. It is the radical politics of the avant-garde, suppressed in definitions of high modernism, to which postmodernists return in order to counteract the effects of affirmative culture.

Geisel is an appropriate figure to place in this debate. Not only does his life (1904–1991) span the years of the modern and the postmodern, but he always had a foot in each camp. That is, he was a modernist in both "high modern" and "avant-garde" terms and a postmodernist inasmuch as his work follows the legacy of the avant-garde. Much of this essay has investigated Geisel's investment in avant-garde techniques, but now let us turn for a moment to the idea of Geisel as a "high modernist" author. Geisel originally began publishing cartoons under his mother's maiden name—Seuss—because he was saving his surname—Geisel—for the "Great American Novel" he would someday write. Evidence suggests that this novel would have been high modernist in form. Ruth MacDonald's description of it as "an unpublished manuscript of a virtually undecipherable, stream-of-consciousness novel written in his mid-twenties" (3) suggests the complexity of a work by Faulkner or Joyce. Add to the case for Seuss-as-high-modernist that his attention to form is legendary. For example, the revising and rewriting of *The Cat in the Hat* took him about a year. Geisel credited his editor, Saxe Commins—who also edited Ernest Hemingway, William Faulkner, and Eugene O'Neill—with stressing the importance of form (Steinberg 87; Morgan and Morgan 138). Perhaps as a testament to Geisel's success at mastering formal qualities for which high modernism has been praised, the modernist critic Hugh Kenner wrote a tribute in Seussian verse ("Ode to Dr. Seuss," 1991).

To return to the question posed by Seuss's location in the history of modernity and postmodernity: Will the ongoing marketing bonanza diminish the avant-garde energies in Dr. Seuss's work? If the new Dr. Seuss books based on the Nickelodeon television show are any indication, the answer has to be yes. *The Song of the Zubble-Wump* (1996), for example, has tamed the wily Cat in the Hat, turning him into a moralizing preacher; instead of the provocative questions we have come to expect from Dr. Seuss, the book offers amens. In this respect,

The Song of the Zubble-Wump recalls Jameson's comments on pastiche: "it is a neutral practice of . . . mimicry, without any of parody's ulterior motives, amputated of the satiric impulse" (*Postmodernism* 17). Although pastiche can be affirmative or critical, *Zubble-Wump* is pastiche in the former, more Jamesonian, sense. The book brings in Horton to help save the Zubble-Wump egg, the Grinch to play the role of the villain, and the Cat in the Hat to be the book's moral center. Whatever adversarial roles these characters played in the books written by Geisel, their edges have been dulled for *Zubble-Wump*. The edginess that marks Seuss's style is missing, as is the malleability of the moral universe of Seuss's books.

By *malleability* I mean that these books suggest a certain instability in the moral world: instead of good and evil or black and white, Seuss's characters are more complex, inhabiting a world of better and worse, perhaps—but a world that has many shades of gray. For example, the Once-ler changes his mind about industry's effects on the environment, but only after his industry has already destroyed it. On one hand, he changes too late; on the other, he does change, which suggests possibilities for other changes in the future. In *The Song of the Zubble-Wump,* however, moral instability has been banished. Here, the Grinch—who, oddly, resembles a cross between *Sesame Street's* Grover and Oscar the Grouch—is the villain: "That Grinch is all broken, that Grinch is all bent. / His heart's full of hurt and his soul is cement," Megan's grandfather tells her. On the contrary, as Geisel has said of the Grinch, he "is the Hero of Christmas. Sure . . . he starts out as a villain, but it's not how you start out that counts. It's what you are at the finish" (Morgan and Morgan 276). Like Dickens's Scrooge, the point of Seuss's Grinch is that he has within him the capacity to change. *Zubble-Wump* denies the possibility of any ambiguity in the Grinch's character. The Grinch thwarts the plans of the good guys, and at the story's end the narrative promises us that the evil Grinch will be back once again: "But you all know the Grinch / He'll be back / before long." Ambiguity animates Seuss's work and enables his reader to see the inconsistencies and contradictions of the world. *Zubble-Wump,* however, merely reflects a staid, bourgeois status quo.

Whereas this new book moralizes instead of provoking, "Seuss!"— a recent exhibit at the Children's Museum of Manhattan—used pastiche to provoke the imagination.[20] Unlike the *Zubble-Wump* travesty, the "Seuss!" exhibit was not part of a corporate tie-in to Seuss Enterprises; rather, the curators of the museum (which has produced many literature-based exhibitions for children) had long wanted to present an exhibition on Dr. Seuss. The museum's executive director, Andrew Ackerman, explained, "We would always ask ourselves, 'If we had a choice to do any books at all, what would they be?' It always came down to Dr. Seuss" (Graeber C1). In contrast to the first publication from the Wubbulous World of Dr. Seuss series, "Seuss!" provoked thought instead of pronouncing morals, opened children's minds instead of lecturing to them. Using characters and situations from a variety of Seuss's works, the exhibit encouraged active engagement on the part of its visitors. As the critic Brian Sutton-Smith has said of Seuss's books, this exhibit encouraged "flexibility and possibility" because "flexibility of thinking . . . [is] what mental development is about these days" (Cott 14).

In one part of the exhibit, there were cylinders "decorated with Seussian creatures holding a letter," followed by "a word root like 'up' or 'all' or 'at.'" When children spun the cylinders, they formed new words (Graeber C26). Using chance to create new words or sentences was a favorite game of the surrealists. In this game—known as "The Exquisite Corpse"—each person would add words (starting with an article and an adjective, then a noun, and so on) to make random sentences such as "The exquisite corpse shall drink the new wine" (Brotchie 25). The cylinders in the "Seuss!" exhibit may have had the liberating effect that surrealists found in nonsense: by showing children how language works, "random" sentences gave them the power to experiment. Another portion of the exhibit reproduced some of Seuss's drafts in order to show children the art of revision. Ackerman explains, "Children often get frustrated if they can't do something perfectly, so it's a big relief to know that even the best artists used drafts." The same space included a place for visitors to "do some creative experimentation, devising new characters by combining pieces in the shape of Seussian animals' heads and bodies" (Graeber 26). Again, the exhibit used Seuss's work as Seuss would have wished—to empower children to use language and their imaginations.

Power over language and imagination may not enable a child to challenge all of the world's faulty logic, but it does provide a starting point. In providing this starting point, "Seuss!" achieved what Geisel wanted children's museums to accomplish. As dada and fluxus artists wanted to break down the boundary between art and audience, so Geisel wished to break down the boundary between exhibit and visitor. As E. J. Kahn tells us, in 1955 Geisel "wrote and acted in an

'Omnibus' television show devoted to an imaginary Seuss Museum. It differed from the general run of museums in that children going through it were not forbidden to touch the displays; on the contrary, the exhibits were all marked 'Do Touch.'" Seuss explained, "I want a museum that will have a real, operable printing press alongside a shelf of books, and blocks of wood and chisels alongside woodcuts, so that children can watch and work at the same time" (Kahn 80). With Geisel's help, by 1967, one wing of La Jolla's Museum of Art had been devoted to an interactive museum, the philosophy of which seems to have been "Do Touch." As a *Newsweek* article reported, "grade-school kids excitedly picked through piles of Barbie-doll heads, eyeballs, limbs, and torsos for parts to build an abstract model of a city. Elsewhere, they lugged $2,100 movie cameras about to film the summertime activity at the museum" ("Logical Insanity" 58). "Seuss!" and Seuss's own museum ideas develop a kind of avant-garde for kids.

At this point, it is too early to say which version of Seuss will predominate—the one with avant-garde leanings, as exemplified by the "Seuss!" exhibit, or the affirmative pastiche, as represented by *The Song of the Zubble-Wump*. Let us hope for the former version, because exhibits such as "Seuss!" and books such as *The Cat in the Hat* can give children some of the cognitive tools necessary for questioning the world in which they live. Although Dr. Seuss's books are didactic, they teach not by delivering a lecture to their readers but by encouraging subversive thoughts and behaviors. If children learn the structures of power as they acquire language, then deconstructing language can have a liberating effect by offering a potential challenge to the structures of power that language bears. Seuss's works license the imagination as a realm in which one can at least *imagine* another world, if not actually realize that world. By providing the impetus to change the world, Dr. Seuss encouraged children to subvert dominant modes of socialization. And it is this skeptical, imaginative version of Dr. Seuss—and not the William Bennett–style "Moralist in a Hat"—that present and future generations of children will need to meet.

Notes

1. Witness, e.g., Microsoft's recent "Where do you want to go today?" commercial; among the images that drift by during the thirty-second advertisement is René Magritte's bowler-hatted man. The image recurs in Magritte's work, but the best-known example is, perhaps, *The Man in the Bowler Hat* (1964), in which a dove flies in front of the face of a man in a bowler hat. The figure also appears in *The Musings of the Soli-*

tary Walker (1926–27), *In the Land of Night* (1928), *The Song of the Violet* (1951), *Siren Song* (1952), *Golconda* (1953), *The Poet Rewarded* (1956), *The Ready-Made Bouquet* (1957), *The Month of the Grape Harvest* (1959), *The Good Faith* (1962), *The Son of Man* (1964), *The Open Door* (1965), *Decalcomania* (1966), and many others—including photographs of Magritte himself (he often wore a bowler hat). The Microsoft commercial was not the first time Magritte was appropriated by commercial culture. Corporate use of Magritte's images goes back at least to 1951, when designer William Golden appropriated Magritte's *The False Mirror* (1928) for the CBS "eye" logo: although now merely a silhouette of its original version, at that time the CBS logo featured blue sky and clouds behind the pupil of an eye—exactly as in Magritte's painting. Indeed, in December 1963, Magritte wrote his lawyer and friend Harry Torczyner that he was considering legal action against CBS: "Columbia Broadcasting has registered the image as a 'trademark,' and I think it was inspired by 'Le Faux Miroir.' I have already collected all the documentation on the presence of 'Le Faux Miroir' in the United States since 1936, whereas the trademark only dates from 1952! 'Le Faux Miroir' was reproduced in the 1936 catalogue of the Museum of Modern Art (1936 Exhibition of Dada and Fantastic Art) and on view to the New York public at that time (logically, the logo's designer, who died in 1959, must have seen it!)" (Magritte and Torczyner 93).

2. For example, when writing *How the Grinch Stole Christmas!* he worked hard to avoid "sound[ing] like a second-rate preacher or some biblical truism" (quoted in Morgan and Morgan 159). Tish Rabe and David Stephen Cohen (who wrote the script of *Zubble-Wump*), however, seem less concerned.

3. As Tim Wolf suggests in "Imagination, Rejection, and Rescue: Recurrent Themes in Dr. Seuss," Seuss consistently associated cats with the imaginative and the anarchic. Wolf notes the appropriateness of having "Patrol Cats" (as opposed to dogs) as guardians of "the roots of childlike imagination" in *The King's Stilts* (1939): "To defend our childlike imagination and joy, Seuss seems to say, we must be like cats toward society, not dogs. (This may also look forward to the anarchistic Cat in the Hat saving two children from a dull adult-ruled afternoon.)" (149).

4. Unfortunately, *Zubble-Wump* seems to be the beginning of a trend in Seuss marketing. *Seuss-isms: Wise and Witty Prescriptions for Living from the Good Doctor* (1997) transforms Seuss from a figure who encourages the questioning of authority into a moralist who affirms the status quo. The small book takes Seussian verses out of context and transforms them into homilies for living. For example, whereas *Oh, the Places You'll Go!* addresses both hope and despair, *Seuss-isms* includes only the more hopeful verses.

5. Although Geisel once said, "I'd rather go into the *Guinness Book of World Records* as the writer who refused the most money per word," after his death the hypercommercialization of Dr. Seuss began. Seuss's characters now appear on boxer shorts, t-shirts, and hats by Esprit; Universal City in Orlando is building a twenty-five-acre Seuss theme park in Orlando, Florida; and Steven Spielberg is developing a *Cat in the Hat* movie (Smith B1). During his life, Geisel restricted the marketing of his work to books and a few television specials. In their biography, *Dr. Seuss and Mr. Geisel*, Judith and Neil Morgan write of several occasions on which Geisel resisted attempts to market his work. Once Robert L. Bernstein, then sales manager at Random House, suggested many "promotional ideas, including 'Cat's pajamas' in all sizes, but Ted resisted. He was wary of anything—product franchising, most of all—that might cheapen the Dr. Seuss image" (161). Another time Geisel "set up a sculpting studio next to the pool house in La Jolla and created the Cat, Horton and four 'Seuss multi-beasts'—one named Roscoe—to be marketed as self-assembly polyethylene kits for the March toy show in 1959. But no one else's version of a Dr. Seuss creature satisfied Ted," and so the creatures were never made (164).

6. Sawin's *Surrealism in Exile* (1995) traces the influence of the exiled avant-garde on American artists and posits the period (1937–45) as a crucial hinge between the Euro-

pean dada and surrealism of the first half of the century and the artistic movements that followed, such as abstract expressionism and pop art.

7. The Morgans report, "Ted had written a script about modern art for a half-hour Ford Foundation television workshop in the *Excursion* series, and it was broadcast live over NBC on Sunday afternoon, January 31 [1954]. Burgess Meredith was the host, and [Hans] Conreid was cast opposite Ted as an art connoisseur" (145–46).

8. As Jon Agee notes in his review of *The Secret Art of Dr. Seuss* in the *Los Angeles Times* (3 December 1995), "A couple of strange, hallucinogenic landscapes recall the paintings of Max Ernst or Yves Tanguy—except that in each case, somewhere in the scene, there's a cat. Surrealism, even Cubism, is apparent, as in the fractured perspective of a city where a feline detective pursues its quarry. The titles of the paintings ('The Rather Odd Myopic Woman Riding Piggyback on One of Helen's Many Cats') are comparable to those of the Dadaists."

9. A sensitivity to gender has never been one of the surrealists' strong points (see especially Helena Lewis's *The Politics of Surrealism* 71–76). Although Geisel has been rightly criticized for his books' treatment of women—as in Alison Lurie's essay "The Cabinet of Dr. Seuss" (1990)—he never quite approaches the levels of misogyny in, say, some of Salvador Dalí's work. That said, the topic of Seuss and gender should not be ignored. To give a sense of the debate, here is the evidence, both critical of and in defense of Seuss. Lurie points out "the almost total lack of female protagonists" and adds that "when little girls appear they play silent, secondary roles" (51). She also cites the vain female characters Gertrude McFuzz in the story of that name (from *Yertle the Turtle and Other Stories*, 1958) and the bird Mayzie in *Horton Hatches the Egg* (1940). Finally, Lurie notes that, in "The Glunk That Got Thunk" (a story included in *I Can Lick 30 Tigers Today!*, 1969), a little girl thinks up a dangerous Glunk, which her brother must then unthink. Lurie's conclusion, however—"Moral: Women have weak minds; they must not be ambitious even in imagination" (52)—seems a bit strong, based on just one story. For example, in the posthumously published *Daisy-Head Mayzie* (1994), a little girl named Mayzie McGrew grows a flower on her head. If we take the flower as a metaphorical imagination, the problem is then not the fact that she has ideas but rather that Finagle the Agent exploits them for commercial gain. Also, I think it would be fair to argue that many of Seuss's young protagonists are more "everychild" figures than specifically gendered as male or female children. Geisel's response to Lurie was to note that most of his characters are animals, "and if she can identify their sex, I'll remember her in my will" (Morgan and Morgan 286).

10. According to the Morgans, Geisel would have sold them but his wife Helen prevented him (143).

11. In *Yertle*, a small turtle named Mack topples Yertle, a dictator who, Seuss says, "is Adolf Hitler" (Sadler 249). Mack undoes the hierarchical power structure that enables Yertle to dominate the other turtles, but the book does not conclude with the finality of "they all lived happily ever after." Instead, the book concludes, "And today the great Yertle, that Marvelous he, / Is King of the Mud. That is all he can see. / And turtles, of course . . . all the turtles are free. / As turtles and, *maybe*, all creatures should be" (my emphasis). When asked, "Why 'maybe' and not 'surely'?" Geisel responded, "I qualified that . . . in order to avoid sounding too didactic or like a preacher on a platform. And I wanted other persons, to say 'surely' in their minds instead of my having to say it" (Cott 28). In other words, the *maybe* introduces an element of doubt that compels the reader to respond in the affirmative. *The Lorax* (1971), which tackles the problem of corporate exploitation of the environment, effects a similar response with the word *unless*. Told in the flashback format of *The Butter Battle Book*, *The Lorax* uses the character of the Once-ler to dramatize the negative effects that industry has had on the ecosystem. *The Lorax* concludes with a sense of urgency directed toward the reader: repentant ex-industrialist Once-ler tosses the last Truffula Seed to the narrator (identified only as

"you" in the text). The book concludes with the seed in transit, about to land in "your" hands. As the Once-ler realizes, "UNLESS some like you / cares a whole awful lot, / nothing is going to get better."

12. Another critic claims that, at the end of each Seuss book, "[t]here is an abrupt return to simple diction, and a simple, realistic illustration implicitly declares that Seuss's protagonist was only fantasizing" (Lurie 50). But in Seuss's stories, there is no such thing as "only fantasizing"; on the contrary, his books consistently depict the imagination as a powerful force.

13. A series of Seuss's stories involve a young protagonist telling an increasingly outrageous story and conclude by framing the narrative. His first, *To Think That I Saw It on Mulberry Street* (1937) follows this pattern, as does *McElligot's Pool* (1947), *Scrambled Eggs Super!* (1953), *If I Ran the Zoo* (1950), and *If I Ran the Circus* (1956). But even here the narrative frame often (though not always) leaves either an element of doubt or simply a weak sense of closure. For instance, in *Mulberry Street*, the momentum that Marco's tale has developed over the preceding forty pages is not effectively checked by the sudden decision not to tell his father about it. The cumulative effect of Marco's imaginative enterprise outweighs his two-line disclaimer that he saw only "a plain horse and wagon" on Mulberry Street. Similarly, by the conclusion of *If I Ran the Circus*, Morris McGurk's idea for a circus has begun to startle Mr. Sneelock, the owner of the store behind which the proposed circus would take place. When we first see Sneelock, he remains calm, smoking his pipe—and because he enters Morris's imagination as calm he remains that way throughout the tale. But during Morris's imagined circus, Sneelock's role becomes more and more dangerous: being lassoed by a Wily Walloo, having a crab apple shot off his head by a blindfolded bowman, skiing on Roller-Skate-Skis through Stickle-Bush trees, standing in the mouth of a Spotted Atrocious, wrestling a Grizzly-Ghastly, and diving into a goldfish bowl. At the end of the tale, when we reenter the world outside Morris's story, Sneelock's eyes are suddenly wide open, suggesting that the imagined feats of "brave Sneelock" have rattled him a bit.

14. In the same essay, first published as the introduction to *Surrealism* (1936, including essays by André Breton and Paul Eulard) and later in Read's *The Philosophy of Modern Art* (1953), Read argues, "From our point of view, Lear is a better poet than Tennyson; Lewis Carroll has affinities with Shakespeare" (56). As Paul C. Ray's *The Surrealist Movement in England* (1971) suggests, the English surrealists looked to Carroll (1832–98) and Lear (1812–88) as literary ancestors because their techniques seemed allied with the surrealist goal of "discredit[ing] conventional reality" (28). In fact, even though the French surrealists considered Lautréamont to be their primary literary influence, they too were interested in the work of Carroll and Lear: Louis Aragon translated Carroll's *Hunting of the Snark* into French, and Breton saw in Carroll's work a project that intersected with his own (Ray 60).

15. At a writers' conference at Salt Lake City in July 1949, Geisel told the assembled students that he placed his work in the company of nonsense literature: "In the realm of nonsense, there are Mother Goose, (Edward) Lear, Lewis (Carroll), P. L. Travers and Dr. Seuss" (Morgan and Morgan 23–24). Others have noted Seuss's link to the nonsensical, too. The writer and critic Jonathan Cott has suggested Lear as a possible antecedent for Seuss's "fantastical-looking animals and composite beasts" (11), and, perhaps sensing Carroll's influence, the author of an article on Seuss's political cartoons called the piece "Malice in Wonderland" (*Newsweek* 9 Feb. 1942: 58–89).

16. Children's literature as children write and see it shares this characteristic with Seuss's work. As Iona and Peter Opie's collection of traditional rhymes shows, children often use nonsense as a way of criticizing the adult world. The Opies' *I Saw Esau*, published in 1947 and reprinted in 1992 with illustrations by Maurice Sendak, contains many apparently nonsensical (and often rhymed) challenges to authority.

17. The book was sold in bookstores through Random House and to schools

through Houghton Mifflin. The Morgans report that the "Random House trade edition quickly outran Houghton Mifflin's school edition, averaging sales at the start of about twelve thousand copies a month and rising rapidly." They speculate that the Random House edition may have sold more because "spurred by playground word-of-mouth, children nagged their parents to buy it" (156).

18. The ambiguous note on which *The Cat in the Hat Comes Back* ends mirrors Geisel's conflicted relation with the idea of atomic power. On one hand, his interest inspired him to use atomic energy in an early film script. While working for the army's film division at what they called "Fort Fox" in January 1945, he was assigned "to write a film spurring postwar troops to help avoid a third world war." Inspired by a brief story in *The New York Times* that claimed that if the energy from a glass of water could be harnessed, "it could blow up half the world," Geisel "drafted a film treatment that warned of the potential threat of devastating explosions." Afraid that his film script would expose the Manhattan Project (of which Geisel knew nothing), a colonel in Washington ordered him to burn his source—and the film was never made (Morgan and Morgan 115). On the other hand, Geisel was very sympathetic toward the Japanese and troubled by the destruction wrought by the American atomic bombs. His film for American troops in defeated Japan was deemed too sympathetic toward the Japanese people, so RKO pictures edited it to fit the official U.S. position. As MacDonald points out, "Dr. Seuss clearly found the Japanese admirable and America's relations with them worthy of preservation in spite of public pressure in the United States to the contrary" (75). Seuss's trip to Japan in 1953 inspired *Horton Hears a Who!* (1954) and its message that "a person's a person no matter how small" (Morgan and Morgan 144–45). The book, which Seuss dedicated to his "Great Friend," Kyoto professor Mitsugi Nakamura, defends the rights of Whos against the threat of total annihilation of their world.

19. For an opposing view, see Michael Steig's Freudian reading of *I Wish That I Had Duck Feet* in his essay "Dr. Seuss's Attack on Imagination." He calls it "a form of (possibly unintended) propaganda for conformity" (140). Although Steig admits that the message of conformity is "possibly unintended," it seems important to consider *Duck Feet* in the context of not only the rest of Seuss's work but of children's literature as a whole. *Duck Feet* (one of many Geisel works written under a pseudonym other than "Dr. Seuss") engages children's imagination at least as much as other books for young readers and does not fit the category of propaganda.

20. The exhibit opened on February 14, 1997, and closed on February 28, 1999.

Works Cited

Agee, Jon. "The 500 Cats of Theodor Geisel." Review of *The Secret Art of Dr. Seuss*. *Los Angeles Times Book Review* 3 December 1995: 22.

Alexandrian, Sarane. *Surrealist Art*. 1969. Trans. Gordon Clough. New York: Thames and Hudson, 1970.

Anderson, Celia Catlett, and Marilyn Fain Apseloff. *Nonsense Literature for Children: Aesop to Seuss*. Hamden, Conn.: Library Professional, 1989.

Bandler, Michael J. "Portrait of a Man Reading: Theodor Seuss Geisel (Dr. Seuss) Interviewed by Michael J. Bandler." *Washington Post Book World* 7 May 1972: 2.

Barthes, Roland. *Mythologies*. 1957. Trans. Annette Lavers. New York: Hill and Wang, 1994.

Bodmer, George R. "The Post-Modern Alphabet: Extending the Limits of the Contemporary Alphabet Book, from Seuss to Gorey." *Children's Literature Association Quarterly* 14, no. 3 (fall 1989): 115–17.

Brotchie, Alastaire, comp. and ed., and Mel Gooding, ed. *A Book of Surrealist Games*. Boston and London: Shambhala Redstone, 1995.

Bürger, Peter. *Theory of the Avant-Garde.* 1974. Trans. Michael Shaw. Minneapolis: University of Minnesota Press, 1984.

Cahn, Robert. "The Wonderful World of Dr. Seuss." *The Saturday Evening Post* 6 July 1957: 17–19, 42, 46.

Cott, Jonathan. *Pipers at the Gates of Dawn: The Wisdom of Children's Literature.* New York: Random House, 1983.

Duchamp, Marcel. *The Writings of Marcel Duchamp.* Ed. Michel Sanouillet and Elmer Peterson. Various translators. New York: Da Capo, 1989. (Reprint of *Salt Seller: The Writings of Marcel Duchamp,* Oxford University Press, 1973.)

Gablik, Suzi. *Magritte.* 1970. New York: Thames and Hudson, 1985.

Graeber, Laurel. "From Green Eggs to Ham, Hands On." *New York Times* 14 February 1997: C1, C26.

Harvey, David. *The Condition of Postmodernity: An Enquiry into the Origins of Cultural Change.* Cambridge, Mass.: Basil Blackwell, 1989.

Hopkins, Lee Bennett. *Pauses: Autobiographical Reflections of 101 Creators of Children's Books.* New York: HarperCollins, 1995.

Huyssen, Andreas. *After the Great Divide: Modernism, Mass Culture, Postmodernism.* Indianapolis: Indiana University Press, 1986.

Jameson, Fredric. *Postmodernism; or, the Cultural Logic of Late Capitalism.* Durham, N.C.: Duke University Press, 1991.

———. *Marxism and Form.* Princeton: Princeton University Press, 1971.

Johnson, Crockett. *A Picture for Harold's Room.* 1960. New York: HarperCollins, 1988.

Kahn, E. J., Jr. "Children's Friend." *The New Yorker* 17 December 1960: 47–93.

Kenner, Hugh. "Ode to Dr. Seuss." *Art and Antiques* 8 (December 1991): 104.

Lear, Edward. *The Complete Nonsense of Edward Lear.* 1947. Collected and introduced by Holbrook Jackson. New York: Dover, 1951.

Lewis, Helena. *The Politics of Surrealism.* New York: Paragon, 1988.

Lifton, Betty Jean. "*The Butter Battle Book.*" *New York Times Book Review* 26 February 1984: 37.

"The Logical Insanity of Dr. Seuss." *Time* 11 August 1967: 58–59.

Lurie, Alison. "The Cabinet of Dr. Seuss." *The New York Review of Books* 20 December 1990: 50–52.

Lystad, Mary. *From Dr. Mather to Dr. Seuss: 200 Years of American Books for Children.* Boston: Schenkman, 1980.

MacDonald, Ruth K. *Dr. Seuss.* Boston: Twayne, 1988.

Magritte, René, and Harry Torczyner. *Letters Between Friends.* Trans. Richard Miller. New York: Abrams, 1994.

Marquis, Alice G. *Hopes and Ashes: The Birth of Modern Times, 1929–1939.* New York: Free, 1986.

Morgan, Judith, and Neil Morgan. *Dr. Seuss and Mr. Geisel: A Biography.* New York: Random House, 1995.

Motherwell, Robert, ed. *Dada Painters and Poets.* New York: Wittenborn, Schultz, 1951.

Nadeau, Maurice. *The History of Surrealism.* Trans. Richard Howard. Cambridge, Mass.: Belknap-Harvard University Press, 1989.

"The One and Only Dr. Seuss and His Wonderful Autographing Tour." *Publisher's Weekly* 8 December 1958: 12–15.

Quindlen, Anna. "The One Who Had Fun." *New York Times* 28 September 1991: 19.

Rabe, Tish. *The Song of the Zubble-Wump.* Illus. Tom Brannon. New York: Random House-Jim Henson Productions, 1996.

Ray, Paul C. *The Surrealist Movement in England.* Ithaca and London: Cornell University Press, 1971.

Read, Herbert. "Introduction." In *Surrealism.* Ed. Herbert Read. New York: Harcourt, Brace, 1936. Pp. 19–91.

Sadler, Glenn Edward. "Afterword: A Conversation with Maurice Sendak and Dr. Seuss." In *Teaching Children's Literature: Issues, Pedagogy, Resources*. Ed. Glenn Edward Sadler. New York: MLA, 1992. Pp. 241–50. [Interview took place in 1982.]

Sawin, Martica. *Surrealism in Exile and the Beginning of the New York School*. Cambridge: MIT Press, 1995.

Seuss, Dr. [Theodor Seuss Geisel]. *And to Think That I Saw It on Mulberry Street*. 1937. Random House, 1991.

———. *The Butter Battle Book*. New York: Random House, 1984.

———. *The Cat in the Hat*. 1957. New York: Random House, 1985.

———. *The Cat in the Hat Songbook*. Piano score and guitar chords by Eugene Poddany. New York: Random House, 1967.

———. *The Cat's Quizzer*. New York: Random House, 1976.

———. *Daisy-Head Mayzie*. New York: Random House, 1994.

———. *Horton Hatches the Egg*. New York: Random House, 1940.

———. *How the Grinch Stole Christmas!* New York: Random House, 1957.

———. *If I Ran the Circus*. 1956. New York: Random House, 1984.

———. *If I Ran the Zoo*. 1950. New York: Random House, 1977.

———. *The Lorax*. New York: Random House, 1971.

———. *Oh, the Places You'll Go!* New York: Random House, 1990.

———. *On Beyond Zebra!* 1955. New York: Random House, 1983.

———. *The Secret Art of Dr. Seuss*. New York: Random House, 1995.

———. *The Tough Coughs as He Ploughs the Dough: Early Cartoons and Articles by Dr. Seuss*. Ed. Richard Marschall. New York: William Morrow, 1987.

———. "We Always Were Suckers for Ridiculous Hats . . ." *PM* 29 April 1941: 20.

———. *Yertle the Turtle and Other Stories*. 1958. New York: Random House, 1986.

Smith, Dinitia. "A Purist's Creatures Go Commercial." *New York Times* national ed., 13 February 1997: B1, B12.

Steig, Michael. "Dr. Seuss's Attack on Imagination: *I Wish That I Had Duck Feet* and the Cautionary Tale." *Proceedings of the Ninth Annual Conference of the Children's Literature Association*. Boston: Northeastern University, 1983. Pp. 137–41.

Steinberg, Sybil S. "What Makes a Funny Children's Book?" *Publisher's Weekly* 27 February 1978: 87–90.

Torczyner, Harry. *Magritte: Ideas and Images*. Trans. Richard Miller. New York: Abrams, 1977.

Wittner, Lawrence S. *Cold War America: From Hiroshima to Watergate*. New York: Praeger, 1974.

Wolf, Tim. "Imagination, Rejection, and Rescue: Recurrent Themes in Dr. Seuss." *Children's Literature* 23 (1995): 137–64.

The Structure of the Moral Dilemma in Shiloh

Claudia Mills

Children's literature has long had the role of providing moral in-struction and shaping moral development.[1] Some notable children's books, however, go beyond the task of transmitting and inculcat-ing accepted values to portray children engaged in a process of real moral reflection that can itself transcend and challenge our shared values. Phyllis Reynolds Naylor's Newbery-winning novel *Shiloh* is re-markable for its recognition of certain fundamental ambiguities and limitations in the morality we share. The moral dilemma that eleven-year-old Marty Preston faces in the novel is extraordinarily complex, raising challenges both to how we reason about our obligations to members of the moral community and to how we define the scope of that community. The latter may occasion the novel's most significant philosophical triumph in its illumination of how we fail to apply even our most central and unambiguous moral principles to children and to animals.

In "real life," children struggle with sometimes extraordinary seri-ousness to develop into full-fledged moral agents. In *The Moral Life of Children* (1968) and *The Moral Intelligence of Children* (1997), Robert Coles provides moving case studies of children trying to sort through their moral obligations against a background of their parents' beliefs, their religious beliefs, and the transmitted beliefs of their culture. Children also seem to have a natural curiosity about the philosophical dimensions of their lives, as shown by Gareth Matthews's depictions of his successful attempts to engage children in philosophical dialogue (1980). I want to suggest that this capacity for philosophical per-plexity, turned toward the moral seriousness of our lives, makes *Shiloh* a wonderful vehicle for engaging children in sophisticated moral re-flection, for the questions *Shiloh* raises are ones that the professional philosophy literature itself has been struggling to answer.

An earlier version of this essay was presented at the 23d Annual International Con-ference of the Children's Literature Association in Charlotte, N.C., June 6–9, 1996. I am grateful to the audience there for many helpful comments, as well as to Elizabeth Keyser and the reviewers for *Children's Literature*.
Children's Literature 27, ed. Elizabeth Lennox Keyser (Yale University Press, © 1999 Hollins University).

The Generation of Moral Dilemmas

Is there always a right answer to the question "What should I do?" Many of us are tempted by the view that even if it may be difficult to determine what we should do in a given situation, there is indeed a correct answer. The task of moral theory, then, is to array the totality of our correct moral judgments into one systematized framework, providing an explanation and justification of how they fit together into one unified whole. The two leading secular moral theories developed since the eighteenth century are consequentialism (identified in its utilitarian form with Jeremy Bentham and John Stuart Mill) and deontology (identified with Immanuel Kant). According to consequentialism, the right act in any given situation is the act that produces the best consequences, usually understood in terms of the welfare of all those affected by the act. (Important for our purposes is that utilitarian consequentialists such as Bentham historically have defended the extension of moral considerability to all sentient creatures, including nonhuman animals, so that in evaluating actions we must look at their implications for both human and animal welfare.) On deontological (obligation-based) moral theories, the right thing to do is established by invoking moral obligations grounded in some way other than by appeal to consequences. For example, according to Kant, we must act only on maxims (principles) that can be consistently universalized and only with respect for other persons as ends in themselves.

A number of philosophers, however, have asked whether there is indeed always a right answer to the question "What should I do?" They suggest that we may sometimes face real moral dilemmas, which all the resources of moral theory are inadequate to resolve. A moral *dilemma* is more than merely a difficult moral choice. According to one recent definition, a "moral dilemma is a situation in which an agent S morally ought to do A and morally ought to do B but cannot do both, either because B is just not-doing-A or because some contingent feature of the world prevents doing both" (Gowans 3). Here the world presents us not with a merely difficult choice between a right action and a wrong action but with an impossible choice between two simultaneously required but mutually incompatible right actions, or, viewed otherwise, between two wrong actions, since whichever action one chooses, one will leave undone at least one other action equally obligatory from a moral point of view.

Apparent moral dilemmas tend to arise when consequentialism and deontology point in different directions in some problematic cases—when the best consequences can be produced (or disastrous consequences averted) only by violating some important moral principle (for example, by breaking a promise or telling a lie). Defenders of consequentialism or deontology usually reply to such challenges by insisting that the apparent moral dilemma dissolves when the underlying issues are looked at more carefully and filtered through the "correct" moral theory.

One may also argue in response to such problem cases, however, that no theory is adequate to the task of matching the complex nature of moral reality. Thomas Nagel, for example, in "The Fragmentation of Value," writes that we recognize the legitimate claims of so many diverse types of value that basic and irreducible conflict among them is "ubiquitous" (Nagel 180). Nor can we find a way out of moral conflict by relying on any simple priority rules that would tell us which kind of value to weight more heavily when two different kinds of value conflict, for the absoluteness of such priority rules is simply absurd: "It is absurd to hold that obligations can never outweigh rights, or that utility, however large, can never outweigh obligation" (177).

I argue in what follows that *Shiloh* offers an example of a moral dilemma that simultaneously affirms and undermines both the deontological and consequentialist strands of our ordinary morality. There is no one clear solution to Marty's dilemma available, either to Marty in the course of the story or to the reader in retrospective reflection after reading. The result of the moral inquiry in *Shiloh* is not moral despair, however, nor an abandonment of the attempt to live a morally serious life, but ultimate moral triumph.[2]

Consequences and Moral Obligation in Shiloh

The dilemma Marty Preston faces in *Shiloh* at first glance fits into the familiar framework of consequentialism pitted against deontological respect for moral duty.[3] Marty discovers a dog who is being abused by his owner, Judd Travers, and names the dog Shiloh. When Shiloh runs away from Judd to Marty, Marty decides to hide Shiloh from Judd and from his own family. On one side, we see the concern for welfare characteristic of consequentialism; we see concern for the suffering and happiness of one sentient creature. On the other side, we see respect for familiar moral duties not to lie, steal, and break promises.

So Marty faces the question whether it is permissible to violate these other moral duties in order to produce the morally desirable outcome of saving Shiloh.

Presented in this way, most readers would be initially sympathetic to the consequentialist argument—that Shiloh's welfare outweighs the moral prohibitions against lying, promise-breaking, and stealing. Marty himself at points characterizes his decision in these terms, disregarding the moral standing of the prohibitions in favor of concern for Shiloh. "A lie don't seem a lie anymore when it's meant to save a dog, and right and wrong's all mixed up in my head" (70).

But in Naylor's sensitive treatment of these issues, complexity quickly emerges to temper our first proconsequentialist response. Consequentialism judges acts by their consequences, and the consequences to Shiloh of Marty's hiding him turn out to be worse than the consequences of leaving him with Judd: a neighbor's vicious German shepherd leaps into the pen Marty built to hide Shiloh, leaving him severely injured and, even after he ultimately recovers, permanently lame. Marty reflects on this afterward: "Worst of all, I'd brought Shiloh here to keep him from being hurt, and what that German shepherd done to him was probably worse than anything Judd Travers would have brought himself to do, short of shootin' him, anyways" (96–97). Judd Travers says the same thing when he discovers what has happened: "Look what you done to my *dog!* . . . I sure never caused him an injury like this one. Wouldn't never have happened if you'd brought him back like I told you" (111). Marty closes his eyes: "Nothin' I can say to that" (111).[4]

Moreover, consequentialism insists that the right action is determined not by assessing the consequences to any one party but by looking at the consequences to *all* those affected by the act, extending out as far in time as one can reasonably foresee. Marty's dilemma is sharpened toward the end of the novel when consequentialist considerations, even understood only in terms of animal welfare, begin to extend more widely. Marty comes across Judd shooting a deer out of season; he decides to bargain with Judd not to report him, in exchange for Judd's promise to sell him Shiloh. But this means that future deer will now be in danger from Judd's careless bloodthirstiness, which Marty himself recognizes: "I'm so glad to be gettin' Shiloh, I can hardly think straight. But I'm thinkin' straight enough as I help drag that doe to Judd's to know that by lettin' him get away with this, I'm putting other deer in danger. He kill this one out of season, he'll figure maybe he can kill some more. To save Shiloh, I'm making it harder for deer" (125–26).

Likewise, as she decreases the attractions of the consequentialist solution, Naylor also increases the attractions of the deontologically based obligations that Marty must violate. These are not presented as items on some arbitrary and unmotivated list of commandments to be obeyed blindly. Instead, respect for moral obligation, in the world of *Shiloh,* both reveals and shapes moral character. We see Judd Travers for what he is not only through his cruelty to animals but also through his cheating Mr. Wallace at the corner store (22), through his breaking the antipoaching law, and through his breaking his promise at the end of the book to sell Shiloh to Marty. Marty begins to feel his own character warp as he continues his ever-escalating series of lies to protect Shiloh: "Funny how one lie leads to another and before you know it your whole life can be a lie" (60). Outer adherence to truth-telling and to promise-keeping can be a sign of inner integrity.

Moral duties are also situated within a larger social fabric. They are justified because of how they structure our interactions with others. Lies and broken promises lead to a loss of trust, to a rending of the fabric that binds together families and communities.[5] It is for this reason that Marty's mother doesn't want to lie to Marty's father about her discovery of Shiloh: "I never kept a secret from your dad in the fourteen years we've been married. . . . He ever finds out about this dog and knows I knew but didn't tell him, how could he trust me? If I keep this one secret from him, he'll think maybe there are more" (83). She does keep Marty's secret, though, with the result of a subsequent strain in the marriage. And Marty experiences at first hand the loss of his father's trust when his father asks him,

". . . What else you keeping from me?"

"*Nothing,* Dad!"

"How do I know that's not another lie?"

" 'Cause it's not."

"You saying so don't make it true." (93)

Thus, the reader is left rooting for Shiloh and hoping that Marty will be able to save him, but realizing that the costs of Marty's trying to do so are genuine—costs that do not evaporate with correct theoretical understanding of the situation.

Perhaps highlighting the contrast between philosophy and literature more generally, *Shiloh* ends up offering a profoundly antitheo-
retical response to the moral theorist, for moral theory is largely use-
less in resolving Marty's dilemma. Instead, what turns out to matter is
a heightened sense of moral particularity.[6] Marty's father twice challenges him as to why he is so concerned to save Shiloh when there are
thousands of other equally mistreated animals whose welfare—on a
strictly consequentialist view—should matter just as much as Shiloh's:
"If this dog's mistreated, he's only about one out of fifty thousand
animals that is" (24); "You think Judd Travers is the only one around
here hard-hearted toward his animals? . . . Open up your eyes, Marty.
Open your eyes!" (94). But Marty rejects this insistence that he be able
to generalize his concern for Shiloh to a concern for all mistreated
animals. It is perhaps the most troubling sign of Judd's moral blind-
ness that he does not see the particularity of his animals, signaled by
his refusal to name them: "Never name any of my dogs. Dogs one,
two, three, and four is all. . . . 'Git,' 'Scram,' 'Out,' and 'Dammit':
that's my dogs' names" (35). Dogs for Judd are interchangeable units:
"Lose one, I'll buy another" (35). It is when Marty names Shiloh as a
distinct individual that he acquires his particular and personal obligation toward him. Marty is not trying to save the world but to save
Shiloh—though perhaps saving him is the first step toward saving the
world. Moral judgment proceeds case by case, and it is never easy.

Persons Versus Animals

While *Shiloh* lays bare some of the complexities at the heart of ordinary morality, both affirming and challenging our consequentialist
and deontological commitments, it also offers a crusading challenge
to ordinary morality in the questions it raises about our treatment of
those who are not fully members of the moral community—particularly nonhuman animals but also to a certain extent children.

At three different points in the novel, Marty compares animals to
children: it has been a familiar tactic in the history of moral philosophy to try to extend moral consideration to some hitherto excluded
group by stressing its relevant similarity to some included group.
"What if [Shiloh] was a child? . . . If some kid was shaking like this
dog is shaking, you wouldn't feel no pull for keeping an eye on him?"
(24). To this his father replies simply, "This here's a dog, not a child,
and it's not our dog" (25). The other two points of comparison, how-

ever, raise questions about whether we fail as a society in protecting children just as we fail to protect animals. When Marty tells Judd, "I figure a dog's the same as a kid. You don't treat a kid right, he'll run off first chance he gets, too" (64), Judd responds with stories of how he was abused as a child by his father and still "turned out." Marty asks, "Turned out how?" The answer is clear: turned out to be himself an abuser. Finally, when Marty, desperate for some solution to his struggle to keep Shiloh, debates reporting Judd to the authorities for animal abuse, he thinks to himself, "Tyler County hasn't hardly got the money to investigate reports of children being kicked, Dad says, much less dogs" (113), highlighting the lack of value we, as a society, place on the welfare of both.[7]

Just as *The Adventures of Huckleberry Finn* more than a century earlier challenged existing notions of African Americans as property, capable of being bought and sold, so *Shiloh* raises parallel questions about our treatment of animals as property.[8] But whereas the character Huck shares the racist assumptions of his culture, Marty is an animal rights advocate from the first page of the novel, where he shows his squeamishness about eating the rabbit his father shot that day. Although he is not a vegetarian (and the issue of eating meat is never raised at any point in the novel), he is personally opposed to hunting, telling the reader that he shoots only at tin cans: "Never shoot at anything moving, though. Never had the slightest wish" (12).

Marty extends his concern for animals to the farthest fringes of animal creation, explicitly defending the rights of even insects and snakes. He is uncomfortable when his little sisters capture lightning bugs: "Seeing those bugs in a jar reminds me of Shiloh all chained up at Judd's, a prisoner as sure as those bugs" (31). He tells his sisters, "They'll die if you keep 'em in a jar" (32). Later, after having pretended to his sisters that he has seen a snake nearby in order to keep them from finding Shiloh's hideout, he responds to Dara Lynn's cry, "Kill it! Git your gun and blow its head off," with "Even snakes got the right to live" (62).

Throughout, Marty's parents insist to Marty that Shiloh is Judd Travers's property and that it is none of Marty's business how Judd chooses to treat him: "If it's Travers's dog, it's no mind of ours *how* he treats it" (24); "Judd Travers has the right to name his dog anything he likes or nothing at all. And you've got to get it through your mind that it's *his* dog, not yours, and put your mind to other things" (37); "You've got to go by the law. The law says that a man that pays money for a dog owns that dog" (94). In contrast, Marty claims that it is love, not money, that should establish the relation of belonging. When his mother points out to him yet again, "This dog don't belong to you," Marty shoots back, "Mine more than Judd's! . . . He only paid money for him. I'm the one who loves him" (82).

Marty is ultimately able to save Shiloh when he accidentally stumbles upon Judd in the act of killing a deer out of season; he can now blackmail Judd into agreeing to sell Shiloh to him in exchange for his promise not to report Judd (out-of-season killings carry with them a $200 fine). Although this point is not highlighted in the novel, it is clear that our societal and legal concern for animals extends only so far as establishing *when* they may be killed, not *whether*. It is a crime to kill a deer out of season; it is no crime to kill a deer in season. Although somewhat more protected by anticruelty laws, domestic animals in a sense lack even this much protection:

"What if a man shoots a dog?" I ask.

Dad looks over at me. "Dogs aren't ever in season, Marty. You know that."

"But what if a man shoots one, anyway?"

"That would be up to the sheriff to decide what to do, I guess." (38–39)

Shiloh does not try to settle the question of how much weight we should give to animal rights or interests or how these should be weighed against human interests when the two conflict. But in a novel that is extraordinarily sensitive to moral ambiguity, the moral considerability of animals emerges as a point beyond doubt or question. Through Naylor's skill as a novelist, the reader comes to care about Shiloh as deeply as Marty does and so to reject the premise that morality should be indifferent to how animals are treated.

Morality, Law, Culture, Religion

Most moral theories begin by trying to separate out, within the realm of the normative, that which is distinctively moral or ethical from action-guiding prescriptions based on law, culture, or religion. What we morally ought to do is not identical with what we legally ought to do, or with what most people in our culture usually do, for both law and culture could be wrong, as history showed us in Nazi Germany. Nor can what we morally ought to do be identified simply with what our religion tells us to do, for that will ground a legitimate ethical prescription only if we have some independent reason for accepting religious authority—and often we accept religious authority only because we think God is good, as shown by our independent moral evaluation of his commands.

In *Shiloh* we find Marty trying to separate what is right from what is legally, culturally, and religiously required. But even as Marty draws these familiar distinctions, in the end he finds that all four domains—morality, law, culture, religion—are in his world inextricably woven together.

Marty repeatedly challenges the authority of a law that would allow a man to own and mistreat an animal as Judd mistreats Shiloh. "What kind of a law is it, Ma, that lets a man mistreat his dog?" (82). When his father tells him that if he objects to the law, he should obey it while he works to change it, Marty asks, "What if there isn't time, Dad? Shiloh could be dead by the time somebody looked into the way Judd treats his dogs" (94). The law is neither infallibly correct in the line it draws between permitted and proscribed behavior nor able successfully to deter the behavior it proscribes.

Marty's world in *Shiloh* is the world of a close-knit rural Appalachian community with its own clearly defined code of conduct, to which Marty makes frequent reference in the novel. The code consists chiefly in neighborliness within boundaries set by an ethic of each minding his own business. When Marty's lies lead others in the community to think that his family has come on hard times, people pitch in to help with donations of food. Even Judd Travers stops to give Marty a ride into town. But the central organizing principle of the ethic of Friendly, West Virginia, is that "folks keep to their own business. . . . In Tyler County that's important. Way it's always been, anyhow" (23). This means that Marty would cause a serious rupture in the community should he decide to take Judd to court for animal abuse: "Around here it's serious business when you got a quarrel with your neighbor and you got to carry it as far as the law. Folks ain't that fond of Judd, and most of 'em likes my dad, but when it comes to taking a man's property I figure they'll side with Judd" (117). But Marty challenges this ethic, at least inwardly: "Dad wouldn't report Judd even if *he* saw him shoot a doe out of season, because that's the way it's always been around here. That don't necessarily make it right, of course . . ."

(130). Marty finds himself wondering, too, about "whose business it is when someone breaks the law. Wonder if Dad wouldn't never tell on Judd no matter what he done. Bet he would. There's got to be times that what one person does is everybody's business" (132–33).

Marty's own moral code is also steeped in religion. One does not sin, according to Marty's deeply devout mother, because one does not want to be "separated forever from God's love." Thus, when Marty eats his sister's chocolate Easter rabbit and later lies about it, his mother tells him, "Dara Lynn don't know who ate the ear off her candy rabbit and I don't know who did it, but Jesus knows. And right this minute Jesus is looking down with the saddest eyes on the person who ate that chocolate" (56). The memory of this episode leads Marty to offer his own prayer on what he should do in his dilemma over Shiloh: " 'Jesus,' I whisper finally, 'which you want me to do? Be one hundred percent honest and carry that dog back to Judd so that one of your creatures can be kicked and starved all over again, or keep him here and fatten him up to glorify your creation?' " (57). Marty answers this question himself: "If Jesus is anything like the story cards from Sunday school make him out to be, he ain't the kind to want a thin, little beagle to be hurt" (57).

But later Marty distances himself from a religiously based resolution to his problem. In a passage that strikingly parallels Huck Finn's famous declaration—if he has to go to hell for helping Jim to escape, "All right, then, I'll *go* to hell" (272)—Marty reflects on whether he'll go to hell for the lies he tells to save Shiloh: "I don't feel good about the lies I tell Dara Lynn or David or his ma. But I don't feel exactly bad, neither. If what Grandma Preston told me once about heaven and hell is true, and liars go to hell, then I guess that's where I'm headed. But she also told me that only people are allowed in heaven, not animals. And if I was to go to heaven and look down to see Shiloh left below, head on his paws, I'd run away from heaven sure" (73).

Yet even as Marty separates the question of what is right for him to do from the question of what is legally, culturally, and religiously required, in the course of *Shiloh*, law, culture, and religion play an essential role in arriving at the solution to the novel's central moral dilemma.

Marty is able to force Judd to make the agreement to sell Shiloh only by threatening to report him to the legal authorities for poaching. Marty retains his allegiance to law generally, even if he wishes that the law could go farther than it does toward the protection of animals or, for that matter, children. The law against poaching exists to protect pregnant and nursing does, to protect some kind of natural balance. And it is the sanctions attaching to violation of this law that allow Marty to negotiate his final bargain with Judd. In a world where men are not always good, law, with its attendant sanctions, is an important tool for ensuring moral compliance.

But it is one thing for Judd to make the agreement; it is another thing for him to keep it, and to keep it over the long term. The sanctions attending law—legal condemnation and punishment—cannot guarantee compliance with what the law requires. Marty knows that if he cannot win Judd over as a friend, Shiloh will be forever vulnerable to an "accident": "I don't want to make him mad. No use having a winner and loser, or the bad feelings would just go on. Don't want to have to worry about Shiloh when he's running loose and I'm in school. Don't want to feel that Judd's so sore at me he'll think up any excuse at all to run his truck over my dog" (140). In order to ensure enduring compliance, Marty must cultivate a continuing relationship with Judd as a neighbor, as a member of the moral community, rather than shunning and ostracizing him as a moral outcast. Marty comes to understand and even to pity Judd as he puts in his promised twenty hours' worth of work on Judd's property. Even though at one point he says of Judd, "I hate him more than the devil" (134), the novel is remarkable in its ultimate unwillingness to demonize its villain. Judd's moral failings, however grievous, are placed in a human context; we understand why Judd is the way he is, and we find ourselves rooting not for his damnation but for his redemption.

Finally, the novel concludes with a return to what I see as implicitly a religiously based morality. Halfway through Marty's promised twenty hours of work, Judd sneers that he is working for nothing, that their written agreement is worthless because it was signed without a witness. When Marty asks his parents that evening, "What's a witness?" his mother responds with the religious rather than the legal sense of the word: "Somebody who knows the Lord Jesus and don't mind tellin' about it" (138). His father supplies the legal sense: "Somebody who sees something happen and signs that it's true" (138). Marty decides that all he can do, in the face of Judd's renunciation of their contract, is to continue to follow through on it himself: "You and me made a bargain, . . . and I aim to keep my part of it" (139). He tells himself, "I got no choice. All I can do is stick to my side of the deal and see what happens. All in the world I can do" (140). The resolution of the stand-off comes when Marty, in essence, stands witness, in his mother's religious sense of the term, for an ethic of love, crystallized in his love for Shiloh. When Judd asks Marty, "What you going to do with that dog once he's yours?" the answer is just "Love him" (142). This answer finds a comfortable home in the novel's explicit invocation of one particular love-based ethic — Christianity.

Conclusion

At the end of *Shiloh* the moral ambiguity that has characterized Marty's dilemma throughout has been resolved into a desperate kind of moral certainty. Earlier, when Marty's father tells him, "I want you to do what's right," Marty shoots back at him the question, "What's right?" And for once in Marty's eleven years, "I think I have my dad stumped" (94). But the resolution of Marty's dilemma comes when, in the end, he witnesses for what is right in the face of Judd's refusal to do what is right. Here deontology and consequentialism at last come together. Marty does what he has to do to produce the consequence of saving Shiloh, and he does it not by telling a lie or breaking a promise but by keeping his word and living up to his half of a covenant, by continuing to stand by what he believes to be right.

How is this to be determined if not by appeal to any particular moral theory? Naylor shows Marty doing what Nagel argues that we must do, in the absence of any other alternative — we must rely on our best judgment: "I contend that there can be good judgment without total justification, either explicit or implicit" (180). This judgment is, for Nagel, an Aristotelian-style practical wisdom "which reveals itself over time in individual decisions rather than in the enunciation of general principles. It will not always yield a solution. . . . But in many cases it can be relied on to take up the slack that remains beyond the limits of rational argument" (180). In the novel's final paragraph, Marty reports that he has learned that "nothing is as simple as you guess — not right or wrong, not Judd Travers, not even me or this dog I got here" (144). But although right and wrong are seldom simple, in the end we can witness to the right as we see the right, a right identified with great difficulty and no guarantees, through attention to moral particularity, through a willingness to take seriously the diverse claims of law, culture, and love. Indeed, in the end, as Marty says, it is all that we can do.

Notes

1. See, e.g., Ann Scott MacLeod's fascinating discussion in *A Moral Tale,* as well as many of the works reprinted in *From Instruction to Delight,* edited by Patricia Demers and Gordon Moyles.

2. In thinking about the relation between moral dilemmas and moral seriousness, I am indebted to my colleague Ann Davis's "Moral Dilemmas."

3. As is common among philosophers, I use *duty* and *obligation* interchangeably.

4. It should be noted here that a reasonable consequentialism will need to judge acts not by their actual consequences but by their expected consequences, since it seems unfair and unreasonable to hold agents responsible for outcomes that they could not have foreseen. But here we can say that Marty should have had reason to doubt that his hiding Shiloh in this way would lead to an optimal outcome.

5. For a discussion of the fundamental moral significance of trust, see Annette C. Baier, "Trust and Antitrust."

6. In this Naylor may be giving voice to what some feminist writers have called "an ethics of care," which values concreteness rather than abstraction and particularized others rather than generalized others. See, for example, Nell Noddings, *Caring.*

7. As an interesting historical aside, a reviewer of this essay notes that it was the founding of the Society for the Prevention of Cruelty to Animals that heightened awareness of the abuse of children and led to various legal protections for them.

8. I do not mean here to be equating Shiloh with Jim in any other sense than that both are perceived as property, for Jim is clearly a moral agent in a way that Shiloh of course is not.

Works Cited

Baier, Annette C. "Trust and Antitrust." In *Moral Prejudices: Essays on Ethics.* Cambridge: Harvard University Press, 1994.

Coles, Robert. *The Moral Intelligence of Children.* New York: Random House, 1997.

———. *The Moral Life of Children.* Boston: Houghton Mifflin, 1968.

Davis, Ann. "Moral Dilemmas: Introductory Remarks." 1995. Typescript.

Demers, Patricia, and Gordon Moyles, eds. *From Instruction to Delight.* Toronto: Oxford University Press, 1982.

Glover, Jonathan, ed. *Utilitarianism and Its Critics.* New York: Macmillan, 1990.

Gowans, Christopher W., ed. *Moral Dilemmas.* New York: Oxford University Press, 1987.

Kant, Immanuel. *Grounding for the Metaphysics of Morals.* 1785. Trans. James W. Ellington. Indianapolis: Hackett, 1981.

MacLeod, Ann Scott. *A Moral Tale: Children's Fiction and American Culture 1820–1860.* Hamden, Conn.: Archon, 1975.

Matthews, Gareth. *Philosophy and the Young Child.* Cambridge: Harvard University Press, 1980.

Nagel, Thomas. "The Fragmentation of Value." In *Moral Dilemmas.* Ed. Christopher W. Gowans. New York: Oxford University Press, 1987.

Naylor, Phyllis Reynolds. *Shiloh.* New York: Atheneum, 1991.

Noddings, Nell. *Caring: A Feminine Approach to Ethics and Moral Education.* Los Angeles: University of California Press, 1984.

Twain, Mark. *The Adventures of Huckleberry Finn.* 1884. New York: Grosset and Dunlap, 1948.

Reviews

Sacred Text and Secular Values

Gillian Adams

The Bible for Children: From the Age of Gutenberg to the Present, by Ruth B. Bottigheimer. New Haven: Yale University Press, 1996.

For years, historians of children's literature have only given lip service to the importance of Bible stories for children, if they mention them at all. As Ruth Bottigheimer herself comments, with the recent exception of Patricia Demers's *Heaven upon Earth* (1993) and articles by such critics as Mitzi Myers, "scholars and intellectuals have scorned moral and religious literature for children since the early nineteenth century" (226 n. 29). Bottigheimer has corrected this serious omission with a fascinating book—winner of the 1996 Children's Literature Association Book Award—that is the fruit of extensive research for more than ten years in forty-three libraries, personal collections, and bookstores in eight American and European countries and in at least five languages. As a look at her fifty-page bibliography of primary and secondary sources attests, she has consulted works ranging from the medieval period to books and articles published as late as 1993. Yet, in spite of its erudition, *The Bible for Children* avoids modern academic-speak, indeed is so clearly written and generally reader-friendly (with, for example, all foreign-language quotations translated and the original text relegated to the end notes), that it is suitable for interested undergraduates as well as graduate students and professors. This is not to say that the work lacks critical sophistication. Bottigheimer wrestles here with a number of difficult theological and social issues, including the woman question, and has initiated paths of inquiry that should provide provocative material for many further discussions.

Bottigheimer's major claim is that children's Bibles through the

Children's Literature 27, ed. Elizabeth Lennox Keyser (Yale University Press, © 1999 Hollins University).

ages do not, as one might assume, simply retell Bible stories in simpler
language. Rather, by means of additions, omissions, and the choice
of illustrations, "children's Bible stories teach far more than Bible
content . . . [they are] an important part of the transmission of cultural norms and values from one generation to the next" (xi–xii).
Bottigheimer begins her book with a look at the means of transmission of biblical material, which can include such items as catechisms,
summaries, poems, riddle books, puzzles, and coloring books. Her
working definition of what her book is about, however, is "prose re-
workings of the narrative sections of the Bible for child readers" (4).

The first of these prose re-workings, or "precursor texts," that Bottigheimer discusses is by a twelfth-century lecturer in the cathedral
schools, Peter Comestor (c. 1100–1178). His *Historica Scholastica* consisted of only the narrative parts of the Bible, based on the Latin
Vulgate, but also included material from other sources such as Jose-
phus, Eusebius, and early and contemporary commentaries. The *Historica Scholastica* was an immediate success and translated into French
by Guiart Desmoulins in 1289, with a number of alterations, and
vernacular versions soon existed all over Europe. As Bottigheimer
makes clear, Comestor's was a fluid text, and multiple copies exist
in a variety of versions, illustrated and unillustrated, cheap and ex-
pensive, glossed and defaced by many hands. Although Bottigheimer
states in this book that the *Historica Scholastica* was originally intended
for university students (15), she now suspects that younger children
may have been part of the intended audience (letter, 25 February
1997), as the simple language indicates. It is also well to remember
that Comestor was a schoolteacher and that the actual age of most
twelfth-century university students was between thirteen and sixteen.
Printed for school use as late as the sixteenth century, by that time the
Historica Scholastica was already well on its way to oblivion. Nevertheless, much of its content had become an integral part of popular culture, and the impact of some of Comestor's extrabiblical details has
lasted well into the twentieth century. For example, in his account of
Noah's drunkenness, Comestor added the word *irridens* ("mocking")
to the Bible's neutral presentation of Ham's response to his father's
nakedness, making the tale into one of filial disrespect (see 104 ff.).
Thus Comestor provides a justification for Noah's curse on Ham and
his descendants and, ultimately, for the enslavement of blacks.

Bottigheimer's second precursor or "model" text is Martin Luther's
Passional (1529), a fifty-two-page printed pamphlet on the life of Christ

in German. It was intended for "children and simple folk" (23) and illustrated with simplified woodcuts based on Albrecht Dürer's *Small Passion.* Unlike the *Historica Scholastica,* it consisted only of words from the Bible, a concept well ahead of its time, and was only in print for thirty-seven years. After Luther's death it dropped out of use, but it prefigured an important genre.

After a general survey of the variety of children's Bibles to be found from the early modern period to the present in Europe (including Russia) and the United States (chapter 3), the second, and major, section of *The Bible for Children* examines a series of problematic Bible stories and looks at what their different versions can tell us about the children for whom they were published and the societies in which they lived. Given the mass of material with which Bottigheimer has to deal, a limited choice is a necessary strategy, and it leaves room for researchers to investigate a number of other stories and their permutations that are necessarily beyond the scope of this book. Bottigheimer discusses (after a chapter on the changing nature of God and a later chapter on the injunction to work) the sacrifice of Isaac, the death of Absalom, Lot's incest with his daughters, Noah's drunkenness, Joseph and Potiphar's wife, David and Bathsheba, the rape of Dinah, the rape and murder of the Levite's wife, Jael and Sisera, the Tower of Babel, the parting of the Red Sea, the marriage at Cana (miracles), the Crucifixion, and, perhaps the most controversial account of all, that of Adam and Eve in the Garden of Eden.

Until we get to the Tower of Babel, then, the stories discussed here have to do with the death of children, sex, and violence. Bottigheimer's choice of passages appears to be based on the Bible stories that she feels are especially problematic in regard to child readers, particularly girls. This is not to say that such stories are unimportant, but only to note that a different researcher might have come up with a different set of choices. In fact, as a prepubescent child reader of Bible stories both in a large, illustrated volume (title forgotten) and in the versions in classic comics, I was familiar with these stories, but they were by and large not the ones—with the exception of the sacrifice of Isaac, the Crucifixion, and the Fall—that puzzled or bothered me. These murders, rapes, and incestuous relationships were not central to my concerns at the time. Rather, I worried about what I perceived as the unfair and arbitrary judgments of the God of the Old Testament, for example the story of Jepthah's daughter, which Bottigheimer does discuss as an example of the rule that adult sin seems to result in child death (72). And they were not the stories that I (along with other children, I suspect) was most interested in, such as those about the ark and the flood, or Joseph and the coat of many colors (of which the Potiphar's wife section is only a minor part), David and Jonathan and David and Goliath, Moses, Ruth, or Jonah.

The thorny question of children's responses to Bible stories at any period is perhaps largely unresolvable, given the many variables and the paucity of published research on the subject. But we must be careful not to assume that those responses will be identical to our adult ones. If I was not bothered by these stories, would today's children (one of Bottigheimer's concerns), who are more familiar with sex and violence, if only through the media, be affected by them? Likewise, children of earlier periods grew up faster and were more exposed at an earlier age to material and experiences that we now consider offensive and unacceptable. Indeed, it is often argued that the "innocence" of children is only a Romantic construction. Thus I also wonder what impact the stories that Bottigheimer examines and is offended by had on the children of the past.

Nevertheless, Bottigheimer provides ample evidence that as time progressed, at least some providers of children's Bibles came to the conclusion that certain stories were less than suitable and made an effort to soften lurid material, particularly in regard to sex, by changing the story, omitting parts of it, or leaving it out altogether. These efforts, however, as well as the promotion of values such as filial obedience at all costs, were always subject to the variables of period, religious group (Catholic, Protestant, Jewish, and reformed congregations of various sorts), nationality, social class, intellectual climate, and the sources of the children's Bible in question—which, until recently, were not the Bible itself but other children's Bibles. One has to admire Bottigheimer's skill in juggling these variables in order to arrive at her conclusions regarding what the versions of each story reflect about the cultural values being promoted at the time. But a caveat is in order here. Although each chapter is more than sufficient unto itself, Bottigheimer has published since 1990 twelve or so articles in scholarly journals on aspects of the material in *The Bible for Children,* which are referred to in the endnotes. The serious researcher on a given subject would do well to consult these further explorations.

One of the most important features of this book, and one not included in articles by Bottigheimer that I have seen to date, is the illustrations. She provides a number of pictures of different versions of the same scene for most of the stories discussed, and she uses them to good effect to demonstrate how societal responses to the stories change: for example, in the display of Noah's genitals or in the foregrounding, backgrounding, or softening of the gory details of the Crucifixion. Discussions of this latter event and of the story of Adam and Eve's fall comprise the last two chapters of the book, and whatever the importance to individual child readers of the earlier biblical episodes Bottigheimer deals with, no one could argue with the centrality of the last two chapters. Here we see the difference between the "cerebral tone" of the prototypical Catholic portrayal by Fontaine (182) and the "narrative of violence" and new phrasings "stitched together" by the Lutheran Hübner (183). At the end of the twentieth century, both Protestants and Catholics have chosen to shift their focus to the Resurrection as the culminating event in the Christian narrative, and recent collections of Bible stories have found a number of ways to diminish the former emphasis on the Crucifixion.

Bottigheimer ends her book with a discussion of the changing perspectives on who is to blame for the Fall: Adam, Eve, or the serpent. This chapter is informed by recent feminist discussions such as those by Elaine Pagels and Mieke Bal, discussions that have yet to be fully reflected in versions of the Fall written for children. In fact, Bottigheimer notes that "the closer we come to the nineteenth and twentieth centuries . . . the greater Eve's share of guilt" (203) in such versions. She also notes the stark contrast between the sin-based Christian interpretations of Genesis 3 and those in Jewish Bibles, which gloss over the episode or omit it entirely. Bottigheimer ends her discussion with very recent attempts at down-playing the centrality of the Fall, as well as at ecumenism and at returning to the Bible's actual words stripped of centuries of additions and rephrasings.

Bottigheimer's seminal work is a vital beginning to research in a long-neglected area of popular culture in general and children's culture in particular. Countless authors have detailed the importance of religious matters in the formation of their character, as, for example, Frank McCourt in his 1996 award-winning memoir, *Angela's Ashes*. Studies by Robert Coles and others also testify to the centrality of religious, ethical, and philosophical questions in children's thinking. The number of children's authors who address these questions, either overtly or covertly, is legion. Moreover, children are part of the audience for media presentations of Bible stories that now may be their major or only way of learning about them. Although such presentations are beyond the scope of Bottigheimer's book, they certainly should be addressed by children's literature critics.

Finally, Yale is to be congratulated for publishing this handsome book with so many illustrations. If some are not as clear as others, it seems likely that the antiquity of the source is to blame. There are a few typos in the Works Cited, and I am puzzled by the statement on 199–200 that Anne de Vries's children's Bible reached a large number of European children from 1948 onward when later in the text and in the Works Cited its publication date is given as 1989. Nevertheless, these are quibbles. Bottigheimer's *The Bible for Children* should be on the library shelves of every institution that has a program in children's literature, education, or religion, and serious scholars of children's literature will want to own, and to ponder, a copy for themselves.

Three Ways of Looking at Victorian Fantasies

Jan Susina

An Expression of Character: The Letters of George MacDonald, ed. Glenn
Edward Sadler. Grand Rapids, Mich.: Eerdmans, 1994.

The Literary Products of the Lewis Carroll-George MacDonald Friendship, by
John Docherty. Lewiston, N.Y.: Mellen, 1995.

*Inventing Wonderland: The Lives and Fantasies of Lewis Carroll, Edward
Lear, J. M. Barrie, Kenneth Grahame, and A. A. Milne,* by Jackie Wullschläger. New York: Free, 1995.

These three books cover the same general subject: the life and literary works of major Victorian fantasy writers for children. Since
Sadler, Docherty, and Wullschläger use different critical approaches
to their topic, it is fascinating to realize how little these books as a
group have in common with one another. The George MacDonald
who emerges from Sadler's massive collection of letters barely resembles the George MacDonald whom Docherty shows to be a writer
involved in an intense and extended literary wrestling match with
Lewis Carroll. Only one single letter to Carroll appears in Sadler's
volume, a brief response to Carroll's request for an introduction to
Noel Paton, whom Carroll was considering as a possible illustrator
for *Looking-Glass.* The Lewis Carroll who provides the title for Wullschläger's group biography of five pivotal Victorian and Edwardian
fantasy writers is not the same Carroll who Docherty claims was involved in a long-standing literary and religious debate with MacDonald that, he suggests, resulted in their children's books being filled
with reciprocating allusions. MacDonald is excluded from Wullschläger's master list of fantasy writers and barely makes a mention in her
book.

Sadler's *An Expression of Character* is a much-needed collection of
letters of George MacDonald, perhaps best known by children's literature scholars for *At the Back of the North Wind, The Princess and the Goblin,*
and *The Princess and Curdie,* as well as his many visionary fairy tales.
Sadler has also edited the outstanding two-volume *The Gifts of the Child*

Children's Literature 27, ed. Elizabeth Lennox Keyser (Yale University Press, © 1999
Hollins University).

Christ: Fairy Tales and Stories for the Childlike (Eerdmans, 1973), which is the standard edition for MacDonald's fairy tales. *An Expression of Character* will undoubtedly find an important and useful place next to *The Gifts of the Child Christ* and William Raeper's *George MacDonald* (Lion, 1987) as essential scholarly texts for anyone wishing to do serious critical work on MacDonald. Sadler has chronologically arranged more than three hundred letters divided into six major periods of MacDonald's life. Sadler provides necessary annotations to the correspondence, an accurate register of the letters, and an index to the people and places mentioned in the collection. Although not as extensive or detailed in its scholarly notes as Morton Cohen's two-volume *The Letters of Lewis Carroll* (Oxford, 1979), *An Expression of Character* is a treasure trove for those interested in MacDonald's religious beliefs.

There is one great limitation to this volume, however, although the fault lies not with Sadler but with MacDonald. MacDonald's withdrawal into total silence during the final years of his life is well known, as is the complexity of his highly mystical and mythopoetic prose. Any reader hoping to find the "golden key" to unlock the mysteries of his intricate fantasies will be sorely disappointed. In one letter to a cousin, MacDonald explains, "A man whose business is writing is seldom fond of letters" (328). Although MacDonald dutifully wrote hundreds of letters, they are surprisingly flat and impersonal when compared to his emotionally and erotically charged fiction. The only two letters that equal MacDonald's published work are a touching letter to John Ruskin written four days after the death of Rose La Touche and a guiltily penned note to Thomas Carlyle begging him to duplicate a letter written to a mutual friend that MacDonald had inadvertently misplaced. MacDonald avoids analysis of his work in the letters; as he wrote to A. P. Watt, his literary agent, "I will do nothing to bring my personality before the public in any way farther than my work in itself necessitates" (355).

Occasionally there is a brief reference to his own work, such as the letter to his wife in which he suggests that *The Princess and the Goblin* is "as good work of the kind as I can do, and I think will be the most complete thing I have done" (174). But those seeking insights to MacDonald's fantasies are better off reading his "The Fantastic Imagination" than the letters collected in *An Expression of Character*.

A strikingly different look at MacDonald is provided when Docherty places MacDonald's literary works next to those written by Lewis Carroll and argues forcefully that for forty years the two writers engaged in a spirited "literary game with each other," confirming William Blake's dictum that "Opposition Is True Friendship" (xii). The mention of Blake reveals much about *Literary Products,* since this study resembles a wildly hermeneutical study that promises to reveal the meaning behind all of the esoteric symbolism and personal mythology that are imbedded in Blake's poetry. Several of Docherty's charts, which are meant to illuminate "the structure of Alice's Wonderland trials as a caduceus" (115) or "Alice's trials and transformations superimposed upon the cycle of the year" (172), for example, are worthy of the visual imagery of Blake, or at least that of Harold Bloom's interpretation of Blake.

Since Lewis Carroll makes up half of this dense study, which is restricted to the influence of the two writers on each other, I must say this is the most curious interpretation of Carroll that I have read since Abraham Ettleson's *Lewis Carroll "Through the Looking Glass" Decoded* (Philosophical Library, 1966), which maintains that *Looking-Glass* is a result of Carroll's close reading of religious writing of Baal Shem Tov and that it has more in common with the *Jewish Daily Prayer Book* than with chess. I have serious reservations with Docherty's analysis and yet, as the King of Hearts says in *Alice in Wonderland,* "I seem to see some meaning in them, after all" (155). This is no parody of scholarship like Frederick Crews's *The Pooh Perplex,* but an amazingly detailed, overly convoluted, yet highly insightful book that is woefully in need of editing.

The friendship between MacDonald and Carroll, and their admiration for each other's writing, have been long acknowledged, although no scholar has ever attempted as rigorous or extended a comparison of the texts as does Docherty. The Novalis epigraph that MacDonald used for the concluding chapter of *Phantastes*— "Our life is no dream; but it ought to become one, and perhaps will" (180)—is revised to "Life, what is it but a dream?" (347) in the final line of the valedictory poem that concludes *Looking-Glass.* The epigram, which MacDonald was fond of citing throughout his work, clearly influenced much of Carroll's writing, including *Alice in Wonderland, Looking-Glass,* and *Sylvie and Bruno.* Docherty suggests that MacDonald modeled the figure of the bad knight, who is Anodos's double in *Phantastes,* on Carroll. Docherty calls this portrait a "character assassination" of a "helper of girl children" (301) that eventually pressured Carroll into producing his positive image as the White Knight in *Looking-Glass.* MacDonald followed up his allusion to Carroll in *Phantastes*

with "My Uncle Peter," a short tale in which a lonely, older man
befriends a young girl but her family puts an end to their relationship. Uncle Peter falls into depression, but proper theology revives
him; Docherty sees the story as intended as both a warning to and
an attempt to comfort Carroll, who was beginning to involve himself
with the Liddell family. Carroll responded to MacDonald's "My Uncle
Peter" with the poem "Stolen Waters," which is an attempt to address
MacDonald's criticism. These short texts then lead to fairy tales by
both that feature Alice exploring her unconscious: Carroll's *Alice's
Adventures Underground,* which would later become *Alice in Wonderland,* and MacDonald's "Cross Purposes." Docherty continues to find
example after example of allusions to Carroll in MacDonald's writing
and vice versa.

Docherty's most astonishing claim is that *Alice in Wonderland* has
as many and as significant references to *Phantastes* as it does to Alice
Liddell. As audacious as this sounds, Docherty compellingly shows
that the structure of *Alice in Wonderland* both parallels that of Mac-
Donald's "Cross Purposes" and then inverts the structure of *Phantastes.* The study continues in this cross-referencing fashion, stating
that Carroll's "Bruno's Revenge" was written in response to *Phantastes* and MacDonald replied to "Bruno's Revenge" with "The Giant's
Heart." Throughout their careers, Docherty claims, MacDonald and
Carroll continued the complicated literary call-and-response, Carroll's *Looking-Glass* being written in reaction to MacDonald's *Adela
Cathcart* and MacDonald's *Lilith* being an answer to *Looking-Glass.*

This is a difficult and frequently perplexing book, and by the conclusion, the reader might think that Docherty has uncovered so many
hidden passageways between the two writers that, like the city of
Gwyntystorm in MacDonald's *The Princess and the Curdie,* the entire
structure seems to collapse of its own weight. The chief limitation is
that Docherty examines MacDonald and Carroll almost myopically
and does not sufficiently place them in the wider context of the Victorian sphere. Although I have no doubts that both writers read each
other with as much care as Docherty claims, both read widely in multiple areas and were undoubtedly influenced by other writers. But
if even half of what Docherty claims about the literary relationship
between MacDonald and Carroll is correct, then this is one of the
most original and significant analyses of Carroll produced in the past
twenty years.

Whereas Docherty's book suffers from overambition, the opposite is true for Wullschlèger's *Inventing Wonderland*. Using the lives and works of Lewis Carroll, Edward Lear, J. M. Barrie, Kenneth Grahame, and A. A. Milne, she makes the case that the Victorian and the Edwardian periods constituted a golden age of fantasy writing for children. This is hardly an original concept. Humphrey Carpenter's *Secret Gardens: The Golden Age of Children's Literature from Alice in Wonderland to Winnie-the-Pooh* (Houghton Mifflin, 1985) made a similar point ten years earlier and in a far more convincing fashion. One wonders who the intended audience for this book is, since it is primarily a synthesis of previous research. Admittedly, there are some slight variations between the two books: Wullschlèger includes Edward Lear, who is missing from *Secret Gardens,* but Carpenter includes chapters on Charles Kingsley, George MacDonald, E. Nesbit, and Beatrix Potter in his survey. Wullschlèger and Carpenter do not do as good a job as Stephen Prickett (*Victorian Fantasy* [Indiana University Press, 1979]) and Gillian Avery (*Nineteenth Century Children* [Hodder and Stoughton, 1965]) do in placing these fantasy writers in the broader and more carefully examined literary context of Victorian and Edwardian culture that includes texts written for children and adults.

Moreover, Wullschlèger's book is riddled with errors. It is unclear why her chapter on Carroll precedes the one on Lear whereas the rest of the book follows chronologically. She argues that these five writers created "between 1865 and 1930" a "radical new literature for children" (4), although Lear published *A Book of Nonsense* in 1846. Wullschlèger reports that Catherine Sinclair's *Holiday House* is "a collection of stories about fairies and giants" (102), which seems to suggest that she has read not the novel but only the frequently reprinted interpolated fairy tale that Uncle David tells Laura and Harry. She maintains that "the golden age of Victorian and Edwardian children's books appeared to come from nowhere" (97), which sounds as though she has chosen to ignore how fairy tales and literary fairy tales modified the content of children's literature during the first half of the nineteenth century, as shown in the scholarship of Jack Zipes, U. C. Knoepflmacher, and Brian Alderson. She repeats the charming but discredited story that the dormouse of Carroll's *Wonderland* was based on Dante Gabriel Rossetti's pet wombat.

Many of Wullschlèger's conclusions seem equally flawed. She argues that Lear's limericks reveal "classlessness" (73). Other critics suggest that the limericks reveal inflexible codes of Victorian society personified as the unnamed "they" in the final line who regularly punish individuals who dare to vary from accepted behavior. Wullschlèger examines this group of writers and argues for their childhood unhappiness and disappointments as the basis for their creation of fantasies that idealized childhood, although she acknowledges that A. A. Milne simply doesn't fit the pattern, since he was a "happy child" who became "a charming young man excelling in the adult playground of prewar London" (181).

Despite the many problems with this book, Wullschlèger does make some valuable connections. Her chapter on J. M. Barrie is the strongest in the study; she situates Barrie's *Peter Pan* among the numerous literary Pans that were part of the cultural landscape of the period, including Robert Louis Stevenson's essay "Pan's Pipes," Maurice Hewlett's play "Pan and the Young Sheperds," Rudyard Kipling's *Puck of Pook's Hill,* and Aubrey Beardsley's *Under the Hill.* Wullschlèger's pairing of Kenneth Grahame and Thomas Hardy as the two great writers of the period engaged by "the rural myth" and championing rural tradition against the modernist enemy that would eventually defeat them (168) is equally persuasive.

Each of these books contains serious limitations, although they are different in nature and varying in degree. Of the three, Docherty's study, although it is the most complicated of the group, is also the one that will most reward the reader who is willing to engage in its argument.

Works Cited

Carroll, Lewis. *Alice's Adventures in Wonderland* and *Through the Looking-Glass.* 1865, 1872. New York: Puffin, 1962.
Docherty, John. *The Literary Products of the Lewis Carroll-George MacDonald Friendship.* Lewiston, N.Y.: Mellen, 1995.
MacDonald, George. *An Expression of Character: The Letters of George MacDonald.* Ed. Glenn Edward Sadler. Grand Rapids, Mich.: Eerdmans, 1994.
———. Phantastes *and* Lilith. Introduction by C. S. Lewis. 1858, 1895. Grand Rapids, Mich.: Eerdmans, 1964.
Wullschlèger, Jackie. *Inventing Wonderland: The Lives and Fantasies of Lewis Carroll, Edward Lear, J. M. Barrie, Kenneth Grahame, and A. A. Milne.* New York: Free, 1995.

Louisa May Alcott: New Texts and Contexts

Christine Doyle

Norna; or The Witch's Curse, by Louisa May Alcott. General editor Juliet McMaster. Edmonton, Canada: Juvenilia, 1994.

A Long Fatal Love Chase, by Louisa May Alcott. New York: Random House, 1995.

The Inheritance, by Louisa May Alcott. Edited by Joel Myerson and Daniel Shealy. New York: Dutton, 1997.

Louisa May Alcott on Race, Sex, and Slavery. Edited and introduced by Sarah Elbert. Boston: Northeastern University Press, 1997.

Louisa May Alcott: An Intimate Anthology. New York Public Library Collector's Edition. New York: Doubleday, 1997.

Louisa May Alcott in the twentieth century may remind one of the Energizer bunny: she keeps going and going—and going. Spurred on by the collections of Alcott's sensation fiction uncovered and published under the direction of Madeleine Stern beginning in 1975 (a new "omnibus" volume containing all the recently uncovered short stories, *Louisa May Alcott Unmasked,* was published by Northeastern University Press in 1995), interest in what *else* the author of *Little Women* wrote continues more than a hundred years after her death in 1888. Two adult novels, *Work* and *Moods,* were reprinted in 1977 and 1991, respectively, after being out of print for decades. Volumes of Alcott's letters and journals more complete than Ednah Dow Cheney's *Life, Letters, and Journals* (1889) had included appeared in 1987 and 1989. Neither popular nor scholarly interest in Alcott's work shows any signs of abating; although *Little Women* remains Alcott's one true masterpiece for most scholars, several newly available works demonstrate anew her considerable talent and her wide-ranging interests, providing ever more glosses on her classic novel and her phenomenal career.

Considering the newest publications first demonstrates just how many ways there are of looking at Louisa May Alcott. The New York

Children's Literature 27, ed. Elizabeth Lennox Keyser (Yale University Press, © 1999 Hollins University).

Public Library uses *An Intimate Anthology* to showcase some of its fascinating collection of photographs, illustrations, and manuscripts featuring Alcott, her work, and her Concord home. The volume reprints some generally available materials, such as *Hospital Sketches,* "Transcendental Wild Oats," letters, journal entries, and two sensation stories, but also some much less accessible materials, including five poems and several recollections of Alcott from around the turn of the century. The many photographs, manuscripts, and illustrations in this handsome volume tantalize enough to make one consider a trip to New York to view the collection in person.

Sarah Elbert's intriguing *Louisa May Alcott on Race, Sex, and Slavery* draws together four of Alcott's Civil War stories and an 1864 article from the *Commonwealth* in which Alcott discusses letters from "several members of one of the colored regiments" (41) who had been taught rudimentary literacy by female volunteers while they were encamped at Readville. She frames the letters with her own commentary on the soldiers' courage and more particularly on their eagerness for education: she praises their courage in entering "the double battle they must fight against treason and ignorance" (44). The volume concludes with a chapter from the United States Sanitary Commission report, also published in 1864, delineating conditions among the freed men and women in what were essentially Civil War refugee camps. As Elbert demonstrates, Alcott drew liberally from such reports for her own Civil War stories. That the collection includes a children's story, "Nelly's Hospital," testifies to the fact that critics increasingly are looking at the larger context of Alcott's whole career and the interconnections between her works in several genres for several audiences—a concept for which Elizabeth Keyser's *Whispers in the Dark* (1993) must be acknowledged as a groundbreaking model.

Because two of the stories, "M. L." and "My Contraband," have been reprinted elsewhere recently, the most important value of this particular collection lies in Elbert's provocative but well-grounded introduction. Issues of "race, sex, and slavery" come together most forcefully around considerations of miscegenation or "amalgamation"; Elbert convincingly demonstrates the threat that public fear of sexually mixing the races posed to the abolitionist movement and how that fear was used against abolitionists. Her application of the "gendered bodies" work of critics such as Lora Romero and Nancy Bentley to the stories in the collection (several of which do have cross-racial sexual implications) makes for fascinating reading, as does the less controversial but equally interesting examination of Alcott's propensity for using her fiction as a social project.

Two works of Alcott juvenilia have surfaced or resurfaced in recent years, the first thanks to Juliet McMaster and her students in a course called "Classics of Children's Literature," the second due to a fortunate find by Joel Myerson and Daniel Shealy at Harvard's Houghton Library. *Norna; or, The Witch's Curse* is a melodrama written by Alcott (with at least some contributions from her sister Anna) at about age fifteen and immortalized as the Christmas theatrical in *Little Women*. McMaster's students have previously published juvenile works by Jane Austen, Charlotte Brontë, and Lady Wortley Montagu; they prepare and edit text, write introductions and textual notes, and illustrate the volumes they undertake.

Norna is a story of disguise, murder, and vengeance, the latter with the assistance of the title character, a witch. Alcott's interest in the Gothic romance (is the "castle of Rodolpho" a take-off on Radcliffe's Udolpho?), as well as her knowledge of Shakespeare, are evident in the plot, characters, and trappings of the play. Norna herself, a witch working to bring a remorseless murderer to justice, may foreshadow Alcott's lifelong interest in powerful female characters, at least one of whom, Jean Muir of *Behind a Mask,* is repeatedly referred to as a witch. Also of interest here are the collaborative nature of the playwriting, although there is only Anna's word on what she wrote ("the love part," [5]), and the commentary on the intricacies of performing the plays, particularly when only Louisa and Anna could be depended upon, and the other two sisters only occasionally prevailed upon, to perform.

No doubt McMasters's series is an exciting and worthwhile enterprise for burgeoning scholars, but sometimes the scholars' inexperience works against them. The introduction, for example, paints a picture of Alcott's life with only the broadest strokes, makes factual errors, and does not seem to be aware of Alcott's immersion in sensation fiction during the 1860s. The two illustrators do not seem to have been able to decide whether the play is a lush melodrama or a cartoon; in their art, it wavers back and forth between the two. The endnotes repeatedly refer to parallels to Marlowe's *Dr. Faustus* when one of the great obsessions of Alcott's literary life was not Marlowe's but Goethe's version of the tale. It seems that many of these limitations could have been avoided by a stronger editorial hand, possibly one with more background in Alcott studies than the students could be expected to have. (Why, for example, did someone not notice that this is a work of Alcott "at about fifteen" in the preface and at sixteen on the last page?) Notable for the high quality of their contributions to the volume are Erika Rothwell, whose essay connects *Norna* to Alcott's other works in some fine and insightful ways, and Michael Londry for his textual history, a well-researched and informative appendix. Alcott scholars may find little new here, especially since the larger volume from which the play is taken, *Comic Tragedies*, is generally accessible though out of print, but the project itself is certainly a worthy undertaking.

Joel Myerson and Daniel Shealy came across *The Inheritance*—which a note in Alcott's hand called "my first novel written at seventeen"—while working on *The Selected Letters of Louisa May Alcott* at the Houghton Library. The media hype about the book was and is off-putting: Dutton's dust cover recounts an incident from *Little Women* that is clearly a fictionalized reference to *Moods*, her first *published* novel, but says "Here at last [*The Inheritance*] is the book 'Jo' wrote"; the television movie broadcast when the book first appeared Americanizes the tale and ultimately bears little resemblance to Alcott's text beyond the title. Once one gets past these annoyances, however, the book itself is an interesting piece of juvenilia.

For one thing, it provides early evidence of Alcott's fascination with Charlotte Brontë's *Jane Eyre*, published just two years before Alcott wrote *The Inheritance* and always one of her favorite books. The plot concerns a young woman who functions as a governess to the youngest daughter of a wealthy English family, a beautiful but proud rival for an older lord's affections, revealing tableaux along the way and an inheritance that comes along just in time to turn all the tables at the end. Perhaps Alcott was reading *Wuthering Heights* as well: Edith Adelon's "status incongruence" (Peterson 15) results from the fact that she was originally picked up as an orphan in Italy and brought to the family "as a playmate" (10) by the now-deceased Lord Hamilton; when the novel opens, she is neither quite a member of the family nor a servant.

Unresolved attitudes toward class issues, to which neither Alcott nor Brontë was a stranger, complicate the point of view in this novel; despite clear indications that Edith is as noble as any of the wealthy Hamiltons, even more so than cousin Ida, and despite sacrificing her inheritance twice—first to protect a downtrodden young man and then to protect and be a part of the family she loves—Edith still cannot accept Lord Hamilton's marriage proposal until she has been proved to be of the proper social class. Alcott may have been a democrat, but she was also a New Englander.

Finally, although the language of the text is heavily melodramatic and sentimental, advertising its author's immaturity, the character of Edith intrigues the reader as an early version of the active Alcott heroine. She is noble, self-sacrificing, and self-effacing, and she sings like an angel (rumor has it that her mother was an Italian opera singer), but it is she who climbs over a cliff to rescue her charge, Amy, when she falls while the Hamiltons and their friend Lord Percy are on an outing. In another episode, she proves a formidable horsewoman when the jealous Ida whips her horse, sending it racing wildly toward a stone wall. In some respects, Edith seems to be Jo and Beth March combined, a telling characterization in view of those two sisters' closeness in *Little Women* but a bit odd when combined into one character as it is here. Alcott apparently never tried to publish *The Inheritance*, which even a cursory reading would pronounce a wise choice, but the fact that she preserved the manuscript probably indicates a lasting affection for her "firstborn," an affection that the modern reader, if not expecting too much of a seventeen-year-old, can share.

Certainly, and not unexpectedly, the most complex and best written of the new Alcott novels is the most mature work, *A Long Fatal Love Chase*, another manuscript that sat gathering dust for years at the Houghton Library before being offered on the rare books market and purchased by the New Hampshire educator and collector Kent Bicknell. Alcott wrote *Love Chase* after returning from her first trip to Europe in 1866, probably intending it for anonymous publication, but "[publisher James R.] Elliott would not have it, saying it was too long & too sensational!" (*Journals* 153, September 1866). Manuscript markings and another manuscript at the Houghton entitled "Fair Rosamond" indicate that Alcott attempted to revise the story, but it was never published until 1995. Alcott used its original title ("A Modern Mephistopheles") for another work in 1877.

The *Love Chase* is certainly long, covering nearly all of Europe that Alcott had seen on her 1865–66 journey, and it is certainly sensational—in a twentieth-century, as well as a nineteenth-century, sense. The far-ranging plot features gambling, attempted bigamy, a custody battle, an obsessed stalker, the imprisonment of our heroine in a madhouse, and struggles with priestly celibacy. (In a stroke of genius, the *New York Times* had Stephen King review the novel when it appeared.) Alcott proves herself a master of intertextuality in this work, playing with references to "Fair Rosamond," *The Tempest, Faust,* and *Jane Eyre,* among others. The book begins with eighteen-year-old Rosamond Vivian, who lives alone with her invalid grandfather on an island off the coast of England, lamenting from her window seat, "I'd gladly sell my soul to Satan for a year of freedom" (3). Almost immediately, Philip Tempest, who looks a great deal like a picture of Mephistopheles that the Vivians just happen to have hanging in their hallway, appears at the door, ready to make Rosamond's wish come true. Tempest soon becomes as much Rochester as Satan; perhaps Alcott's point is that they much resemble one another, particularly when it comes to manipulating human hearts—Hawthorne's (and to a large extent, Alcott's) unpardonable sin.

After a month's blissful courtship, Tempest brings Rosamond to tears as he explains to her how he has found her a position as a companion, far away from where he will be, then finally confesses that he wishes her to be *his* companion—reminiscent of the proposal scene in *Jane Eyre.* Tempest "marries" Rosamond with the help of a phony cleric, since he already has a wife (though not locked in an attic). It takes Rosamond a year to uncover Tempest's secret, but when she does, she flees, and he pursues her all over Europe. When he inadvertently kills her at the end, he fatally stabs himself over her corpse, declaring, "Mine first—mine last—mine even in the grave!" (242).

Although first and foremost an unabashed page-turner, *Love Chase* also encompasses some of Alcott's most pervasive literary themes. Early on, Rosamond has a plaintive conversation with Tempest delineating the societal limitations on women's self-reliance. When Rosamond later flees from Tempest, she is forced to explore these limited options one by one: she sews, she becomes a nurse-companion for a time, she pretends to be a nun (and typical of Alcott, the real actress portrayed in the novel, Madame Honorine, is a kind and helpful character), and she ultimately relies on family—her husband's ex-wife and son, ironically—for support. The fact that Tempest ultimately destroys her may merely further the sensational plot or it may be one of Alcott's more pessimistic commentaries on women and nineteenth-century culture.

Regardless of the ultimate outcome, Rosamond is another active heroine, similar to her only slightly younger "sister" Jo March. She takes daring walks on parapets, climbs across rooftops, cuts her hair and disguises herself as a boy, all to escape her pursuer. When Tempest has her imprisoned in a madhouse, her worst suffering stems from idleness, for all books and writing materials are forbidden to her.

Readers who find Alcott's attitudes toward sexual passion problematic in other works will find this one especially intriguing. Although Rosamond professes to be so in love with her husband that it is difficult to leave him and harder to forget him despite overwhelming evidence that he is both a liar and a murderer, there are no indications of children after a year of marriage and no particular indications of intimacy between them. On the other hand, some of the scenes between Rosamond and Father Ignatius, a priest who befriends her during her stay in the convent, are highly charged with sexual energy. When Ignatius helps Rosamond to escape Tempest by rowing her across a river to a safe haven, she comments that he should be a knight, not a priest, whereupon he declares that he "will be, for an hour," removes his cassock, and throws it into the bottom of the boat, vehemently ordering it to "Lie there, detested thing!" (141). Although Rosamond and Ignatius maintain a chaste relationship even as their love for one another increases, and although Alcott seems to borrow from *Faust* the idea that, like Faust and Gretchen, they can take joy in knowing they will be reunited after death for eternity, one must wonder at the seething but unfulfilled passion in this novel.

Finally, though it may seem odd, it is also fitting that a "new" Louisa May Alcott novel should briefly appear on the *New York Times'* best-seller list in 1995, a novel that is at once modern and Victorian, typical of Alcott's serious themes but also an example of the kind of work she threw herself into in the 1860s in order to keep her family solvent. Portions of the proceeds from the book are going to Orchard House, the Alcotts' Concord home, and to the descendants of Fred Pratt, the nephew Alcott adopted before her death in order that he might have the power to retain future rights to her works. Louisa May Alcott's writing continues to support her home and family, even as it continues to provide intriguing new perspectives for consideration by modern readers and critics.

Works Cited

Alcott, Louisa May. *The Journals of Louisa May Alcott.* Ed. Joel Myerson, Daniel Shealy, and Madeleine B. Stern. Boston: Little, 1989.
Peterson, Jeanne. "The Victorian Governess: Status Incongruence." *Victorian Studies* 14 (1970): 7–23.

Instruction and Delight: Letters from a Father to His Children

A. Waller Hastings

Dearest Chums and Partners: Joel Chandler Harris's Letters to His Children: A Domestic Biography, ed. Hugh T. Keenan. Athens: University of Georgia Press, 1993.

In a common critical and historical formulation, children's literature is located between the poles of instruction and delight. Depending on historical period and individual predilection, adult critics have valued children's books variously by the extent to which they teach children proper values or useful knowledge, or by their entertainment value. In a world that includes both William Bennett's *Book of Virtues* and R. L. Stine's *Goosebumps* series, it seems safe to assert that both poles continue to define the literary landscape for young readers today.

Along the spectrum defined by these poles, Joel Chandler Harris has always seemed to me decidedly on the "delight" end. Notwithstanding the possible folkloric value of his Uncle Remus tales, their primary purpose seems to be to amuse, not to teach. It is the anarchic energy of Br'er Rabbit, the trickster who outwits larger and more powerful opponents, that remains in one's imagination rather than any moral or practical lessons one might derive from the tales. It comes as something of a surprise, then, to discover that Harris exhibits the impulse both to instruct and to delight in this volume of letters. Writing to his children whenever they were away from home, he provided entertainment in his comical accounts of everyday happenings at home and diligently sought to improve his children's minds, giving advice on how to improve handwriting and to follow boarding-school rules, discoursing on good and bad literature, or sending his eldest son Julian a book on Emerson in order to stimulate "a little interest in thoughtful things" (22).

In 1890, when the letters begin, Harris was already well established professionally. His literary reputation had been made ten years earlier with the first volume of Uncle Remus stories. Additional col-

Children's Literature 27, ed. Elizabeth Lennox Keyser (Yale University Press, © 1999 Hollins University).

lections of folklore, sketches, and stories followed, firmly placing him as a regional humorist and writer, and he held a respected editorial post at the *Atlanta Constitution*. With the proceeds of his writing he had settled his large family (wife, mother, and seven children) in a comfortable house in an Atlanta suburb, where he would remain for the rest of his life. For the next eighteen years, he would continue a high rate of literary production while watching his children make the transition to adulthood and making his own transition to patriarch and eventually grandfather.

Because of the time period covered by this collection, the reader seeking illumination of Harris's best-known work, the Uncle Remus stories, will be disappointed, and indeed, there is little direct reference to his own copious writing activities. Harris casually inquires whether one of his daughters received a new volume he has sent her or alludes to the need to finish a story commissioned by some magazine—the reader must consult the footnotes to get a clue to which book he might mean. Seemingly significant family events such as the marriage of a child or the birth of a grandchild also receive comparatively slight attention. Such momentous events seem of less interest to the writer and his audience than comical reactions to the family's circle of acquaintance or solicitous inquiries about the children's financial situation, travel plans, and failure to write (a recurrent theme).

There is little here, then, of a conventional "literary" nature. Rather, the collection's aim is, as one of its subtitles suggests, to provide a picture of the author's home life. Harris is revealed as a devoted father, constantly concerned about his children's welfare and paying attention to the smallest details of family existence that might interest the particular correspondent to whom he is writing. He delights in the comic possibilities of everyday life in such accounts as the epic mystery of a Christmas fruitcake (spun out through several letters to his daughters in anticipation of a break from their convent boarding school) and this "sad story of a piece of cheese":

> Well, here was the cheese and close by was an elderly old man who should have known better than to get on speaking terms with this piece of cheese in its overcoat of French mustard. But he was reckless; age doesn't give some elderly old people judgment and discretion. . . . He introduced himself to the piece of cheese with a large smile of affection. This was on Friday night.

The next day the cheese reminded him that it was his guest. Sunday it told him so in still plainer language; so that it was not until Monday night that the elderly old man was able to seat himself at his Georgia mahogany desk, and write of his desperate conflict with the cheese in its mustard overcoat. (to Lillian and Mildred Harris, 10 April 1899, p. 280)

The humorous view of life that Harris here directs against himself was, of course, one tool of his literary success. So, too, was the close observation of the follies and foibles of those around him, manifest in his sharing of the latest Atlanta gossip with his children as well as in his experiments with dialect. Today, with heightened sensitivities to possible ethnic slurs, dialect humor has fallen from favor, but that too was a part of Harris's literary success. The thick "Negro" accents of Uncle Remus render some passages nearly unreadable today and reflect casual racial stereotyping that, for instance, led Harris to attribute one of his wife's headaches to "hiring a negro and paying him to watch her work" (to Mildred Harris, 20 January 1901, p. 371). At the turn of the century such dialect was a common feature of popular entertainments, both on the stage and on the newsstand, and Harris was one of the best-known practitioners of this kind of humor. Several stories for the amusement of his children hinge on supposed black or German speech patterns and on recognizably stereotypical behavior.

Much of the humor in Harris's letters appears in those addressed to his daughters Lillian and Mildred while they attended St. Joseph's Academy in Washington, Georgia. Letters to his sons Julian and Evelyn, both of whom followed their father into literary careers, are more commonly in a serious vein, offering advice on writing and on proper conduct. The latter often appear aphoristic, as in this from a letter to Julian, who was visiting his grandparents in Quebec: "Remember that learning is merely an accomplishment and not a virtue, and if [your grandparents] seem to you to be ignorant, bear in mind that, in time, you will seem to be ignorant to your descendants" (July 1890, pp. 4–5), or later: "Do you know what genius is? It is large talents united with the ability to take pains—native ability wedded to persistent industry" (27 July 1890, p. 10). Writing instruction in the letters, developed at greater length, may suggest Harris's own reporting and composition practices: "Do you know what would be a good thing to do? Keep a journal, and write in it your experience and observation each day, and all the incidents that occur. Make notes of the patois, or dialect that the farmers speak. To do this would seem monotonous to you now, but it would be invaluable to you hereafter, and some of the simplest notes would be of great aid to you, particularly if you propose to get your bread by the sweat of your mind" (to Julian Harris, 26 October 1890, p. 21). As they grew older, the girls, too, were offered nuggets of advice about life and writing, but generally in smaller doses than Harris administered to his sons.

There is, then, a variety of material in this collection to interest both the casual reader and the serious Harris scholar. It seems to fall short of Keenan's goal of creating a domestic biography, however, primarily because the letters themselves are sporadic. Harris wrote to his children only when they were away from home, and then addressed the particular interests of whomever he was writing; both limitations create gaps in the record that are only partly filled by the editorial notes. More extensive editorial additions to bridge these gaps and to provide context for the letters might make the book function more effectively as biography.

Keenan provides several pieces of useful critical apparatus to aid the reader in navigating through the epistolary mass. A brief introduction outlines the major themes of Harris's letters, and a chronology of Harris's life enables the reader to situate the small, day-to-day incidents of domestic life related in the letters against the more "public" events associated with his literary career, including book publications and involvement in various editorial activities. There is also a genealogical chart of Harris's family, an essential in view of his nine children and twelve grandchildren. (Two of the children died before the period covered by the letters, and only half of the grandchildren were born before Harris's death in 1908.) The letters typically allude to marriages and births only obliquely, assuming that the correspondent already knows that he or she has acquired a new in-law, niece, or nephew; the family tree thus serves as a framework for the reader to place these references.

No such convenient guide to the rest of a large cast of characters exists, however. Footnotes provide identification for many individuals mentioned, but they are inconsistent and can frustrate the reader who is less familiar with Harris's family affairs than the original recipients of the letters were. Keenan offers the letters as a "domestic biography" and, as with any biography, tries to identify significant players on their first appearance. But a more typical reading pattern for a volume such as this is to dip in at various points, savoring a few letters at a time, rather than reading continuously from beginning to end. That the identity of a visitor to the Harris household was established in a footnote appearing twenty-five or one hundred pages earlier is little consolation when one has not recently read that note, and there is no cross-referencing to help find the identification.

The index provides some help, but rarely enough, since it catalogues people by their last names, whereas Harris more often refers to family friends only by their first names. For example, one of his daughters' school friends, Burdeene Biechele, was evidently a great favorite of the writer, as attested by her frequent appearance in Harris's letters. References to her are scattered across hundreds of pages of text; only occasionally is she identified in footnotes. The reader trying to place Burdeene is not likely to know enough to find her indexed under "Biechele." It would, of course, be absurd to footnote every person mentioned on every appearance, but it might perhaps have been useful to include an appendix identifying all of the characters who move in and out of these letters.

In the end, such frustrations do not, however, overwhelm the letters' ability to surprise, delight, and inform the reader interested in one of the significant figures in American children's literature of the nineteenth century. Harris wrote to Julian, "I don't like to write letters myself, and I never do unless I feel it to be my duty" (3 August 1890, p. 11). This collection demonstrates how often and how well he obeyed the call of that duty, and it will provide significant insights into this period of the writer's life.

Additional "Variations": Further Developments in Feminist Theory and Children's Literature

Anne K. Phillips

Harvesting Thistles: The Textual Garden of L. M. Montgomery, ed. Mary Henley Rubio. Guelph, Ontario: Canadian Children's Press, 1994.

Nancy Drew and Company: Culture, Gender, and Girls' Series, ed. Sherrie A. Inness. Bowling Green State University Popular Press, 1997.

Waking Sleeping Beauty: Feminist Voices in Children's Novels, by Roberta Seelinger Trites. Iowa City: University of Iowa Press, 1997.

When the *Children's Literature Association Quarterly* began running a column on literary theory and children's literature in 1988, the initial article in that column was Perry Nodelman's "Children's Literature as Women's Writing." Summarizing the winter 1982 *Quarterly* special section, "Feminist Criticism and the Study of Children's Literature," Nodelman noted that many of the authors in that issue collectively imply "the intriguing idea that children's literature as a whole is actually a kind of women's writing" (32). In her landmark 1987 essay, "Enigma Variations: What Feminist Theory Knows About Children's Literature," Lissa Paul suggests "powerful implications about the content and language of children's literature and children's literature criticism; something to do with 'inside' stories; something of our own fractured sense of the distinctions between self and other; something in tune with our particular moment in Western culture—something articulated in feminist theory" (186). Nodelman's and Paul's essays are among the most frequently cited scholarship on feminist criticism and children's literature, and issues of language, power, and identity remain the focus of much children's literature scholarship. The following reviewed books—two essay collections and one full-length theoretical study—manifest these concerns as well.

Originally released in connection with the First International Symposium on L. M. Montgomery at the University of Prince Edward Island in June 1994, *Harvesting Thistles* is a collection of eighteen

Children's Literature 27, ed. Elizabeth Lennox Keyser (Yale University Press, © 1999 Hollins University).

essays that seeks to reestablish Montgomery as the "Jane Austen of Canada" (Rubio 4). The title of the collection originates in Montgomery's novel *The Blue Castle* (1926). The heroine, Valancy Sterling, is confined to a home in which her mother and cousin watch her every move; they only allow her to read a library book titled *Thistle Harvest* because it is ostensibly a nature study. She finds it empowering, however, and thus "dangerous." As editor Mary Rubio explains, "Montgomery's own books, like *Thistle Harvest,* are books which amuse and soothe, but are also filled with subversive, prickly shafts. Montgomery writes trenchant social satire within the containers of her 'romances'" (1–2). Taken together, the essays included in this collection seek "to put to rest the untenable assumption that L. M. Montgomery writes only about an 'unblemished bucolic paradise' for undiscriminating women and children. This is the first collection of a growing body of Montgomery scholarship to focus on thistles in her landscape. To read her as a rosy-hued optimist who only wrote romances with happy endings is to misread her profoundly" (6). In addition, Rubio aims "to present new interpretations by critics who have had the advantage of reading Montgomery's journals and thus deepening their reading of the novels" (7).

The collection includes material originally delivered at academic conferences; it also contains essays that the editor has solicited. A few essays are book excerpts. The contributors range from leading Montgomery scholars such as Elizabeth R. Epperly and Elizabeth Waterston to scholars who wrote graduate theses or dissertations on Montgomery. With only a few exceptions, the articles are informed by feminist theory and criticism: for example, three of the essays focus on Montgomery and issues of autobiography; two study sisterhood in Montgomery's life and work; others examine the representation of the female voice and the female experience in Montgomery's fiction and journals. Although the collection as a whole is weakened by individual essays that are incomplete or undeveloped (or, occasionally, inaccurate), several of the essays extend Montgomery scholarship in significant new directions and are a welcome addition to the Montgomery canon.

Some of the essays are marred by errors that should have been rectified by the editor. In Marie Campbell's essay, "Wedding Bells and Death Knells: The Writer as Bride in the Emily Trilogy," she studies "how the domesticity Emily embraces, symbolized as it is by the 'Disappointed House,' serves to negate the possibility of future literary output or success" (137). Attempting to establish a literary tradition for her argument, Campbell refers to Alcott's *Little Women:* "Interestingly, Professor Bhaer—that consummate symbol of patriarchal protection and authority that Jo March eventually marries in Louisa May Alcott's *Little Women*—also demands that 'his' wife give up her lucrative writing career" (138). Campbell's reference is so general that it is inaccurate. The difference between Jo's sensational fiction and her other literary endeavors should be more carefully delineated if the author wishes to be convincing. Other essays, perhaps originally conference presentations, should have been refocused and revised more substantially in preparation for publication. The folklorist Edith Fowke's contribution is merely a lengthy quotation from *Emily Climbs* with a frame discussion of only a few paragraphs; Rubio should have encouraged her to develop in some more significant way the final paragraph, in which she suggests the significance of Montgomery's presentation of this "urban legend." Finally, in "Anne Shirley's American Cousin: *The Girl of the Limberlost*," Clara Thomas compares the American ethos in Stratton-Porter's fiction to a Canadian ethos in Montgomery's works; however, Thomas's reference to the second half of Stratton-Porter's novel as "Elnora, Part II, or success at College, and Part II, Success in Love" (61) is simply bizarre. Stratton-Porter's heroine never attends college, choosing instead to accept a teaching position in the Onabasha schools. A more accurate assessment of the novel would enhance Thomas's thesis. In addition, less summarization of Stratton-Porter's life and more development of her argument about the fiction would make it much more compelling. In all these instances, more deliberate editorial involvement—or a more rigorous refereeing of the manuscript—would have made for a better book.

Nonetheless, there are many fine essays in the collection. Denyse Yeast provides a satisfactory combination of theory and practice in her essay, "Negotiating Friendships: The Reading and Writing of L. M. Montgomery"; after exploring the theories of Patrocinio Schweickart and Sidonie Smith in connection with Montgomery's journals, she then studies aspects of *Anne of Green Gables*, the *Emily* trilogy, and *Rilla of Ingleside* to show that "Montgomery's self-definition through her writing is intensely relevant" (124). The Scottish historian Owen Dudley Edwards's contribution to the collection, "L. M. Montgomery's *Rilla of Ingleside*: Intention, Inclusion, Implosion," is especially useful in placing *Rilla* in a compelling historical and literary context that bolsters Montgomery's own impression, late in her career, that *Rilla* was her best novel (Edwards 127). Elizabeth Waterston studies Montgomery's development of a younger protagonist than either Anne or Emily in "Marigold and the Magic of Memory," an essay that capably demonstrates how *Magic for Marigold* was very much influenced by Montgomery's experiences as a mother, contemporary educational theory, and "years of radical change in ideas about early childhood and about fiction" (155). Rounding out the collection, Jennie Rubio argues in " 'Strewn with Dead Bodies': Women and Gossip in *Anne of Ingleside*" that "*Anne of Ingleside* is loosely structured as a domestic romance with a sentimental ending, but its central metaphors and internal logic deny the possibility of women's experience ever being contained in this kind of fiction. A closer examination reveals that even the genre itself . . . becomes a symbol both of women's silence and their alternative forms of discourse" (171). Focusing on the stories told and elided in the quilting bee episode, Rubio contributes a most useful and interesting discussion of this too-often-overlooked Montgomery novel.

Harvesting Thistles, like the beginning of spring, whets the scholar's appetite for digging. Elizabeth R. Epperly's contribution to the volume, "Approaching the Montgomery Manuscripts" (74–83), is a survey of the fifteen manuscripts owned by the Confederation Centre of the Arts in Charlottetown: "Collectively the manuscripts suggest how Montgomery spent a lifetime creating, rewriting, and reading texts that vibrate with the tension between what is and what could be" (83). Although Rubio and her contributors convincingly demonstrate the significance of studying that tension, readers come away from the volume newly aware of how much more there is to be harvested from Montgomery's manuscripts, fiction, and journals.

In North America, much contemporary attention to girls' series fiction is directed either at Montgomery's heroines (Anne Shirley, Emily Byrd Starr) or at Nancy Drew. In the wake of the 1993 conference at the University of Iowa (and subsequent publications such as the June 1994 issue of *The Lion and the Unicorn* and *Rediscovering Nancy Drew,* edited by Carolyn Stewart Dyer and Nancy Tillman Romalov), Nancy Drew has become the most well-studied heroine in American series fiction. The original producer of Nancy Drew books, the Stratemeyer Syndicate, has also received critical attention, including Carol Billman's *The Secret of the Stratemeyer Syndicate* (Ungar, 1986) and Deidre Johnson's *Stratemeyer Pseudonyms and Series Books* (Greenwood, 1982) and *Edward Stratemeyer and the Stratemeyer Syndicate* (Twayne, 1993).

Nonetheless, there are still great gaps in our understanding of other American series fiction. To date, only a few scholars have approached the subject: Faye Riter Kensinger, in *Children of the Series and How They Grew* (Bowling Green University Popular Press, 1987); Paul Deane, in *Mirrors of American Culture: Children's Fiction Series in the Twentieth Century* (Scarecrow, 1991); Jane S. Smith, in "Plucky Little Ladies and Stout-Hearted Chums: Series Novels for Girls, 1900–1920" (*Prospects* 3 [1977]: 155–74); and *Girls' Series Books: A Checklist of Hardback Books Published 1900–1975* (University of Minnesota, Children's Literature Research Collections, 1978). Hence, serious critical attention to this often overlooked and underestimated literature is a most welcome addition to the American children's literature canon.

Nancy Drew and Company: Culture, Gender, and Girls' Series, edited by Sherrie Inness, contains nine essays on series fiction heroines ranging from Anne of Green Gables, Betsy-Tacy, Cherry Ames, and Nancy Drew to less well-known ones such as Isabel Carleton and Linda Lane. Inness argues in her introduction that "studying girls' reading is an important building block in understanding how girls are socialized" (1); in devoting an entire volume to essays on series fiction for girls, Inness explains, "[m]y point is not to claim that series books are always shining examples of literary art, but to show that . . . they are still engaged in important cultural work" (11, n.2). A number of the essays in *Nancy Drew and Company* therefore demonstrate how series books both seek to liberate the adolescent female and at the same time "help to perpetuate traditional gender relationships and class stereotypes" (Inness 10).

In one of the strongest essays in the collection, "Gender, Class, and Domesticity in the Isabel Carleton Series," Kathleen Chamberlain studies the way Margaret Eliza Ashmun encodes "a rhetoric of class" (41) into her series fiction. Her reference to Ashmun's own composition text, particularly the section on "vulgarisms," convincingly demonstrates that "[t]o Ashmun, language is one of the signs that separates the middle from the working class" (41). Chamberlain's ensuing discussion of money, household commodities, and other economic and social indicators throughout the series is provocative. It can be difficult to write effectively about a series that isn't well known, yet Chamberlain provides an admirable balance of plot summary and analysis.

Other essays in the collection are not as well developed or convincing. It is difficult to distinguish K. L. Poe's thesis in "The Whole of the

Moon: L. M. Montgomery's *Anne of Green Gables* Series," an essay overwhelmed by references to other critics as well as by extensive plot summary. Deidre Johnson's "Community and Character: A Comparison of Josephine Lawrence's Linda Lane Series and Classic Orphan Fiction," is marred by some curious assumptions about the orphan literature that she compares with the Linda Lane series, including Jean Webster's *Daddy-Long-Legs*. Johnson mistakenly refers to the male lead of *Daddy-Long-Legs* as "Jarvis" (though his name is Jervis)—an error originated by Mary Cadogan and Patricia Craig in their derogatory discussion of *Daddy-Long-Legs* in *You're a Brick, Angela! A New Look at Girls' Fiction from 1839 to 1975*. Perpetuating their error, Johnson causes readers to wonder whether she actually studied the orphan fiction she refers to in her article or whether she is merely working off Cadogan and Craig's characterization of it. The remainder of Johnson's essay, an analysis of the tensions associated with authority inherent in Lawrence's work, is much more convincing. In "Nancy Drew as New Girl Wonder: Solving It All for the 1930s," Deborah L. Siegel draws on Martha Banta's *Imaging American Women: Ideas and Ideals in Cultural History* to show how Nancy is an adolescent New Woman. The final section of her essay, however, in which she argues that "Nancy undoes the work of the Great Depression," is not as developed and convincing as it could be. Perhaps a few references to the way later books in the series reflect different goals or ideology would help make her case that the early volumes are distinct and significant.

Two of the essays in the collection manifest a broader focus on girls' series fiction, and both conclude with similar claims about the conservative nature of series fiction. Nancy Tillman Romalov is represented by "Mobile and Modern Heroines: Early Twentieth-Century Girls' Automobile Series," in which she demonstrates that "girls' adventure series is a genre often at odds with itself, replete with contradictory impulses and convoluted narrative strategies, meant, it seems, to reconcile greater freedom and fitness for girls with their continued subordination to a patriarchal, genteel order" (76). Inness contributes "Girl Scouts, Camp Fire Girls, and Woodcraft Girls: The Ideology of Girls' Scouting Novels, 1910–1935," in which she argues that "[a]lthough scouting in fiction and in reality might offer girls a fleeting feeling of agency, ultimately scouting is only one of many state-sanctioned institutions that produces more malleable subjects for the nation" (91). Both essays are thought-provoking, but their lack of specific textual analysis may frustrate the reader. For instance, though

Inness briefly cites the titles of four different series books to support her thesis about imperialism, her essay might be more successful if it incorporated more substantial and sophisticated close readings from one or more of those examples.

The project of *Nancy Drew and Company* is a worthwhile one; readers will come away from the volume with a greater awareness of the variety and complexity of American twentieth-century series fiction for girls. At the end of the volume, one wishes that there were more of a conclusion, perhaps some dialogue along the lines of the scholarly exchanges following the articles in *Children's Literature* 22 and 23, in which authors read and responded to each other's essays. For instance, one wonders how Maureen Reed might have approached class, gender, and race in the Betsy-Tacy books after reading Chamberlain's piece. Alternatively, Poe's essay on Montgomery might have benefited from Johnson's work on the female community in the Linda Lane series. A final section in which Inness or even all of the authors included in this volume commented on their project, and on the connections between essays, would give readers even more to consider about series fiction and feminist approaches to children's and adolescent literature.

Inness's collection focuses on books that appeared from approximately 1910 to 1950. Roberta Seelinger Trites's *Waking Sleeping Beauty: Feminist Voices in Children's Novels* incorporates substantial analyses of even more contemporary fiction, primarily from the 1960s to the 1990s. Her study is an accessible yet substantive examination of feminist theory and children's literature. The theory is engaging and the selection of relevant texts is especially impressive, because it draws on both well-known and less familiar works and because so many of the texts discussed here are by women of color.

Trites explains in her preface that "[t]his book is intended as an introduction for novices to the field of children's literature, to the theories of feminism, or to both as a demonstration of how feminism as a social movement informs children's novels and how feminism as a literary theory can help us understand those texts. I have geared the study specifically to those who work with or will work with children as teachers because it seems imperative to me that educators understand the nuances of feminism at work in literature if they are to adapt successfully feminist practices in their classrooms" (ix–x). Thus the text is political: it encourages readers who may not already define themselves as feminists to begin to understand literature, and the world of interpersonal relationships, through a feminist lens. A "feminist children's novel," according to Trites, is one "in which the main character is empowered regardless of gender" (4); "[s]ome of the most poignant feminist children's narratives are those which recognize that traditional gender roles have been as limiting for boys as they have for girls: MacLachlan's *Arthur, for the [Very] First Time* (1980), Cleary's *Dear Mr. Henshaw* (1983), and Avi's *Nothing But the Truth* (1991) are just a few of the novels that address these issues" (5). Trites suggests that "the greatest distinguishing mark of the feminist children's novel is that the character who uses introspection to overcome her oppression almost always overcomes at least part of what is oppressing her. Feminist children's novels, on the whole then, constitute a triumphal literature" (3).

In each chapter Trites provides an initial section in which she explains her theory, followed by a section in which she applies that theory to several texts. For instance, in the second chapter, "Subverting Stereotypes: Rejecting Traditional Gender Roles," Trites examines the way feminist children's novels demonstrate "a clear textual effort to revise those traditional gender roles that mandate female submissiveness" (12). She then contrasts Cynthia Voigt's *On Fortune's Wheel* with Robin McKinley's *The Blue Sword;* Janet Lunn's *The Root Cellar* with Jean George's *Julie of the Wolves* and Nicholasa Mohr's *Nilda.* Her argument that "the presence of traditionally depicted females could be used to serve as part of the revision, for it is only against the passive female, the silent female, the objectified female, that the feminist protagonist's achievements can be fully understood" (6) is especially effective in the discussion of *Nilda,* in which Trites contrasts the experiences of the (feminist) teenage protagonist with those of her (traditional) mother. Readers come away from Trites's analysis with a richer understanding of both characters and a respect for Mohr's approach.

In Chapter 3, "Subjectivity as a Gender Issue: Metaphors and Intertextuality," Trites explores the way in which feminist texts such as Natalie Babbitt's *Tuck Everlasting* embody answers to the questions, "who has agency in a text? and how has language shaped that subject's agency?" (28). Here, Trites also examines the way visual metaphors and metaphors of photography, naming, birth imagery, and intertextuality lend themselves to explaining the difference between the subject and object in works such as Virginia Hamilton's *A White Romance,*

Patricia MacLachlan's *Journey,* Angela Johnson's *Toning the Sweep,* and Francesca Lia Block's *Weetzie Bat.*

Chapters 4 and 5 focus on protagonists' development of their voices, whether in conversation with others or through writing. Chapter 4, "Transforming Feminine Silence: Pro/Claiming Female Voices," focuses on "how feminists have formulated interdependency as a narrative strategy through which females can overcome this socioliterary silencing" (48) in such novels as Mildred Taylor's *Let the Circle Be Unbroken,* Patricia MacLachlan's *Cassie Binegar* and *Baby,* and Minfong Ho's *Rice Without Rain.* In Chapter 5, "Re/Constructing the Female Writer: Subjectivity in the Feminist *Künstlerroman,*" Trites discusses Louise Fitzhugh's *Harriet the Spy* and Mollie Hunter's *A Sound of Chariots;* she argues that "[b]ecause writing and re-visioning have so much potential to help people understand their agency, quite a few feminist children's novels explore what it means for children to write" (63).

In Chapter 6, "Female Interdependency: Literal and Metaphoric Sisterhood," Trites, in reference to community, examines Cynthia Rylant's *Missing May* and Virginia Hamilton's *M. C. Higgins the Great;* in reference to heterosexual relationships, Janet Lunn's *Shadow in Hawthorn Bay* and Barbara Wersba's *Love Is the Crooked Thing;* in reference to female bonds, Nancy Garden's *Annie on My Mind,* among others.

In Chapter 7, "Refuting Freud: Mother/Daughter Relationships," Trites convincingly argues that children's literature critics need to look at not only the daughters' but the mothers' subject positions. Citing numerous examples of relevant theory and criticism, Trites examines both "traditional narratives that allow for the daughter to achieve independence from her mother in the classically Oedipal manner that Nancy Friday describes in *My Mother/My Self,* and those less traditional and less Freudian ones that allow the daughter to mature without necessarily breaking from her mother" (103). Crescent Dragonwagon's *The Year It Rained* is an example of the former; Pam Conrad's *Prairie Songs* and Virginia Hamilton's *Plain City* exemplify the latter. This chapter also deals with what Trites defines as "maternal narrative structures" in which authors "develop themes of birth and/or maternity to enact a positive reproduction of mothering" (112): E. L. Konigsburg's *From the Mixed-Up Files of Mrs. Basil E. Frankweiler,* Hamilton's *Arilla Sun Down,* Paul Fleischman's *The Borning Room,* and, briefly, Sharon Creech's *Walk Two Moons.*

Chapter 8, "Metafiction and the Politics of Identity: Narrativity, Subjectivity, and Community" discusses "language, storytellers, and artist figures, subjectivity, and community" (123) in such texts as Hamilton's *Zeely,* Avi's *The True Confessions of Charlotte Doyle,* and Ursula K. Le Guin's *Tehanu.* Trites concludes her study with Chapter 9, "Afterword: Feminist Pedagogy and Children's Literature," in which she emphasizes the importance of providing students with "a community in which to learn and to voice their opinions"—a community enabled by "the myriad possibilities of feminist expression" (140).

Waking Sleeping Beauty is a valuable addition to the growing body of scholarship on feminist theory and children's literature. I can't think of a better model of well-informed, thoughtful literary analysis of children's literature, for myself, for my students, or for my colleagues. I occasionally want to quibble with Trites, particularly about her treatment of the texts she has identified as "prefeminist" (including *Little Women, Anne of Green Gables,* and *Daddy-Long-Legs*); in addition, I'm curious about how she would expand and support her brief identification of texts such as *Maniac Magee* as "masculinist." Nonetheless, *Waking Sleeping Beauty* is a book to which I will enthusiastically return, both for its excellent scholarship and for its engaging pedagogy.

Works Cited

Nodelman, Perry. "Children's Literature as Women's Writing." *Children's Literature Association Quarterly* 13, no. 1 (spring 1998): 31–34.

Paul, Lissa. "Enigma Variations: What Feminist Theory Knows About Children's Literature." *Signal* 54 (September 1987): 186–202.

It's a Small-Minded World After All: International Perspectives on Children's Literature and Censorship

Carolyn Sigler

Censorship in Children's Literature, ed. Alleen Pace Nilsen and Hamida Bosmajian. *Para•Doxa: Studies in World Literature* 2, nos. 3–4 (1996).

Censorship in Children's Literature is as complex and significant as the issue of censorship. "[B]ecause the concept hovers around the ragged edges of cultural values," writes co-editor Alleen Pace Nilsen in her comprehensive introductory essay, "Focus on Censorship," censorship itself can be difficult to define: "If we didn't have boundaries, we might have to create them just so there would be something to let us know when we had gone beyond them. The problem is that different people want different boundaries" (308). *Censorship and Children's Literature* covers a wide range of issues and perspectives and will provide an invaluable resource for those interested in questions of academic and artistic freedom, children's rights, and the production and consumption of children's and young adult literatures. One of its many strengths is its examination of censorship from many points of view, bringing together articles that address the concerns of authors, publishers, teachers, librarians, and academics, written by an international collection of scholars analyzing censorship issues in Australia, New Zealand, Japan, Canada, the United States, Bulgaria, Sweden, Great Britain, Germany, and Greece. Though the essays contained in this double issue of *Para•Doxa* are occasionally uneven—and at times provide frustratingly brief discussions of complicated cultural, pedagogical, and literary situations—they offer important introductions to a variety of censorship issues and invaluable starting points for further study, including a list of resources on censorship compiled by Hamida Bosmajian and Ken Donelson.

In her own essay, Nilsen organizes the issues addressed by the collection into four interrelated categories of censorship: "political, pedagogical (or educational), economic (or marketplace), and internal (or private)" (308). The articles in the first three categories

Children's Literature 27, ed. Elizabeth Lennox Keyser (Yale University Press, © 1999 Hollins University).

examine censorship as an assertion of hegemonic, institutional authority that "does not protect the individuality of the child; rather, it protects the power of the system itself" (Batycki 325). The collection makes clear, however, that the same patriarchal ideologies that motivate censorship by institutions such as governments, schools, and churches can also inform "private" acts of censorship by parents and other individuals. "If we look at censorship not as a conflict of values but as a way to assert power," writes Sara Fine, "then censorship, particularly when it comes to children, is *not* about their moral development; it is about the fear of losing control over them. Authoritarian parents are more often outraged by books that portray young people defying their parents' values than by the language the book contains. . . . Dirty language is still cleaner—and easier to control—than rebellion" (quoted in Apseloff 481).

Essays such as Christa Kamenetsky's "Censorship in Totalitarian States," Meni Kanatsouli's "Censorship in Greece: 1974 to the Present," Midori Todayama's "Censorship in Japan," and Maria Nikolajeva's "The 'Serendipity' of Censorship" each study governments' political control over and use of children's literature as a tool for disseminating official ideologies and thus influencing behaviors and beliefs. Nikolajeva's insightful essay looks at censorship in the Soviet Union, where she grew up, describing "how children's literature functions under abnormal social conditions, what strategies it establishes in order to survive and how oppression can, paradoxically enough, influence the literary evolution in a positive way" (379). Alexandra Zervou, in her fine essay on Walter Benjamin's Nazi-era radio play for children, "Walks in Berlin," calls this paradoxical relationship "the game of rules and infractions": strategies by which writers may "pretend to conform to some of [an oppressive government's] rules in order to deal with them more effectively, thus creating for themselves a secret means of resistance" (452). Nikolajeva suggests that fairy tales and fantasy are a major form through which children's writers, in "the cat-and-mouse play between the writer and censorship," have best been able to express subversive ideas (382). Indeed, in her analysis of Salman Rushdie's *Haroun and the Sea of Stories,* Millicent Lenz argues that the fantasy genre can enable the writer to "outwit the censor by assuming an iconoclast's mask of innocence or childishness" (377). In "Redeploying the Spanish Lullaby," Elizabeth Rosa Horan shows how another children's genre, the lullaby, has offered Chilean women a means to subvert conventional notions of women as silent and passive subjects and, further, to "assert the importance of women's discourse in national and continental histories still in the making" (418).

Pedagogical censorship is an even more ambiguous and multi-faceted category, since education touches on issues affecting not only teachers and librarians but publishers, parents, and children themselves as students, readers, and consumers. Maj Asplund Carlsson's essay critiques adult reactions to a popular children's book, *Gummy Tarzan,* in school libraries, concluding that "irony in children's literature is not immediately met with acclaim from the guardians of children's literary taste, librarians and teachers" (397). David Russell's outstanding "Hope Among the Ruins" examines three controversial picture books that deal with violent or disturbing subject matter such as the holocaust and the Los Angeles riots. "Is the function of picture books to preserve a 'cozy, rosy view of the world'?" he asks, "Or is that view more an adult fantasy?" (346). Through detailed and lyrical readings of *Hiroshima No Pika, Rose Blanche,* and *Smoky Night,* Russell suggests that children are "often only too aware that they live in a world where death and destruction respect no age" (347). "What children need," he argues, "are books that are honest in their portrayal of the human condition—especially as it relates to children—and books that will demonstrate the human resilience in the face of catastrophe" (355). In an essay on the young adult author Lois Lowry, Marilyn Fain Apseloff quotes Lowry voicing a similar argument: "Pretending that there are no choices to be made—reading only books which are cheery and safe and nice—is a prescription for disaster for the young. Submitting to censorship is to enter the seductive world of *The Giver:* the world where there are no bad words and no bad deeds. But it is also the world where choice has been taken away and reality distorted. And that is the most dangerous world of all" (484).

In her introductory essay Nilsen observes that the third category, economic censorship, "overlaps political and pedagogical censorship because education is big business" and because in many places "publishers vie to have their textbooks approved and purchased by school officials" (310). Midori Todayama's fascinating discussion of censorship in Japan looks at the relation between government and education, demonstrating how the roles of government-funded schools and libraries in "selection and placement decisions can be almost the equivalent of censorship" (388). Indeed, the desire of book companies to gain approval for lucrative government contracts suggests how "all textbooks are censored secretly by the publishers' editors" (391).

Meni Kanatsouli's "Censorship in Greece: 1974 to the Present" and Joan Gibbons's "Censorship and Selection in New Zealand" provide an overview of economic censorship in their countries. Gibbons argues that, although New Zealand is traditionally liberal in its attitudes toward profanity, "children's book reviewers continue to be somewhat coy and even prissy about the coarser language employed in children's books," which in turn "affects the buying policies of some school libraries" (399). These and other essays examine how authors can be led to private or self-censorship by economic considerations raised by the threat of their work being unmarketable or being banned from school or public libraries, the largest consumers of children's books. In Jeri Kroll's "Gillian Rubinstein's *Beyond the Labyrinth*," Rubinstein, a young adult author, warns that writers for young people "run the risk of censoring ourselves, of writing what we know will not upset any publishers' readers, or children's librarians, along the way. We feel the need to tread warily to get past these guardians, for it is they in most cases who dictate what books will reach young people, not the young people themselves" (335). In Apseloff's "Lois Lowry: Facing the Censors" Lowry recalls how, after a couple of her books had been the subjects of challenges, "I began to consider each bad word that appeared from my typewriter, later from my word processor, and to question whether it needed to be there" (481). Similarly, co-editor Hamida Bosmajian argues convincingly in "Children's Literature and Censorship" that literature for the young is "very much part of the consumer society which tends to censor out before publication those texts that do not, presumably, meet the expectations of the consumer" (315). John Stephens's and Robyn McCallum's essay, "Pruning *The Secret Garden* in 1990s Film," shows how this kind of consumer marketing strategy, intended to lead to a film's or a book's reaching the widest possible audience, can also lead to internal or "anticipatory" censorship.

One weakness of this international collection is that, for all its diversity, the essays are primarily Western in focus. There are no essays on or by African or Middle Eastern writers, and there is only one written from an Asian perspective. Also, although many essays acknowledge that race is a central factor in censorship, this topic is underrepresented among the essays focusing on political, pedagogical, and economic issues. Todayama's essay touches on how a controversy over a depiction of the minority Buraku people in Japan led to the conscious exclusion from school textbooks of depictions of ethnic and other minorities "because people might be offended and blame the textbook for promoting discrimination" (391). In "Cultural Censorship?" Rod McGillis points briefly to ways in which the marketplace functionally censors by giving the works of dominant-culture writers visibility while keeping books by minority writers in obscurity. McGillis argues for the need "to encourage work that deals with culturally specific contexts to be the product of those who live in that culturally specific experience first hand" (428). In "Censorship vs. Selection in Australia" Maureen Nimon observes that current "censorship debates correlate with the complexity of social, cultural and religious groupings within communities. . . . They are in part the outcome of the social will of past decades that has sought to give more recognition to the views of minorities" (506). Although a number of the pieces in *Censorship in Children's Literature* do touch on issues of race and censorship, recent cases such as the removal of Toni Morrison's *Song of Solomon* and Maya Angelou's *I Know Why the Caged Bird Sings* from a public school curriculum in Maryland suggest how much critical work has yet to be done.[1]

I had hoped to find some discussion in this collection of current debates about new questions of "appropriateness" and censorship in children's mass culture on television and on the Internet. Recent debates in the United States over such controversial measures as the television rating system or the Communications Decency Act of 1996—which criminalizes a broad range of constitutionally protected communications on the Internet if made "available" to minors and deemed "indecent" or "patently offensive"—are shifting debates about children and censorship to even more public and far-reaching arenas than schools and libraries.[2] With its focus on print literature, however, this collection is already broad and diverse. The pervasiveness and rapidity of change in mass culture suggest that children's discourses in electronic environments require their own collection.

Though *Censorship in Children's Literature* illustrates that censorship battles are ongoing and, indeed, show signs of escalating around the world, many of the essays observe that the increasing willingness of nations to permit such battles, whereas heretofore they might have been repressed, is a sign that openness and freedom of speech are in ascendance. Indeed, the collection's authors suggest that for such debates to vanish any time soon may not be possible or desirable: "Censorship struggles are evidence of the increasing interdependency of our daily lives," notes contributor Maureen Nimon; "they will dis-

appear only when we all reach unanimity of opinion on every significant matter that confronts us" (506).

Notes

1. After reading two pages of Morrison's acclaimed novel *The Song of Solomon*, St.
Mary's County commissioners unanimously agreed with the school superintendent's
decision to remove it from the curriculum, describing the novel as "repulsive" and
"trash." Angelou's autobiography, *I Know Why the Caged Bird Sings*, was removed from a
ninth-grade curriculum in Anne Arundel County by the school superintendent after
a small group of parents complained that the book is "sexually explicit" and presents a
"slanted portrayal of whites." See Annie Gowen, "St. Mary's Commissioners Back Removing Morrison Novel from Curriculum," *The Washington Post* 18 January 1998: B4.
2. See Kay Vandergrift's "Censorship, the Internet, Intellectual Freedom, and
Youth" site at http://www.scils.rutgers.edu/special/kay/censorship.html for pages of
essential information and links to sites devoted to First Amendment rights, particularly
as they affect children.

Dissertations of Note

Compiled by Rachel Fordyce

Batten, Martha Jacks. "Societal Values and Family Environment Reflected in Selected Current Young Adult Literature and Young Adult Literature of the 50s." Ph.D. diss. University of South Carolina, 1996. 280 pp. DAI 57:2955A.

Batten's dissertation examines "family environment and selected societal values in popular young adult literature in order to determine the differences between current works and works popular in the 50s." Her goal is to identify specific works that "engender and enhance moral and social values." She finds that societal values varied widely between the 1950s and the present.

Benson, Linda Gayle. "The Constructed Child: Femininity in Beverly Cleary's Ramona Series." Ph.D. diss. Illinois State University, 1997. 247 pp. DAI 58:3116A.

While applying feminist theory to the seven Ramona books, Benson finds that there are considerable conflicts between implicit and explicit depictions of gender. "The conclusion provides a discussion of constructivist composition theory that suggests pedagogical strategies by which students may interrogate ideological constructs which position them as subjects within the dominate hegemony."

Berger, Paula Silverman. "Peter Pan as a Mythical Figure." Ph.D. diss. University of Chicago, 1994. 262 pp. DAI 55:422A.

Berger examines how Barrie used characters, themes, and motifs "of Greek mythology to create a magical, imaginary world in which his contemporary counterparts of the gods reenact the Greek myths in contemporary guise." He notes that Kenneth Grahame and Edith Nesbit also "idealized and glorified childhood"; analyzes the Spielberg film based on *Peter Pan;* and concludes with a discussion of passages from childhood to adulthood based on a comparison of the authors with Shakespeare (*A Midsummer Night's Dream*), Tchaikovsky (*The Nutcracker*), Mozart (*The Magic Flute*), and Strauss (*Die Frau ohne Schatten*).

Bongco, Mila Francisca. "Reading Comics: Analyzing Language, Culture, and the Concept of Superheroes in Comicbooks." Ph.D. diss. University of Alberta, 1995. 312 pp. DAI 57:1115A.

Using semiotics and culture studies as a framework, Bongco identifies comics as a product of popular culture and focuses on the superhero comic book. Although it is commonly held that "popular culture enforces the values of some dominant ideology," she finds that "the presence and polarity of superheroes and the superhero genre involve a critique rather than a celebration of a given society's judicial system . . . ; many recent comicbooks portray justice and law as provisional, incomplete and virtually unenforceable by a state increasingly incapable of understanding its complexity."

Boyle, Virginia A. "An Analysis of Issues Involved in the Compilation and Publication of *Facets Non-Violent, Non-Sexist Children's Video Guide.* Ph.D. diss. Union Institute, 1997. 372 pp. DAI 57:4972A.

Boyle discusses the production of the guide she published with Facets, which evaluates "violence and gender bias" in video, film, and television. Eight hundred and fifty titles are listed in the guide, which includes a "significant listing of multicultural videos, representing thirty cultures."

Children's Literature 27, ed. Elizabeth Lennox Keyser (Yale University Press, © 1999 Hollins University).

Brown, Malore Ingrid. "Multicultural Youth Materials Selection." Ph.D. diss. University of Wisconsin, Milwaukee, 1996. 132 pp. DAI 57:4970A.

Brown questions how librarians develop a collection of multicultural materials and literature and what selection procedures they use. She finds that the ethnic background of a community has "a great effect" on selection and that librarians generally use the same criteria for building a multicultural children's collection as they use for other collections. She concludes that there is a continuing "need for staff development training."

Cadden, Michael Joseph. "Dialogues with Authority: Children's Literature, Dialogics, and the Texts of Ursula K. Le Guin." D.A. diss. Illinois State University, 1996. 234 pp. DAI 57:2473A.

Cadden is concerned with "the degrees and kinds of narrative and ideological authority" Le Guin employs in both children's and adult literature and with "the ways narrative can construct or confute authority." He believes that Le Guin's "unique use of genre as a type of audience . . . has implications for the ways we think about children's literature in relation to 'adult literature,' and for the ways we think about writers who 'cross-over' any genre boundaries." He concludes with suggestions for applying his theory to the teaching of children's literature.

Coleman, Esther Meyers. "The Effects of Teachers Reading Orally from Literature by Award Winning African-Americans to Sixth Grade Students in Monoethnic Urban School Settings." Ph.D. diss. Oakland University, 1996. 178 pp. DAI 57:2414A.

Coleman's results indicate "significantly positive relationships among the oral reading time, name recognition [of award-winning authors and illustrators], reading comprehension, and attitudes toward reading."

Comtois, Rita J. "A Qualitative Study of the Perceived Impact of Fairy Tales on a Group of Women." Ph.D. diss. Boston College, 1995. 319 pp. DAI 56:5761B.

This study, in psychology and women's studies, indicates that women who perceive themselves as nontraditional had trouble identifying with "the circumstances of fairy tale heroines," particularly if they read the tales literally and compared them to their own lives. This reading left them "disillusioned and disenfranchised." The study may have implications for child readers.

Crossland, Rodney Bert. "A Content Analysis of Children's Historical Fiction Written About World War II." Ph.D. diss. University of North Texas, 1996. 107 pp. DAI 57:2916A.

Crossland questions whether portrayals of protagonists and written accounts in children's historical fiction about World War II have changed since 1943. Notable changes are a difference in the gender of the protagonists and an increase in violence and how graphically it is portrayed; works written during the 80s and 90s have "a stronger American perspective." And although much of the war took place in the Pacific Rim, "a deficiency remains in the number of novels set in the Pacific Rim countries," and details about the bombings at Hiroshima and Nagasaki are scarce.

Dobson, Warwick. "Truth in Dialogue: A Knowledge-Centered Approach to Drama in Education." D.Phil. diss. University of Sussex, 1997. 302 pp. DAI 58:322C.

Dobson believes that "since the early nineteen-seventies, a number of theorists and practitioners have sought to advance the claim that drama in education represents a form of radical pedagogy which empowers young people." He analyzes "state-centered, child-centered, and knowledge-centered" approaches to child drama and concludes that "only the knowledge-centered approach," based on the work of Dorothy Heathcote and Gavin Bolton, "is capable of synthesizing the cognitive, artistic and aesthetic dimensions into a form of practice which fulfills some of the claims" practitioners have made, and that "classroom drama, in its knowledge-centered manifestation, can be viewed as a polyphony of unfinished dialogues which open students to new and enlightened understandings."

Donnelly, Mary Elizabeth. "Erin's Children at the Crossroads: Adolescence and Oedipal Narratives of the Insurgent Nation." Ph.D. diss. University of Miami, 1996. 300 pp. DAI 57:5162A.

Donnelly analyzes Irish adolescent characters under colonialism in twentieth-century literature. Three types of literature are prevalent: "epic, which posits a homogenous sense of nation and is often performed in violence; novel, which expresses a sense of the colonized nation . . .; and romance, which endlessly defers the traditional envisioning of the nation, but within that deferment reinscribes the politics of sexuality."

Edgington, William Douglas. "Teaching Character Education: The Values in John R. Tunis's Sports Books for Children and Adolescents." Ed.D. diss. Oklahoma State University, 1996. 113 pp. DAI 57:5035A.

Edgington is concerned with the "core values" in the Tunis books written between 1938 and 1973. The values are compassion, kindness, courage, perseverance, courtesy, fairness, respect, honesty, loyalty, and responsibility. He finds that Tunis's writing was consistent over the thirty-five, year period, that the values were not "portrayed didactically," and that the books "should be considered for use in values education."

Fisher, Bonnie Elizabeth. "Writing as a Social Act: Social Influences on the Writing of Marion Dane Bauer and Katherine Paterson." Ph.D. diss. University of Minnesota, 1997. 227 pp. DAI 58:1623A.

Based on the two women's books, papers, and correspondence, housed in the Kerlan Collection, and on personal verification and additional data and interpretations that both Paterson and Bauer supplied, Fisher compares and contrasts their writing and what influences it. "Ideas the study illustrates include: writing is influenced intertextually, writing is dynamic and dialectic, writing is a tool used by members of communities to create meaning, [and that] there are multiple literacies that interplay" in the works of both women.

Glessner, Marci Miller. "Children's Choice in an Elementary School Classroom: Ownership in the Making." Ph.D. diss. University of North Dakota, 1997. 256 pp. DAI 58:3428A.

Glessner is concerned with the ownership of the learning process and with the factors that affect sixth graders' sense of ownership. Four factors emerge: the amount of time children can find to read, the amount of money necessary to buy them an adequate number of books, administrative support for teachers and flexibility in suiting students' needs, and the "community of the classroom, including the maturity of students."

Groch, John R. "Corporate Reading, Corporate Writing: MGM and CBS in the Land of Oz." Ph.D. diss. University of Iowa, 1996. 240 pp. DAI 57:2103A.

Groch argues that the continued popularity of the film *The Wizard of Oz* and "its privileged position in American popular culture" are directly related to the way it has been consciously positioned at different periods in time. In 1939, MGM was selling "quality" that "mollified reformers concerned with the effects of motion picture content on child viewers." In the 1950s, as the film became available on television, it was represented as encouraging family viewing. By 1989 it had become a source of "nostalgia [in] a postmodern condition." The work is significant because it deals with the continual redefinition of popular culture, as well as with "the role entertainment corporations play not only as producers of texts under capitalism but also, and necessarily, as producers of culture."

Hannon, Carole J. "Aging with Disney: Depiction of Gender and Age in Seven Disney

242   RACHEL FORDYCE

Animated Fairy Tales." Ph.D. diss. University of Oklahoma, 1997. 374 pp. DAI 58:331A.

Because Disney's productions are considered "wholesome," many parents use them as "a harmless babysitter." Consequently, "very young children are bombarded with images and ideas that may influence their entire lives." Hannon's findings concerning recent Disney films and their social and cultural message point to a "very real crisis within our media-dominated cultural environment"—for example, male protagonists outnumber female major characters two to one; only one mother (in a nonspeaking role) appears in the seven films she studied; young males are violent (in order to win a fair maid) and older males are greedy; young females "are all romantically involved"; older females are wicked; plots are singularly unfaithful to original texts; sidekick animals "bear the brunt of violence and abuse"; and most female characters are deleted from the film version of the fairy tale. "These alterations are made for both ideological and commercial reasons to sell the Disney product." Because there is practically no scholarship about full-length animated motion pictures, this is a very significant work.

Haupt, Clyde V. "Never the Twain Shall Meet: The Novel and Film Adaptations of *Adventures of Huckleberry Finn.*" Ph.D. diss. State University of New York, Buffalo, 1992. 296 pp. DAI 53:1159A.

Haupt demonstrates that virtually all of the film adaptations of *Huckleberry Finn* (from 1920 through 1985) depart from the text but that not all departures are unfaithful to the text. "In fact . . . most film versions of Huck Finn are film counterparts of the King and Duke, [and] 'humbugs and frauds' who cheat their audiences and debase the novel because they strain for laughs and 'flapdoodle' [may actually provide] substance and honesty, if not authenticity."

Hefflin, Bena Ruth. "African-American Children's Literature and Its Connections to Enriching Learning." Ed.D. diss. University of Pittsburgh, 1997. 194 pp. DAI 58:2209A.

Hefflin studies the response of African American students to discussions about "culturally conscious African American children's literature [to determine] the influence of literature on student self-concept, writing, and attitude toward reading." She finds the results of working with a "mixed-ability" group of children rewarding and concludes that it is "essential to incorporate culturally specific literature into [the] school curriculum."

Hixon, Martha Pittman. "Awakenings and Transformations: Re-Visioning the Tales of 'Sleeping Beauty,' 'Snow White,' 'The Frog Prince,' and 'Tam Lin.'" Ph.D. diss. University of Southwestern Louisiana, 1997. 232 pp. DAI 58:857A.

Hixon's dissertation deals with Western classic and contemporary literature and is predicated on the assumption that fairy tales, past and present, are used for "socialization and education," although contemporary tales usually involve media other than oral story telling, especially print and visual media. She also analyzes the way contemporary storytellers and story writers either adapt or reinterpret old fairy tales "to suit contemporary political and social paradigms. . . . [S]uch 're-visioned' tales say much about the society that produced them." She examines the classic and contemporary tellings of four tales and assesses the ways they have been retold, as well as the impact of their retelling on children's literature. She concludes that the fact that "these tales are still so familiar and powerful despite being retold in a variety of forms indicates that literary variations, like variations in the oral tales, contribute to the longevity of a tale and prove its universal qualities."

Hundley, Clarence Carroll, Jr. "Fairy Tale Elements in the Short Fiction of Nathaniel Hawthorne." Ph.D. diss. University of North Carolina, Greensboro, 1994. 237 pp. DAI 56:553A.

Hundley suggests that Hawthorne was quite aware of specific fairy tales and their tellers and that he consciously worked them into his writing of short stories as well as into *A Wonder-Book* and *Tanglewood Tales*. The dissertation also includes a history and definition of fairy tales. It concludes with a summary of "the major changes that Hawthorne made in his use of fairy tale elements."

Jenkins, David Omar. "The Moral Adventure of Childhood: A Critical Study of the Works of Robert Coles." Ph.D. diss. Duke University, 1994. 242 pp. DAI 55:1004A.

Jenkins raises the question "of whether Robert Coles, in spite of his best intentions, adequately displays children's 'moral lives' and moral character, given the psychiatric models of human behavior which remain compelling for him." He also questions Coles's ability to write to a popular audience and remain faithful to his discipline and his subjects. His study is informed by Alasdair MacIntyre, Ludwig Wittgenstein, Stanley Hauerwas, and Dorothy Day. Jenkins believes that Coles needed the latter "to help him tell Ruby Bridge's story faithfully."

Kerosky, Maria Baka. "Afterwards They Lived Happily Together: A Study on Relational Development in Fairy Tales." Ph.D. diss. California School of Professional Psychology, 1994. 293 pp. DAI 55:577–78B.

Kerosky studies the relation between human psychodynamics and fairy tales. Results indicate "that the most common themes in fairy tales reflect the main assumptions of the theory of relational development," which "focuses on the importance of relationships in successful human development."

Kiner, Henrietta Pauline. "The Social Structure of Children's Twentieth Century Literature." Ph.D. diss. The Claremont Graduate School, 1997. 215 pp. DAI 58:814A.

In her context analysis, based on "the sociology of knowledge," of seventy-five Newbery Award–winning books, Kiner asks the question "Does literature for children incorporate ideologies that are reflective of their contemporary culture?" She finds that post–World War II texts demonstrated "an objectified other, progress, universality, and individualism." Texts shifted to "paradigms of isolation and powerlessness" as the United States became more industrialized. They shifted again around 1950, when authors began to show children in "the role of protagonists [and] as thinking and socially interacting entities capable of self-determination and free-will." In essence "the early books sought to shape their readers' reality, the latter books sought to critique it. . . . This discursive movement also parallel[s] a shift in value structure and morality" during the middle and later decades of the twentieth century.

Knapp, Keith Nathaniel. "Accounts of Filial Sons: Ru Ideology in Early Medieval China." Ph.D. diss. University of California, Berkeley, 1997. 455 pp. DAI 58:554A.

Knapp's dissertation deals with filial piety stories, which are often assumed to have been written originally as literature for children, and demonstrates that they were, in fact, intended for "educated adult males" and that they "flourished because they embodied both the social and political ethos of the great clans" while preaching "subordination and self-sacrifice."

Lesnick-Oberstein, Karin Beate. "Principles and Practice in Critical Theory: Children's Literature." Ph.D. diss. University of Bristol. 243 pp. DAI 52:2915A.

"Rather than offering 'solutions' to the self-defined problems of children's fiction and children's fiction criticism, this thesis wishes to explore the operation of purposes within children's literature criticism, and the way these purposes direct and define the use of texts on, and ideas of, education, childhood, and children." She argues that criticism of children's literature did not originate from a split between school books and children's fiction and concludes with a discussion of the relation between children's literary criticism and adult literary criticism.

Lockhart, Robert Lee. "Literary Art as Experience: Teaching Young Adult Literature, Moral Inquiry, and the Personal Journey Toward Meaning." Ph.D. diss. Virginia Polytechnic Institute and State University, 1996. 247 pp. DAI 57:2835–36A.

Lockhart is concerned with "the gap that exists between theory and practice, where those who work in the classroom find little relevance in the theory discussed and researched on the university level." In his critique of higher education, where, he believes, personal experience can be sublimated by theory, he dis' ısses his reactions to the work of John Knowles and Katherine Paterson and th use of their works in a middle-school classroom.

Luton, Mary Katherine. "'Les Malheurs de Ségur': An Examination of Accusations of Sadism Against La Comtesse de Ségur." Ph.D. diss. University of Virginia, 1997. 234 pp. DAI 58:899A.

Because of her use of violence and corporal punishment, Ségur has, since the middle of the twentieth century, been accused of sadism by some critics, and her work has been deemed inappropriate for child readers. Luton gives a brief history of Ségur criticism, places her work within the history of French children's literature, shows how some critics have "misused" the term *sadism,* and "argues that Ségur's novels provide historical documentation on the use of corporal punishment during her lifetime in both her native Russia" and France. "By comparing Ségur's portrayal of corporal punishment" with contemporary testimony, Luton concludes "that it would be more accurate to consider Ségur a social critic and a reformer than a sadist."

Malone, Martha Louise. "Opera for American Youth: A Practical and Analytical Study." D.M.A. diss. University of Cincinnati, 1994. 385 pp. DAI 55:2632A.

Malone discusses "the most effective approaches currently used for introducing young people to opera," especially those that were specifically written for children. She analyzes "the suitability of the libretto . . . , text-setting, harmony, melody, rhythm, level of difficulty, and vocal ranges and tessituras" of the following "exemplary" works: *The Toy Shop* by Seymour Barab, *The Wayfarers* by John Joubert, *Sid the Serpent Who Wanted to Sing* by Malcolm Fox, *The Elves and the Shoemaker* by Maurice Bailey, *The Fire Maid* by Robert Long, *Marko the Miser* by Thea Musgrave, *The Dead Moon* by Jeffrey Bishop, and *A Muskrat Lullaby* by Edward Barnes.

McCrary, William. "The Fairy Tale Operas of Seymour Barab." D.A. diss. University of Northern Colorado, 1997. 215 pp. DAI 58:1146A.

Since the mid-1960s Seymour Barab has been writing fairy-tale operas (scores and libretti) for children. Five of these are discussed: *Little Red Riding Hood; Who Am I* (based on the Grimms' version of "The Goose Girl"); *The Maker of Illusions* (based on Andersen's "The Snow Queen"); *Snow White;* and *Sleeping Beauty.* The dissertation provides a stylistic analysis of the operas and an appendix with a catalog of Barab's stage, vocal, and instrumental compositions and a transcript of a Barab interview.

Melanson, Lisa Stapleton. "The Hero's Quest for Identity in Fantasy Literature: A Jungian Analysis." Ph.D. diss. University of Massachusetts, 1994. 225 pp. DAI 55:2407A.

"As a genre, fantasy seeks to validate the unconscious world of dreams, to insist not merely on its existence in the human psyche, but on its essential, vital presence." Melanson's premise is that "the quest for identity takes shape according to the hero's place in the life cycle." She discusses the work of Lewis Carroll, John Ruskin, Edmund Spenser, Ursula K. Le Guin, George MacDonald, C. S. Lewis, and H. Rider Haggard.

Monteiro, Katia Canton. "The Fairy Tale Revisited: A Survey of the Evolution of the Tales, from Classical Literary Interpretations to Innovative Contemporary Dance-Theatre Productions." Ph.D. diss. New York University, 1993. 325 pp. DAI 54:2567–68A.

"Because of their enduring popularity worldwide, fairy tales can be considered the paradigm of human narrative." In discussing their origins, Monteiro denies the commonplace that fairy tales are "universal, ageless and anonymous." She believes that the tales have authors who constantly reshape and reconfigure their versions based on "their own socio-historical contexts and their moral, cultural, [and] political values." She discuses Perrault and the Brothers Grimm and the influence of fairy tales on Petipa, Maguy Marin, Pina Bausch, and the American dance group Kinematic.

Morgan, Trevor James. "Acknowledging the Lie: Extreme Self-Consciousness in Contemporary Fantasy Fiction." Ph.D. diss. Texas Tech University, 1995. 243 pp. DAI 56:3952–53A.

Morgan believes that "both our societies and the literature coming out of those societies have moved toward an extreme self-consciousness," particularly in terms of "fantastic" literature. He discusses metafiction and how a narrative becomes self-conscious, and he defines myth, legend, and folktale. He focuses on the works of J. R. R. Tolkien, C. S. Lewis, and Peter S. Beagle.

Nix, Elizabeth Morrow. "An Exuberant Flow of Spirits: Antebellum Adolescent Girls in the Writing of Southern Women." Ph.D. diss. Boston University, 1996. 243 pp. DAI 57:1140A.

In a work based on novels, diaries, and periodicals—and, in Chapter 1, on Caroline Gilman's *The Rose-Bud* (a juvenile periodical) and her novel *Recollections of a Southern Matron*—Nix examines "the processes by which girls were socialized into ladies." She concludes that girls not only resisted conformity but that their culture tolerated that resistance.

Reardon, Daniel Charles. "Up the Dragon: A Study of Rosemary Sutcliff's *Sword at Sunset,* Parke Godwin's *Firelord,* and Selected Arthurian Romance and Fantasy Novels Since 1960." D.A. diss. State University of New York, Albany, 1993. 259 pp. DAI 54:2568A.

Reardon believes that the works of Sutcliff and Godwin differ from other Arthurian romances and historical fiction published since 1960 "in their attention to historical detail and psychological complexity" of character. He also demonstrates the considerable influence Sutcliff has had on writers who followed her.

Rush, Randy Fernandese. "A Survey of African-American Fantasy Literature with Case Study Analyses of the Responses of Four African-American Adolescents to Young Adult Heroic Fantasy Literature That Features Protagonists of African Origin." Ph.D. diss. Ohio State University, 1996. 336 pp. DAI 57:4297A.

Rush identifies fifty works of African American fantasy, and the results suggest that the body of work is limited. Children who read the works "related most strongly to protagonists with similar cultural origins, and their preferred reading genres were mystery, horror, and poetry."

Saad, Shahnaz Christine. "The Portrayal of Male and Female Characters with Chronic Illnesses in Children's Realistic Fiction." Ph.D. diss. University of Pennsylvania, 1996. 240 pp. DAI 57:3013A.

Saad's sample includes fifty-four children's books published between 1970 and 1994, each of which she paired with a child reader "who had the same chronic illness as the character in the book." Most readers found the books "at least slightly unrealistic," although the more "a reader could identify with a book's characters or events, the more the reader enjoyed the book." More than four-fifths of the chronically ill characters were female, reflecting "the traditional societal view that female bodies are inherently pathological." She concludes that although each book might not have been "sexist, racist, or heterosexist in itself," those patterns emerged.

Shastri, Hope. "The Picture Book Dragon." Ph.D. diss. Texas Woman's University, 1993. 122 pp. DAI 54:3624A.

Shastri examines 151 children's books published in the United States between 1950 and 1992 to determine whether dragons, as some critics say, have lost "much

of their mythic power and [have] become stereotyped, denatured and domesticated" and whether "the changes are necessary to make dragons safe for children."
She finds that except for breathing fire, most dragons have become benign; "ge-
nial dragons do not fly. . . . The friendlier the dragons become, the more likely
they will be in a subservient position."

Shea, Victor Norman. "Reading Adventure, Reading Empire, Reading 1884." Ph.D.
diss. York University, 1996. 781 pp. DAI 57:5167A.

In his study of adventure, Shea examines the work of Robert Louis Stevenson, George Henty, and H. Rider Haggard "as both genre of gendered fiction and
rhetorical trope in the language, history, and literature of the British Empire in
1884." He reads adventure "dialectically, in the tension between high and popular
cultural and literary norms" and draws on postcolonial, feminist, and poststruc-
turalist methodologies.

Sheehan, Kevin James. "Two Childhoods." Ph.D. diss. University of Pennsylvania, 1995.
166 pp. DAI 56:1797-98A.

In an analysis of Kingsley's *The Water Babies* and Carroll's *Alice's Adventures in
Wonderland* Sheehan asserts that these two Anglican priests "debate the origin and
end of evil. . . . [Because they] shared the premise that ontogeny recapitulated
phylogeny, their debate was in effect a debate about the relation of childhood to
adulthood." Each believed that *The Origin of Species* supported his argument, although they read Darwin differently. For Kingsley, God is omnipotent, a father to
evolving life, and *Water Babies* "is a Fall-story . . . : all life evolved from a few simple
forms . . . , punishment of sinners is only temporary, [and] all fallen souls will ultimately be united with God in heaven." *Alice in Wonderland* "is a Fall-story which argues that the Malthusian abyss over which life dances is the result of Original Sin."

Sherer, Susan Ellen. "Secrecy in Victorian Fiction." Ph.D. diss. University of Virginia,
1996. 153 pp. DAI 57:3951A.

Sherer addresses secrecy and childhood in both children's and adult Victorian fiction. In them, she observes that the "child's mind, for the adult gazer, is
often either a place of edenic bliss, lost forever and therefore secret to the adult,
or a Pandora's box of evil secrets, or a disturbing admixture of both." Works discussed are Carroll's Alice books, Dickens's *Hard Times, A Tale of Two Cities,* and *A
Christmas Carol,* Andersen's "The Princess and the Pea," and Housman's "Rocking-
Horse Land." In Chapter 15 he concludes that "secrecy, as its etymology makes
clear, implies secretion, parting, which in turn implies lost contact, which, in
another turn, implies some desire or at least possibility for return." In essence,
secrecy is "the search for identity, which in literature inevitably becomes the story
of a journey homeward, or a return."

Simpson, Robin Smith. "Fairy-Tale Representations of Social Realities: Madame D'Aulnoy's *Contes des fees* (1697-1698)." Ph.D. diss. Duke University, 1996. 197 pp. DAI
57:5175A.

In an interdisciplinary study that combines historical and literary scholarship,
Simpson demonstrates that d'Aulnoy's fairy tales "express concrete, seventeenth-
century French social realities," something most scholarship has ignored as readily
as it ignores the role of the fairy in her tales. Simpson contends that if one reads
the tales from the fairy's point of view then "these fairies are more than stereotypical fairy godmothers—they problematize social issues which were important
to d'Aulnoy's contemporaries." Major social issues in which fairies intervene are
"intergenerational relationships, marital relationships, choice of a spouse, patronage, and royal authority."

Stan, Susan Marcia. "A Study of International Children's Picture Books Published in
the United States in 1994." Ph.D. diss. University of Minnesota, 1997. 160 pp. DAI
58:2572A.

Of the 257 international picture books published in the United States in 1994, 72 percent "contained no identifying features to place the geographical setting, making the setting American by implication." In fact, only twenty-seven of the books "contained enough information in the text or illustrations to prompt a discerning reader to recognize that the story did not occur in the United States," but there was not enough information to "anchor" a story in a known place. And of the thirty-two books that had settings outside the United States, only fifteen "were actually set in the country in which they originated."

Swartz, Mark E. "Before the Rainbow: L. Frank Baum's *The Wonderful Wizard of Oz* on Stage and Screen to 1939." Ph.D. diss. New York University, 1996. 536 pp. DAI 57:931A.

Some of the dramatic adaptations highlighted in this dissertation are a 1902 stage version, with a script by Baum, which was a "lavish musical extravaganza" that continued to tour well into the teens; a 1908 multimedia show that Baum toured himself that included "several stereopticon slides and brief motion pictures"; a 1910 one-reel motion picture that was produced by Selig Polyscope Company; and a 1925 slapstick version that was a feature-length silent film. Swartz believes that "these important projects laid the iconographic groundwork for the depiction of Dorothy and her world on stage and screen."

Traylor, Gwendolyn Effler. "The Effect of Figurative Language Instruction Using Children's Literature upon the Writing of Fourth Grade Students." Ed.D. diss. University of Houston, 1997. 178 pp. DAI 58:727A.

Traylor analyzes the effectiveness of an "instructional program using children's literature and writing assignments" on children's use of figurative language in their own writing. She found that there was "a statistically significant difference" in the quality of students' ability to produce similes and create personification. There was no appreciable difference in their ability to employ onomatopoeia or metaphors.

Ulrich, Judy A. P. "An Analysis of Selected Play Adaptations and the Original Version of *The Adventures of Tom Sawyer*." Ph.D. diss. Michigan State University, 1988. 306 pp. DAI 50:1851–52A.

Ulrich studies twenty-one theatrical adaptations of *Tom Sawyer* (eleven since 1967) and finds them not particularly faithful to the original work. Plot lines are omitted; new characters or groups of characters are added; Tom's complexity is retained, but "few plays depict his growth and change." She concludes with suggestions on how to be faithful to a text while adapting it.

Vondra, Janet Louise. "Textbooks and the American Indian: A Not So Distant Mirror." Ed.D. diss. University of La Verne, 1994. 356 pp. DAI 56:1140A.

Vondra discusses the portrayal of American Indians in textbooks adopted for use in California from 1850 through 1994. Although there have been significant changes, she finds that pictures of American Indians have been "consistently developed from a framework of White, western values and political constructs and, as such, serve as a 'mirror' which reflects attitudes and values of the dominant society." Essentially, the image of Indians is negative, and it focuses on the "lack of White ways"; it "supports and justifies the treatment of native Americans and is based on political and economic need of the dominant culture"; or it is a "'timeless' image . . . which ignores diversity among Indians."

Wallis, Judith Mayne. "Children's Favorite Novels: An Analysis of Books That Have Won Multiple State Popularity Awards." Ed.D. diss. University of Houston, 1997. 350 pp. DAI 58:782A.

Wallis examines the format, literary features, content, and genre of books written for third through eighth graders that won state awards between 1981 and 1996 and applies Applebee's Vygotskian schema "for describing text structure" and "Havighurst's developmental tasks of middle childhood" to the works. Results suggest that children in this age group like realistic fiction, a single, well-developed character between the ages of ten and twelve, "integral, contemporary settings," omniscient or first-person narrators, an informal style, "memorable language," "person-against-person" conflict, episodic plots, explicit themes, suspense, and resolution in books that are well packaged and visually appealing. She also found that the novels "were reflective of the same social and psychological issues present in the lives of young readers: sense of belonging, independence, conflict about generations, and family relationships."

Weaver, Mary Bronwyn. "Empowering the Children: Theatre for Young Audiences in Anglophone Canada." Ph.D. diss. University of Toronto, 1992. 317 pp. DAI 55:3688A.

Weaver studies Canadian theater for children from the mid-1960s to the present and analyzes what she calls "Commitment Shortcuts": dramaturgical devices that "allow children to commit to the play through emotional identification, or complicity." These include "accessible iconography, playing on emotional associations of place and time, enactment sequences, victimization of child characters, presenting more than one perspective, ineffectual or absent adults, self-reliant child characters, and open ended hopeful resolutions."

Yeoman, Elizabeth. "Tales Told in School: Children, Stories, and Issues of Justice and Equity." Ph.D. diss. University of Toronto, 1994. 228 pp. DAI 56:2634A.

Yeoman deals with "disruptive texts"—"storybooks that seemed to raise questions of equity and justice, particularly concerning issues of race, gender, peace and the environment." Despite the frequent pressure on the academic community to present children with neutral material and thus build "a more peaceful and egalitarian society," Yeoman believes that "choosing or excluding certain kinds of texts for use in schools is no guarantee of long-lasting social change, or even of changed behavior in individual children."

Young, Grace Halstead. "The Role of Animals in Russian Folk Tales." Ph.D. diss. University of Illinois, Urbana-Champaign, 1996. 212 pp. DAI 57:1646A.

Young studies the influence of pagan and Christian philosophies on folk literature and oral folklore, as well as the differences between the philosophies, noting that Christian influences are more obvious in written literature and, hence, it shows less use of animals as "pagan divinities." In "oral folklore, even in religious fairy tales, [the emphasis] is on the positive, whereas in written tradition animals are most often seen as either inferior or wicked." In pagan tales animals are mankind's friends and helpers; they are depicted as "beautiful treasures formed of gold, silver, and precious stones; as superior to man in their magic power; a benevolent force is often seen in the dragon [that is] evil and fearsome in Western folklore."

Also of Note

Ackerman, Kelley Lee. "Listening to Students' Voices About Young Adult Literature: A Phenomenological Approach." Ed.D. diss. West Virginia University, 1995. 122 pp. DAI 57:2395A.

Ackerman finds that the results of exposing ninth-grade students to young adult literature confirm earlier research.

Alpe, Twila Little. "An Analysis of Gender Representation in Caldecott Award and Honor Books, 1972–1996." Ed.D. diss. Mississippi State University, 1996. 81 pp. DAI 57:1611A.

Alpe concludes "that some change in gender representation has occurred, but representation remains unequal, still picturing males more often than females."

Arnold, David Harvey. "Accelerating Language Development Through Picture Book Reading: Replication and Extension to a Videotape Training Format." Ph.D. diss. State University of New York, Stony Brook, 1993. 51 pp. DAI 54:5378B.

> Arnold examines the use of video to teach "dialogic reading" to mothers of preschoolers.

Barce, Jennifer Wilson. "Examining Early Childhood Literacy in Cross-Cultural Contexts: A Case Study in the Transition Between Amish Home Culture and Public School." Ph.D. diss. Indiana University, 1995. 196 pp. DAI 56:4269A.

Bernstein, Susan Naomi. "Writing as Process and Metaphor in Selected Works of Louisa May Alcott, Margaret Fuller, Herman Melville, and Harriet Jacobs." Ph.D. diss. Pennsylvania State University, 1993. 272 pp. DAI 54:1800A.

Boyer, Steven Dwight. "Authority in the Theological Vision of C. S. Lewis." Ph.D. diss. Boston University, 1996. 522 pp. DAI 56:4824–25A.

Bush, Marcella M. "From Mythic History to Historic Myth: Captain John Smith and Pocahontas in Popular History." Ph.D. diss. Bowling Green State University, 1997. 233 pp. DAI 58:3182A.

> Bush attempts to bridge "the gap between popular and scholarly history" and makes a case for "historians who are willing to open themselves to unconventional sources."

Cantrell, Susan Chambers. "Students' Acquisition of Basic Literacy Skills in Kentucky's Primary School Programs." Ed.D. diss. University of Kentucky, 1997. 157 pp. DAI 58:2078A.

Carpenter, Marilyn Gordon. "Preservice Teachers as Readers." Ph.D. diss. University of Arizona, 1997. 332 pp. DAI 58:1248A.

Castillo i Valero, Montserrat. "Il lustradores Catalans del libre per a infants, 1905–1939." [Catalan children's book illustrators, 1905–1939.] Ph.D. diss. Universitat Central de Barcelona, 1993. 336 pp. DAI 57:1049C.

Chapman, Mary (Anne) Megan. "'Living Pictures': Women and Tableaux Vivants in Nineteenth-Century Fiction and Culture." Ph.D. diss. Cornell University, 1992. 230 pp. DAI 53:2812A.

> Chapman discusses Louisa May Alcott.

Chen, Ren-Fu. "Knowledge, Experience, and Perspectives of Teachers Toward Implementing Creative Drama in Taiwanese Kindergartens." Ph.D. diss. Pennsylvania State University, 1997. 186 pp. DAI 58:2466A.

Davis, Janet Marie Gorden. "Dickens's Bestiary: Animals as Expressions of Character and Theme." Ph.D. diss. University of Maryland, College Park, 1992. 251 pp. DAI 53:2378A.

DeBaryshe, Barbara Diane. "Facilitating Language Development Through Picture-Book Reading: Evaluation of a Read-Aloud Package for Parents and Preshoolers." Ph.D. diss. State University of New York, Stony Brook, 1987. 213 pp. DAI 50:2174B.

> DeBaryshe's study confirms that parent-child interaction "during picture-book reading plays an important role in early language development."

Fallin, Donald Niall. "Hero/Heroine Identification, Gender, and Self-Esteem in Adolescents." Psy.D. diss. California School of Professional Psychology, Berkeley-Alameda, 1997. 114 pp. DAI 58:2716B.

> Hero identification remains important and differs between boys and girls and between children with high and low self-esteem.

Gioia, Barbara Emma. "Once Upon a Time . . . : A Collaborative Study of the Storybook Experiences of Three Deaf Preschoolers." Ph.D. diss. State University of New York, Albany, 1997. 238 pp. DAI 58:1640A

Hackett, Jill. "I've Gotta Crow: Women, Voice, and Writing." Ph.D. diss. The Union Institute, 1997. 350 pp. DAI 58:3505A.

Hashway, Susan E. "The Validation of a Hierarchy of Reading Comprehension Skills for

Young Adults." Ed.D. diss. Grambling State University, 1995. 303 pp. DAI 57:2801A.

Hassig, Debra Higgs. "Homo animal est, homo animal non est: Text and Image in Medieval English Bestiaries." Ph.D. diss. Columbia University, 1993. 592 pp. DAI 54:347A.

Holland Biggs, Karin L. "Disturbing (Dis)Positions: Interdisciplinary Perspectives on Emotion, Identification, and the Authority of Fantasy in Theories of Reading Performance." Ph.D. diss. McGill University, 1994. 527 pp. DAI 56:3783A.

    Holland Biggs examines "why we find some narratives, plots, and images compelling and what this phenomenon can tell us about the cultural bases of human motivation."

Hundert, Debra Ann. "Paths of Learning Through *The Forest of Dreams:* Senior Secondary Students and Theater for Young Audiences." Ph.D. diss. University of Toronto, 1996. 421 pp. DAI 57:3450A.

    Hundert describes the production of an original play for children in a senior classroom setting.

Hunsicker, Gerald Edwin. "The Lensgrinder's Stories: A Children's Reader About Virtues and a Guide for Parents and Teachers to Using the Lensgrinder's Stories." Ph.D. diss. Union Institute, 1996. 87 pp. DAI 57:2409A.

    Hunsicker examines the use of realistic stories to describe the virtues of courage, perseverance, responsibility, work, self-discipline, compassion, faith, honesty, loyalty, and friendship.

Irigaray, Ricardo Luis. "Tolkien and Christian Faith." Ph.D. diss. Universidad de Navarra, 1996. 289 pp. DAI 58:367C. [Spanish text]

    Irigaray is concerned with the "implicit theological contents, contributing to the dialogue between theology and literature" in Tolkien's works.

Jeong, Myn-Gyun Kwon. "The Influence of Home and School Reading Experiences on Young Children's Emergent Reading Stances and Responses to Children's Books." Ph.D. diss. University of California, Berkeley, 1996. 243 pp. DAI 57:3386A.

    Jeong is concerned with the reading "stance" of young Korean students and their mothers.

Johnson, Frances Agnes. "The Role of Stance in a Subgenre of Non-Fiction: Junior High Readers' Response Writing and *Anne Frank: The Journal of a Young Girl.*" Ph.D. diss. Texas A&M University, 1994. 198 pp. DAI 56:500A.

Kapsamer, Claudia. "Wirtschaftliche Entwicklung; Carinthian Summer Festival: Cultural Profile and Economic Development." Dr. Phil. Universität Wien, 1991. 324 pp. DAI 57:324C.

    The Carinthian Summer Festival performs church and children's operas.

Kilstofte, Anne Carol. "Matches: An Opera in One Act Based on the Tale by Hans Christian Andersen." Ph.D. diss. University of Minnesota, 1995. n.p. DAI 56:4197A.

    Kilstofte discusses her fifty-minute opera based on "The Little Match Girl."

L'Allier, Susan K. "The Self-Sponsored Reading of Fifth Grade Students: Does Whole Language Instruction Make a Difference?" Ed.D. diss. Harvard University, 1997. 335 pp. DAI 58:1640A.

    L'Allier's findings show that some instructional practices have a beneficial effect on reading, but more study is needed.

Logan, Mawuena Kossi. "Africa Through Victorian Eyes: George Alfred Henty and the Fiction of Empire." Ph.D. diss. University of Iowa, 1996. 313 pp. DAI 57:3038A.

    Logan's study is as critical of empire and the continuing influence of Victorian colonialism on Africa as it is of the literature of George Alfred Henty.

Lonigan, Christopher John. "Environmental Influences on Language Acquisition: An Examination of the Maternal-Input Hypothesis in the Context of a Picture Book Reading Intervention." Ph.D. diss. State University of New York, Stony Brook, 1991. 111 pp. DAI 52:4492–93B.

Lonigan examines "the effects of a one-month, home-based intervention, designed to optimize maternal reading of picture books to young children."

Mahmoud, Mahmoud Mohamed. "Travel and Adventure in the Works of Robert Louis Stevenson." Ph.D. diss. University of Glasgow, 1984. 278 pp. DAI 51:513A.
Mahmoud deals with adventure fiction as well as travel.

McBride, Roxie Ann. "Multicultural Education Utilizing Multiethnic Children's Literature in Fourth Grade Classrooms: A Descriptive Case Study." Ed.D. diss. Oklahoma State University, 1997. 172 pp. DAI 58:3811A.
"[R]eading multiethnic children's literature can have a positive effect on the attitudes and perceptions of students."

McDaniel, Janet Pandorf. "Developing Problem-Solving Skills in Primary Students." Ed.D. diss. University of Cincinnati, 1997. 260 pp. DAI 58:1593A.

Millin, Sandra K. "Effects of Readers Theatre on Oral Reading Ability and Reading Attitudes of Second-Grade Title I Students." Ed.D. diss. West Virginia University, 1996. 133 pp. DAI 57:1002A.

Mirsky-Zayas, Irina. "An Old Fairy-Tale or a New Legend: A Study of [Nikolay Semyonovich] Leskov's Mythologizing Fiction." Ph.D. diss. Brown University, 1994. 171 pp. DAI 55:1985–86A.
Mirsky-Zayas contends that Leskov has created a new literary genre.

Mistretta-Hampston, Jennifer Lyn. "Parent's Beliefs and Practices Regarding Literacy Development in First Grade." Ph.D. diss. State University of New York, Albany, 1996. 209 pp. DAI 57:4308A.

Muhammad, Rashidad Jaamiʿ. "Value and Authenticity: Young Adult Readers Respond to African-American Literature." Ph.D. diss. Michigan State University, 1996. 262 pp. DAI 57:2040A.
Muhammad focuses on Paula Fox's *The Slave Dancer,* Ou Sebestyen's *Words by Heart,* and Mildred Taylor's *Roll of Thunder, Hear My Cry.*

Mungai-Kamau, Murugi Wa. "Story-Listening and Off-Task Contexts' Effects on Both the Performance and Motivation of African-American and European-American Children." Ph.D. diss. Howard University, 1997. 156 pp. DAI 58:3002A.

Murr, Suzanne Lawler. "Parent Behaviors Displayed in Children's Literature: Content Analysis of Picture Storybooks Between 1946 and 1995." Ph.D. diss. Texas Women's University, 1997. 113 pp. DAI 58:2994A.
Murr samples two hundred books written between 1946 and 1995 and finds that depictions of mothers varied little; portrayals of fathers and other caregivers increased toward the end of the time period.

Nauman, April Diana. "Reading Boys, Reading Girls: How Sixth Graders Understand and Are Influenced by Fictional Characters." Ph.D. diss. University of Illinois, Chicago, 1997. 219 pp. DAI 58:1234A.
Nauman finds that children's books "can be an important enculturating mechanism" for learning traditional roles. Books "encourage children to find ways of relating to characters who seem unlike them."

Nolan, E. Katherine. "Teachers' Perceptions of the Use of Children's Literature to Create Context for Mathematics Instruction." Ph.D. diss. University of Alabama, 1997. 167 pp. DAI 58:2080A.

O'Laughlin, Michael Gary. "Writing Lives: The Writing Processes of Children's Authors and Their Characters." Ph.D. diss. University of Wyoming, 1997. 202 pp. DAI 58:2988A.
O'Laughlin analyzes the fiction and poetry of children's authors, as well as their autobiographical works.

Ozcan, Nihal Misket. "The Development of Children's Story Understanding and Its Relation to Their Understanding of Belief-Desire Psychology." Ph.D. diss. University of Iowa, 1997. 160 pp. DAI 58:1586A.

Pak, Meesook Kim. "A Comparative Analysis of Middle-Class Korean and Middle-Class White American Children's Story Production and Comprehension." Ph.D. diss. University of Rochester, 1997. 119 pp. DAI 58:113A.

Pohlabel, Linda. "Lab Reading and the At-Risk Child: Introducing Families to Books." Ed.D. diss. Brigham Young University, 1997. 151 pp. DAI 58:123A.

Pohlabel examines the positive results of a twelve-to-sixteen week study of three families.

Pongratz, Elaine M. "Lifelong Learning in Young Adult Literature." Ed.D. diss. Pennsylvania State University, 1996. 328 pp. DAI 57:3361A.

Pongratz finds 965 references to lifelong learning in the seventeen novels she examines. Examples were both frequent and meaningful.

Price, Debra Patricia. "Code Instruction, Literacy Tasks, and Metacognition in a Literature-Based and a Skills-Based First-Grade Classroom." Ph.D. diss. University of Texas, Austin, 1996. 351 pp. DAI 58:75A.

Prichard, Teri Gail. "Moving Toward a Literature-Based Classroom in a Middle School Context." Ph.D. diss. University of Arizona, 1996. 342 pp. DAI 57:4676A.

Propster, Diane Marguerite. "Adolescents' Methods of Discussion and Perceptions of Topics and Issues in Three Contemporary Films." Ph.D. diss. University of California, Los Angeles, 1994. 219 pp. DAI 56:762A.

Pymm, Robert Anthony. "Australian Fiction in Australian Libraries: The Collection and Preservation of Titles Published Between 1900 and 1970." Ph.D. diss. University of New South Wales, 1996. n.p. DAI 58:1487A.

Richards, Lyn Altman. " 'Pictures in Our Minds': A Narrative Study of the Incorporation of Creative Dramatics as Pedagogy in Elementary Classroom Content Areas." Ed.D. diss. University of Pittsburgh, 1996. 305 pp. DAI 57:2868A.

Richards finds that creative dramatics transforms "the prescribed language arts, social studies, mathematics, and science curriculum" in a second grade classroom.

Sacerdoti, Yaakova. "At the Crossroads: A Study on the Discourse of Children's Literature." Ph.D. diss. University of Michigan, 1997. 298 pp. DAI 58:447A. [Hebrew text]

Sacerdoti addresses the differences between children's and adult literature and child and adult audiences, maintaining that each is a "literary system." The work of Efraim Sidon and Meir Halev, two important Israeli authors, are the focus of the dissertation.

Scoresby, Kevin J. "The Effects of Electronic Storybook Animations on Third Graders' Story Recall." Ph.D. diss. Brigham Young University, 1996. 109 pp. DAI 57:2449–50A.

Scoresby concludes that "any type of animation hindered the recall of non-illustrated textual details, regardless of how well the animations related to the story text."

Shine, Stephanie. "Preschoolers' Response to Picture Books in Small-Group Discussions: The Role of Genre." Ph.D. diss. University of Texas, Austin, 1995. 244 pp. DAI 56:2108A.

Shine analyzes informational, poetic, realistic, and fantasy picture books; she notes different responses to each "and that different knowledge bases were activated by the genres."

Sipe, Lawrence Robert. "The Construction of Literary Understanding by First and Second Graders in Response to Picture Storybook Readalouds." Ph.D. diss. Ohio State University, 1996. 410 pp. DAI 57:4268A.

Sipe treats "traditional literature; contemporary realistic fiction; and contemporary fantasy."

Smith, Janna Kay Homann. "The Impact of Children's Literature on Student Mathematics Attitudes." Ph.D. diss. Saint Louis University, 1996. 134 pp. DAI 57:2928A.

Smith finds that teaching mathematics using children's literature produced "positive changes" and increased a child's "problem solving efforts."

Smith, Meagan. "Characteristics of Picture Books That Facilitate Word Learning in Preschoolers." Ph.D. diss. State University of New York, Stony Brook, 1993. 73 pp. DAI 54:3366B.

Picture book reading promotes language learning; Smith's work focuses on the child rather than the adult reader.

Steury, Cynthia L. "The Effects of a Trade Book on Attitudes and Achievement in Social Studies." Ed.D. diss. Ball State University, 1996. 182 pp. DAI 57:4655A.

Steury's text is Lincoln and Christopher Collier's *My Brother Sam Is Dead;* the results are inconclusive.

Tepper, Nadine C. "Literacy Development: Teacher/Student Interaction in a Whole Language Classroom (Second-Grade)." Ph.D. diss. University of North Dakota, 1997. 122 pp. DAI 58:3424A.

Thomas, Peggy June Watkins. "James Fenimore Cooper's Use of Character Names and Nicknames in the Leatherstocking Tales." Ph.D. diss. University of Mississippi, 1995. 265 pp. DAI 57:222A.

Tyson, Cynthia Aleace. " 'Shut My Mouth Wide Open': African American Fifth-Grade Males Respond to Contemporary Realistic Children's Literature." Ph.D. diss. Ohio State University, 1997. 261 pp. DAI 58:1642A.

Tyson finds that "contemporary realistic children's literature can increase engagement and sustained interest and help the readers develop socio-political awareness and voices that initiate and enact social action."

Walker, Margaret F. "Trail Treasures: A Young Girl's Journey to Oregon in 1846." Ph.D. diss. Union Institute, 1996. 231 pp. DAI 57:4903A.

Walker has produced an original adventure novel for children based on 1,300 diaries, letters, anecdotes, and other primary sources.

Walters, Mary Lightsey. "The Relationship Between Reading Recovery Story-Writing Activity and Student Achievement and Acceleration Rate." Ed.D. diss. University of Southern Mississippi, 1996. 88 pp. DAI 58:55A.

Waters, Rebecca Ann. "Examining the Revision Activity of Writers in the Early Childhood Classroom." Ed.D. diss. University of Cincinnati, 1996. 153 pp. DAI 57:2920A.

Wiest, Lynda R. "The Role of Fantasy and Real-World Problem Contexts in Fourth- and Sixth-Grade Students' Mathematical Problem-Solving." Ph.D. diss. Indiana University, 1996. 331 pp. DAI 57:5091A.

Williams, Patricia Howard. "Home Literacy Portfolios: Tools for Sharing Literacy Information and for Assessing Parents' Awareness of and Involvement in Their Pre-Kindergarten Child's Literacy Development." Ph.D. diss. University of North Texas, 1996. 200 pp. DAI 57:4644A.

Willis, Melinda Richardson. "An Investigation of Second and Third Graders' Oral Responses to Humorous Children's Literature." Ed.D. diss. University of Kentucky, 1997. 202 pp. DAI 58:2117A.

Willis studies humorous picture books that express verbal or effectual "exaggeration, surprise, slapstick," absurdity, human foibles, ridicule, and violence. Children most often identified humor when it involved surprise or absurdity.

Wilson, Catherine. "Reading Against the Lines: Storyreading and Teaching in a Head Start Classroom." Ph.D. diss. University of Missouri, Kansas City, 1997. 242 pp. DAI 58:1574A.

Wolf, Hermann. "75 Jahre Kinder- und Jugendtheater in Salzburg, 1913–1988." (75 Years of children's and youth theater in Salzburg, 1913–1988) Dr.Phil. diss. Technische Universität Wien, 1990. n.p. DAI 57:0798C.

Yenika-Agbaw, Vivian S. "Postcolonialism and Multicultural Literacy: Images of Africa in Literature for Children and Young Adults." Ph.D. diss. Pennsylvania State University, 1996. 240 pp. DAI 57:1529A.

Yenika-Agbaw finds that "Africa is portrayed as natural and romantic" in literature for children, and when both African and Western authors write about Africa in this way "they encourage neocolonial attitudes or inferiority/dependence from Africans, and perpetuate the myth of the west being Africa's benefactor."

Zimmerman, Mary Alice. "The Archaeology of Performance: A Study of Ensemble Process and Development in the Lookingglass Theatre Production of *The Arabian Nights*." Ph.D. diss. Northwestern University, 1994. 356 pp. DAI 56:764A.

Contributors and Editors

GILLIAN ADAMS is the editor of *Children's Literature Abstracts* and an associate editor of the *ChLA Quarterly*. Her most recent essays and papers are on medieval children's literature, a subject she plans to pursue for the next few years.

KAREN COATS is assistant professor of English at Illinois State University, where she teaches children's literature. Her research focuses on children's and adolescent literature and critical theory, as well as children's studies.

R. H. W. DILLARD is professor of English and chair of the creative writing program at Hollins University. The author of several scholarly books, he is also a novelist and poet.

CHRISTINE DOYLE is an assistant professor of English at Central Connecticut State University, where she teaches courses in children's literature, storytelling, American literature, and women writers. Her recent research focuses on literary influences on Louisa May Alcott, on which she has an essay in Little Women *and the Feminist Imagination.*

RACHEL FORDYCE is a professor of English and dean of the College of Humanities and Social Sciences at Montclair State University and is the former executive secretary of the Children's Literature Association. She is the author of five books, on late Renaissance literature, children's theater, creative dramatics, and Lewis Carroll.

PAMELA K. HARER is a retired California attorney whose avocation for the past twenty years has been the study and collecting of children's books of historical interest. She has given occasional talks at California State University San Bernardino about her collection.

A. WALLER HASTINGS is professor of English and coordinator of English and linguistics at Northern State University in Aberdeen, South Dakota, where he teaches a variety of courses on children's literature. He is currently trying to develop two book projects: a critical book on Disney's animated feature films and a children's novel about the devastating 1997 floods in the Dakotas.

ELIZABETH LENNOX KEYSER is an associate professor of English at Hollins University, where she teaches children's literature, American literature, and American studies. She is the author of *Whispers in the Dark: The Fiction of Louisa May Alcott* (1993) and Little Women: *A Family Romance* (1999).

ALICE MILLS is a senior lecturer in literature, including children's literature, at the University of Ballarat in Victoria, Australia. She has published widely in the field of fantasy literature and is the editor of the *Random House Children's Treasury*. She also has a private practice as a Jungian psychotherapist.

CLAUDIA MILLS is an assistant professor of philosophy at the University of Colorado at Boulder, teaching and writing in the areas of ethics, applied ethics, and social and political philosophy. She is the author of more than twenty books for children, including the Dinah series (*Dynamite Dinah, Dinah for President, Dinah in Love,* and *Dinah Forever*) and the Gus and Grandpa series for first readers.

PHILIP NEL completed his doctorate in 1997 at Vanderbilt University and now teaches at the College of Charleston. His current project (until recently, known as his dissertation) studies novelists, popular culture figures, and children's authors as a way to examine the historical avant-garde in diverse media. In addition to transforming this dissertation into a book, he is trying to interest a publisher in printing a selection of the political cartoons that Dr. Seuss wrote during World War II.

JULIE PFEIFFER is an assistant professor of English at Hollins University. Her research interests focus on Milton's influence on nineteenth-century literature.

ANNE K. PHILLIPS is an assistant professor at Kansas State University. Co-editor of *Children's Literature* 21, she is currently collaborating with Gregory Eiselein on *The Louisa May Alcott Encyclopedia*. She is interested in all aspects of American children's literature.

CAROLYN SIGLER teaches courses in children's and young adult literature, women's studies, and popular culture at Kansas State University. She has edited a collection of Victorian imitations and parodies of Carroll titled *Alternative Alices: Visions and Revisions of Lewis Carroll's "Alice" Books* and is completing a critical book on Carroll and his imitators.

KATHARINE CAPSHAW SMITH, whose work has appeared in *Ariel* and *The Southern Quarterly*, is a doctoral candidate at the University of Connecticut. Her dissertation is titled " 'For the Children of the Sun': African-American Children's Literature, 1914–1954."

JAN SUSINA is an associate professor of English at Illinois State University, where he teaches courses in children's literature. He has edited *Logic and Tea: The Letters of Charles Dodgson to Members of the G. J. Rowell Family* and served as book review editor for *The Lion and the Unicorn*.

ETSUKO TAKETANI is associate professor of English at the University of Tsukuba, Japan, where she teaches American literature. Her essays appear in such publications as *ATO, American Periodicals, Concord Saunterer,* and *Journal of the American Oriental Society*.

ROBERTA SEELINGER TRITES is an associate professor of English at Illinois State University, where she teaches children's and adolescent literature. She is the author of *Waking Sleeping Beauty: Feminist Voices in Children's Novels*.

Index to Volumes 1–25

Compiled by Pamela K. Harer

Award Applications

The Children's Literature Association (ChLA) is a nonprofit organization devoted to promoting serious scholarship and high standards of criticism in children's literature. To encourage these goals, the Association offers various awards and fellowships annually.

ChLA Research Fellowships and Scholarships have a combined fund of $1,000 per year, and individual awards may range from $250 to $1,000, based on the number and needs of the winning applicants. The fellowships are awarded for proposals dealing with criticism or original scholarship with the expectation that the undertaking will lead to publication and significantly contribute to the field of children's literature. In honor of the achievement and dedication of Dr. Margaret P. Esmonde, proposals that deal with critical or original work in the areas of fantasy or science fiction for children or adolescents will be awarded the Margaret P. Esmonde Memorial Scholarship. The awards may be used only for research-related expenses, such as travel to special collections or materials and supplies. The annual deadline for applications is February 1. For further information and application guidelines, contact the Scholarship Chair (see address below).

In addition to fellowships and scholarships, ChLA recognizes outstanding works in children's literature annually through the following awards. The ChLA Article Award is presented for an article deemed the most noteworthy literary criticism article published in English on the topic of children's literature within a given year. The ChLA Book Award is presented for the most outstanding book of criticism, history, or scholarship in the field of children's literature in a given year.

The Phoenix Award is given to the author, or estate of the author, of a book for children published twenty years earlier that did not win a major award at the time of publication, but that, from the perspective of time, is deemed worthy of special recognition for its high literary quality.

The Carol Gay Award is presented for the best undergraduate paper written about some aspect of children literature. The annual deadline for applications is January 20.

For further information or to send nominations for any of the awards, contact the Children's Literature Association, P.O. Box 138, Battle Creek, MI 49016-0138, phone 616 965-8180; fax 616 965-3568; or by e-mail chla@mlc.lib.mi.us. This information is also at our web site, address http://ebbs.english.vt.edu/chla.

Order Form   Yale University Press
                   P.O. Box 209040, New Haven, CT 06520-9040
Phone orders 1-800-YUP-READ (U.S. and Canada)

Customers in the United States and Canada may photocopy this form and use it for
ordering all volumes of **Children's Literature** available from Yale University Press. Individuals are asked to pay in advance. All payments must be made in U.S. dollars. We
honor both MasterCard and VISA. Checks should be made payable to Yale University
Press.

Prices given are 1999 list prices for the United States and are subject to change without
notice. A shipping charge of $3.50 for the U.S. and $5.00 for Canada is to be added to
each order, and Connecticut residents must pay a sales tax of 6 percent.

Qty.	Volume	Price	Total amount	Qty.	Volume	Price	Total amount
____	10 (cloth)	$50.00	_____	____	20 (paper)	$18.00	_____
____	11 (cloth)	$50.00	_____	____	21 (cloth)	$50.00	_____
____	12 (cloth)	$50.00	_____	____	21 (paper)	$18.00	_____
____	13 (cloth)	$50.00	_____	____	22 (cloth)	$50.00	_____
____	14 (cloth)	$50.00	_____	____	22 (paper)	$18.00	_____
____	15 (cloth)	$50.00	_____	____	23 (cloth)	$50.00	_____
____	15 (paper)	$18.00	_____	____	23 (paper)	$18.00	_____
____	16 (paper)	$18.00	_____	____	24 (cloth)	$50.00	_____
____	17 (cloth)	$50.00	_____	____	24 (paper)	$18.00	_____
____	17 (paper)	$18.00	_____	____	25 (cloth)	$50.00	_____
____	18 (cloth)	$50.00	_____	____	25 (paper)	$18.00	_____
____	18 (paper)	$18.00	_____	____	26 (cloth)	$50.00	_____
____	19 (cloth)	$50.00	_____	____	26 (paper)	$18.00	_____
____	19 (paper)	$18.00	_____	____	27 (cloth)	$50.00	_____
____	20 (cloth)	$50.00	_____	____	27 (paper)	$18.00	_____

Payment of $_____ is enclosed (including sales tax if applicable).

MasterCard no. _____

4-digit bank no. _____ Expiration date _____

VISA no. _____ Expiration date _____

Signature _____

SHIP TO: _____

_____

_____

See the next page for ordering issues from Yale University Press, London. Volumes
out of stock in New Haven may be available from the London office.

Volumes 1–7 of **Children's Literature** can be obtained directly from John C. Wandell,
The Children's Literature Foundation, P.O. Box 370, Windham Center, Conn. 06280.

Order Form   Yale University Press, 23 Pond Street, Hampstead, London NW3
2PN, England

Customers in the United Kingdom, Europe, and the British Commonwealth may photocopy this form and use it for ordering all volumes of **Children's Literature** available from Yale University Press. Individuals are asked to pay in advance. We honour Access, VISA, and American Express accounts. Cheques should be made payable to Yale University Press.

The prices given are 1999 list prices for the United Kingdom and are subject to change. A post and packing charge of £1.95 is to be added to each order.

Qty.	Volume	Price	Total amount	Qty.	Volume	Price	Total amount
____	8 (cloth)	£40.00	_____	____	18 (cloth)	£40.00	_____
____	8 (paper)	£14.95	_____	____	18 (paper)	£14.95	_____
____	9 (cloth)	£40.00	_____	____	19 (cloth)	£40.00	_____
____	9 (paper)	£14.95	_____	____	19 (paper)	£14.95	_____
____	10 (cloth)	£40.00	_____	____	20 (paper)	£14.95	_____
____	11 (cloth)	£40.00	_____	____	21 (paper)	£14.95	_____
____	11 (paper)	£14.95	_____	____	22 (cloth)	£40.00	_____
____	12 (cloth)	£40.00	_____	____	22 (paper)	£14.95	_____
____	12 (paper)	£14.95	_____	____	23 (cloth)	£40.00	_____
____	13 (cloth)	£40.00	_____	____	23 (paper)	£14.95	_____
____	13 (paper)	£14.95	_____	____	24 (cloth)	£40.00	_____
____	14 (cloth)	£40.00	_____	____	24 (paper)	£14.95	_____
____	14 (paper)	£14.95	_____	____	25 (cloth)	£40.00	_____
____	15 (cloth)	£40.00	_____	____	25 (paper)	£14.95	_____
____	15 (paper)	£14.95	_____	____	26 (cloth)	£40.00	_____
____	16 (paper)	£14.95	_____	____	26 (paper)	£14.95	_____
____	17 (cloth)	£40.00	_____	____	27 (cloth)	£40.00	_____
____	17 (paper)	£14.95	_____	____	27 (paper)	£14.95	_____

Payment of £ _____ is enclosed.

Please debit my Access/VISA/American Express account no. _____

Expiry date _____

Signature _____ Name _____

Address _____

See the previous page for ordering issues from Yale University Press, New Haven.

Volumes 1–7 of **Children's Literature** can be obtained directly from John C. Wandell, The Children's Literature Foundation, Box 370, Windham Center, Conn. 06280.